D1444332

Unemployment

International Perspectives

Unemployment is a pernicious and apparently ineradicable symptom of twentieth-century economic malaise throughout the world. In November 1984 the Centre for Industrial Relations sponsored an international conference in Toronto which brought together economists from Canada and a number of other countries to discuss explanations for the problem and strategies for dealing with it.

The authors pay particular attention to the role of deficient aggregate demand (associated with the restrictive monetary and fiscal policies used to combat inflation), and the role of structural labour-market rigidities (associated with such factors as wage rigidity, collective bargaining, unemployment insurance, regulation, and legislative constraints in labour markets). A key issue is whether such rigidities prevented labour markets from adapting to rapid changes associated with such factors as oil shocks, deindustrialization, technological changes, and trade adjustments.

As unemployment continues to weaken the Canadian economic structure, governments at all levels must explore new approaches. The essays in this collection provide the kind of assessments with which an old and difficult problem can be considered in new and fruitful ways.

MORLEY GUNDERSON is Director of the Centre for Industrial Relations and Professor of Economics at the University of Toronto.

NOAH M. MELTZ is Assistant Dean, School of Graduate Studies at the University of Toronto. He is also Professor of Economics and Industrial Relations in that university's department of Economics and in the Centre for Industrial Relations.

SYLVIA OSTRY is Canadian Ambassador for Trade Negotiations and Personal Representative of the Prime Minister, Economic Summits.

MORLEY GUNDERSON, NOAH M. MELTZ,
and SYLVIA OSTRY, editors

Unemployment:
International Perspectives

Published for
the Centre for Industrial Relations
by University of Toronto Press
Toronto Buffalo London

© University of Toronto Press 1987
Toronto Buffalo London
Printed in Canada

ISBN 0-8020-5710-1 (cloth)
ISBN 0-8020-6636-4 (paper)

Printed on acid free paper

Canadian Cataloguing in Publication Data

Main entry under title:

Unemployment: international perspectives

Papers originally presented at a conference
sponsored by the Centre for Industrial Relations.
University of Toronto, Nov. 28-30, 1984.
Includes bibliographical references.
ISBN 0-8020-5710-1 (bound) ISBN 0-8020-6636-4 (pbk.)
1. Unemployment. 2. Employment (Economic theory).
I. Gunderson, Morley, 1945-   . II. Meltz, Noah M.
III. Ostry, Sylvia, 1927-   . IV. University of
Toronto. Centre for Industrial Relations.

HD5707.5.U63 1987   331.13'7   C86-095100-6

To the memory of Ezio Tarantelli

Contents

ix Contents

REMEDIES

Preface

The origins of this volume go back to a conference held in Toronto 28–30 November 1984, under the auspices of the Centre for Industrial Relations, University of Toronto. The conference was organized by Professor Noah M. Meltz, then director of the Centre, and Dr Sylvia Ostry of the Canadian Department of External Affairs, who was a visiting scholar at the Centre in 1983–4. The papers were assembled by the organizers and revised by Professor Morley Gunderson, current director of the Centre.

The conference would not have been possible without the financial assistance of the following agencies: Canada Employment and Immigration Commission, Economic Council of Canada, Labour Canada, Ontario Ministry of Labour, and Statistics Canada. We would like to express our appreciation to these agencies for their support and assistance.

The editors wish to acknowledge the important contribution made by the assistant to the director of the Centre, Mrs Deborah Campbell, and the Centre's secretary, Mrs Carmela Moltisanti. The Centre's librarians, Mrs Elizabeth Perry and Mr Bruce Pearce, provided background support and references for the volume.

THE EDITORS

Introduction: A summary of the issues

In the 1980s unemployment became the scourge of Western industrialized countries. Not since the Depression did rates reach such high levels. While societies are now better prepared to protect their citizens than during the 1930s, the result is still massive privation and loss of production for millions of people.

To analyse the causes and possible remedies for the situation this volume provides a comparative approach. Unemployment is examined from the perspectives of western Europe, the United States, and Canada. Each section includes an overview and examines labour-market aspects and industrial relations. However, the wide variation in industrial relations practices forces us to focus our discussion of industrial relations on the United States and Canada. The proposed solutions cover a range of traditional macroeconomic policies along with reduced-time programs and social contracts between labour, management and government.

It is our belief that a comparative approach will highlight the similarities and differences surrounding the economic and social policy debates in the various countries. We have chosen these three groupings because there seemed to be a conscensus in the early 1980s that western Europe (except for Britain) was using government intervention to try to solve unemployment while the United States had moved in the opposite direction, with greater reliance on market forces. Canada was perceived to be in between. Such differences seemed to present an ideal laboratory to test opposing theories in a context where it is not possible to hold everything else constant.

One of the primary findings that emerges from the papers in this volume is that all is not as it seems. Perceptions of what is being done are often not borne out by reality. This observation relates to the major policy debate over whether unemployment is caused by deficient demand or structural factors. While this debate may seem to echo the controversy over the cause of unemployment in the late 1950s and early 1960s, it still contains important issues for the 1980s. The answers, however, are more complex than two decades ago.

Two papers, one by James Tobin and one by William Dymond, provide a general overview of the problem, while Michael Ellman, Martin Neil Baily, and Pierre Fortin examine unemployment in western Europe, the United States, and Canada, respectively.

James Tobin, 1981 Nobel laureate in economics, takes a historical perspective on the problem and then focuses on the situation of the United States in the mid-1980s. His conclusion is that American success in reducing unemployment from the 12 per cent range in 1982 to under 8 per cent has been the result of increases in aggregate demand through massive defence expenditures and increases in the national debt. While in the short run unemployment has been reduced, Tobin sees some longer-term problems because of debt accumulation.

Dymond provides a detailed analysis of the incidence and demographic characteristics of unemployment in various OECD countries, particularly western Europe, the United States, and Canada. One of the major differences he observes is that there were increases in employment in the United States and Canada (primarily in the service sector) whereas employment declined in western Europe. In contrast, labour productivity and real labour costs increased much more in Europe than in North America. Dymond concludes that unemployment in Europe is largely conditioned by structural factors complicated by more restrictive fiscal and monetary policies. For Europe he calls for increased flexibility in wage determination, reduction of taxes on employment, and modification of social policy measures to reduce disincentives.

Michael Ellman takes issue with Dymond's analysis. While acknowledging that structural factors (Eurosclerosis) have caused some unemployment resulting from too large a public sector, the welfare states, employment protection legislation, a hostile environment for entrepreneurs, and so on, he nevertheless feels this view is one-sided and partial. The major problem is the long cyclical downturn in investment resulting from leaving investment to market forces. 'Those OECD European countries which have maintained low unemployment rates (Sweden, Norway, Austria) have pursued macroeconomic and labour market policies aimed at this [increasing investment].'

Martin Neil Baily generally supports Tobin's and Dymond's view that cyclical factors were responsible for the increased unemployment in the United States, although he also observes a long-run increase in structural unemployment due to demographic changes (increases in youth and female components of the labour force). He expects that these factors, which have raised the natural rate of unemployment, will be less important by the late 1980s. This will provide additional scope for monetary and fiscal policies without causing an acceleration of inflation.

Pierre Fortin also agrees with Dymond that high unemployment in Canada stems not from unfavourable structural developments but from a large shortfall of aggregate demand. He believes that since the unemployment rate in the mid-1980s is well above the non-inflationary rate of unemployment, macroeconomic expansion would not run any danger of rekindling inflation. Since such a policy could increase the ratio of public debt to GNP, Fortin advocates restrictive fiscal policy and expansionary monetary policy, even though this could lead to a further depreciation of the Canadian dollar against other (particularly American) currencies.

In his comments, Robert Gregory criticizes Dymond's reference to the need for more flexible labour markets since he observes that the supposedly more flexible labour markets in the United States have been unable to deliver significant increases in real wages or labour productivity. In addition Gregory points out that there has been a productivity slowdown in both western Europe and the United States. He concludes that 'high levels of unemployment stem primarily from a deficiency in aggregate demand rather than an upsurge in structural imbalances in the labour market and the economy.'

In his comments, Richard Lipsey suggests that Ellman believes that both Keynesian (deficient demand) and classical (relatively high wage rates) forces are the cause of high unemployment in western Europe. Moreover, Lipsey points out that real-wage unemployment looks like deficient-demand unemployment, not like structural unemployment. Most studies suggest that high wages may be a problem in Europe and that they are probably not a problem in the United States. In the case of Canada there is uncertainty on this issue, and he believes that more exploration is needed. Lipsey also believes that creating a more secure climate for investors in the United States has helped that country, while an unfavourable climate has hurt western Europe. Lipsey also supports Fortin's call for a more expansive monetary policy, although he does not see the need for as large a depreciation in the Canadian dollar as Fortin expects.

Two very different European labour market approaches are examined by

Ezio Tarantelli and David Grubb. Tarantelli focuses on the relation between inflation and unemployment and the implications of a high level of industrial conflict and wage-cost push for what he terms the three cranky cases in Europe: Italy, France, and the United Kingdom. He argues that the degree of neocorporatism (i.e. the extent of centralization of industrial relations) is a crucial factor in the degree to which economic shocks such as the OPEC-induced oil price increases produce inflation and/or unemployment. The higher the degree of neocorporatism the better the shelter against wage-cost push and industrial conflict. Neocorporatism (termed a social contract in a later paper by Maital) can also create greater credibility for an economic policy announcement concerning a lower target rate of inflation. Neocorporatism thereby shifts the short-run Phillips curve (wage-unemployment trade-off) downward and to the left. Countries such as Japan that have successfully adapted to the oil price increase have a high degree of neocorporatism, while the three 'cranky' cases, which have not successfully adapted, have little neocorporatism.

David Grubb observes that policy based on an employment target can give quite different results from policy based on an inflation target. For example, if the policy in the 1970s has been based on restraining inflation rather than unemployment, unemployment would have been lower after 1975 because expansions in demand in 1972–3 and 1978–9 were based on over-optimistic views of the non-inflationary rate of unemployment. In other words, the inflation-unemployment trade-off curve had shifted upward but policy-markers were not aware of this development.

In his comments, Klaus Weiermair discusses the problems of achieving consensus in different economic circumstances. This point is also raised in the later section on industrial relations.

Changes in the institutional framework of the American labour market are examined by David Bloom and Steven Bloom, while Linda Bell and Richard Freeman test the employment impact of flexible wage structures.

The starting-point for Bloom and Bloom's paper is that the relatively better performance of the American economy in terms of employment is the result of institutional changes in the labour market. They conclude that while by the mid-1980s unemployment had dropped from the heights of 1982 and early 1983, as a whole it had worsened from what it was in the 1970s. This worsening was 'at least partly a reflection of the inability of labour institutions to respond quickly enough to changing labour market conditions.' While there has been change, it does not mean that there will not be even more changes. Macro prescriptions must consider the institutional setting within which the policies will operate – one that has in general been characterized by inertia.

Just as Bloom and Bloom do not attribute the post 1982–3 cyclical gains in employment to flexible labour market structures, so Bell and Freeman do not attribute it to wage flexibility. Bell and Freeman also observe that Japan, which had a sizeable expansion of employment, has a wage-setting pattern with little or no flexibility of relative wages among industries.

In his comments Daniel Hamermesh indicates that Bloom and Bloom may not have provided a sufficient theoretical base to determine whether institutions were changing too fast or too slowly. To analyse these changes he says one has to go beyond the (relatively shrinking) unionized sector of the US economy and consider such major developments as industrial safety, retirement, and disability policy. In contrast, Thomas Kochan believes that there indeed is a common pattern in the United States, citing institutional adjustments such as the trading of wage flexibility and flexibility of other terms of employment for greater commitment to investment- and job-creation activities. However, Kochan is pessimistic about whether this type of bargaining will emerge as the dominant outcome of the American industrial relations system in the 1980s.

On the subject of wage flexibility as set out by Bell and Freeman, Kochan argues that wage-setting patterns of the 1970s were not responsible for the job creation experienced during that period; to have positive effects on employment, the fruits of productivity increases need to be diverted to investment rather than to current or future wage increases for existing employees. Hamermesh's reservation is that 'relative wages, on which Bell and Freeman focus, do not adjust well, but economy-wide wage levels, which are what is important for evaluating responses to aggregate shocks, have been more responsive in the United States than elsewhere.' As a result, Hamermesh concludes that the American labour market has been sufficiently flexible to accommodate past developments and will likely be so in the future.

The three papers on the Canadian labour market approach the unemployment problem from differing perspectives. David Foot and Jeanne Li examine the demographic determinants of unemployment; Craig Riddell looks at the consequences of alternative policies to deal with unemployment; and Morley Gunderson and Noah Meltz consider labour-marketing rigidities.

Foot and Li note the inability of job growth to match the extremely rapid labour-force growth resulting from the entrance of the 'baby boom' cohorts into the work-force. However, the demographic patterns suggest downward pressure on unemployment rates in the late 1980s and the 1990s. At the same time, compositional changes are likely to affect particular unemployment rates. Lower participation rates for women will somewhat ease female unemployment, but the slightly higher rates for men will intensify their unemployment. While unemployment will be reduced for youth, Foot and Li call attention to the possibility of an increase for older workers.

Craig Riddell suggests that unemployment can be reduced in the short to medium term without adverse consequences for inflation, since the economy is well below the level of output and employment at which wage and price inflation would begin to rise. He argues that on balance we should accelerate the economy while reorganizing the costs and risks. These include a likely persistence of high real rates of interest and an increase in the federal deficit. The consequences for future inflation and the deficit have to be weighed against the costs of prolonged high unemployment. Riddell advocates a more expansionary monetary policy (as does Fortin) and no change in the current fiscal stance, long-run reduction in the structural deficit, and norms for wage and price increases involving a planned continuation of the existing disinflation. The chances of achieving these norms through a voluntary incomes policy are slim but not zero. Tarantelli and Maital both advocate the same approach.

For Gunderson and Meltz the issue is whether the greater American success in reducing unemployment after the 1982–3 recession was the result of greater flexibility in its labour market associated with deregulation, wage concessions, and a weaker labour movement. They suggest that many so-called labour-market rigidities may in fact enhance labour-market efficiency. Also, they examined aggregate measures of labour-market rigidities (structural unemployment) and concluded that deficient demand was responsible for the huge increase in unemployment in the 1980s. However, Gunderson and Meltz note a long-run increase in structural unemployment (including the demographic aspects observed by Foot and Li).

In his comments, S.F. Kaliski agrees with Foot and Li that participation rates have to be treated as an endogenously determined result of labour market interaction, but he is not as hopeful as Foot and Li that youth unemployment will decrease by much. Kaliski agrees with Gunderson and Meltz and with Riddell that the increase in unemployment in the 1980s was due more to deficient demand than to structural factors.

Keith Newton also agrees with Gunderson and Meltz and with Riddell that the dominant factor in the early 1980s was cyclical slack, although he urges Gunderson and Meltz to provide theoretical links to connect their empirical measures with their speculation on the implication of labour-market rigidities. Newton commends Foot and Li for suggesting that previous assessments of the contribution of demographic factors to unemployment in Canada may have been underestimated and that ostensibly salutary aggregate outcomes may in fact mask troublesome compositional features. This also helps to underline Riddell's distinction between short-run and long-run aspects of the diagnosis and treatment of unemployment: both cyclical (short-run) and structural (long-run) factors have to be considered.

Given widely divergent practices in industrial relations throughout western Europe, the section on this topic focuses on North America. John Dunlop provides an American perspective, while a round table of practitioners looks at the situation in Canada.

Dunlop sets the stage by indicating that industrial relations cannot be a substitute for optimum macroeconomic policies: 'No industrial relations system can adapt compensation readily to swings in exchange rates or unpredictable macro policies.' While some economists have advocated shorter collective agreements to prevent lags in wage adjustments, Dunlop observes that year-to-year agreements are too expensive in time, effort, uncertainty, and potential conflict to be practical. He sees profit-sharing as only a special-purpose tool of limited applicability not suited for most workers. Collective bargaining, he observes, has always been significantly influenced by the state of demand and competitiveness in the relevant product markets. Accordingly, Dunlop expects collective bargaining, with some lags, to respond constructively to the new environment in sectors experiencing economic trouble (e.g. basic steel, trucking, airlines, meat packing, and construction) and the rapid growth of non-union enterprises. The adaptability in compensation and rules that is taking place also requires major changes in management, especially the need for more co-operative and participatory US management. Along with such a change must come a recognition of the importance of internal labour markets and of the role of training.

The Canadian round table, chaired by John Crispo, consisted of a businessman, Bernd Koken (Abitibi-Price Inc.); a union official, John Fryer (National Union of Provincial Government Employees); Ontario's deputy minister of labour, T.E. Armstrong; and the federal assistant deputy minister of labour, Ray Protti.

Koken believes that there are aspects of collective bargaining that can help to reduce unemployment by assisting organizations in being more competitive and productive. The other side of this proposition is that a negative industrial relations climate (e.g. a proliferation of work stoppages) can encourage firms to invest elsewhere, as happened when US publishers participated in expansion of paper mills in the United States rather than in Canada.

Fryer also believes that Canada's industrial relations system could be used to reduce unemployment, but that it would require basic changes in the system, such as a commitment to full employment, protection of workers' rights in the face of technological change, and consultation between business and labour on labour-market trends and economic issues. Joint problem-solving between labour and management is required on other issues such as productivity and quality of working life. 'If we are going to improve the industrial relations system in Canada, then trade unions must be seen and treated as equal with business and government.'

Armstrong believes that collective bargainers are too often insufficiently aware of the creative role that collective bargaining can play in employment creation. This, however, required a greater involvement of the parties in economic policy-planning mechanisms and systems. We know that on the down side collective bargaining does respond to harsh market facts. But is the recession-induced moderation shared equally among professionals, executives, dividend recipients, and wage earners? 'If wage behaviour is so important an element in economic policy and is so inextricably linked to fiscal and monetary policies, why should labour not be included in advisory undertakings where these policies are discussed and options developed?'

Protti, too, stresses the high degree with which the Canadian collective bargaining system has adapted to changing economic circumstances. Average annual wage increases – including provision for cost-of-living allowance (COLA) clauses – dropped from 13.6 per cent in the fourth quarter of 1981 to 3.1 per cent in the third quarter of 1984. In some parts of Canada, such as Alberta and British Columbia, settlements were running at an even lower rate of 1.8 per cent, while there were also wage freezes or cuts. The structure of bargaining changed from uniform national rates in such industries as meat packing. While this adaptability is important, Protti stresses the need for increased information exchange among labour-market parties. He notes that countries that have experienced a relatively good macroeconomic performance (Norway, Sweden, Austria, Japan) have benefited from what Tarantelli had cited as regular and continuing information exchange and the building of consensus at all levels of society.

John Crispo provides summary comments on the round table and its relation to the other papers. While there is indeed wage-adjustment and work-rule flexibility, it seems to take a very high and sustained level of unemployment to bring it about. Crispo then indicates the mix of policies which could ease this drastic solution, such as appropriate fiscal and monetary policies and a more competitive economy. The latter challenge requires labour and management to work together to make both the country and its enterprises more competitive. The process of joint action is easier to start at the micro level where there is mutual incentive. Individual examples include gains-sharing plans and approaches to change such as the Domtar Industrial Conversion Adjustment Plan. The Canada Labour Market and Productivity Centre could provide a basis for more macro-level consultation between labour and management. As essential element in the joint action 'is the need to stop isolating and ostracizing the labour movement. Neither management nor government nor anyone else should expect trade unions to act more responsibly unless they are treated more responsibly.'

Shlomo Maital proposes a social-contract type of incomes policy to deal with unemployment, and Frank Reid advocates reduced work time.

Maital discusses the theoretical foundations for policies advocated earlier by Tarantelli, Riddell, Armstrong, Protti, and Crispo. He shows, using computer simulations of the US economy, that a simultaneous reduction in both wages and prices produces a more favourable economic situation with greater output and a better inflation–unemployment rate trade-off. Whether the social contract is achieved through voluntary means or is imposed, the economy ends up in a better situation because it is able to escape from the prisoner's dilemma syndrome.

Frank Reid proposes an alternative, though complementary approach to the unemployment problem. He suggests that more attention be paid to three related employment-sharing policies that involve reductions in work time: legislated or negotiated reductions in the standard work week; policies to encourage individual employees to engage in job-sharing, longer vacations, sabbatical leaves, and early retirement; and short-time compensation (STC) policies in which unemployment insurance benefits are used to partially compensate workers for temporary reductions in the work week to avoid layoffs. He indicates that if average hours worked in the 1982 recession had been reduced by 1.3 hours per week, the unemployment rate would have remained at its 1981 level of 7.5 per cent rather than rising to 11.0 per cent during 1982. Reid discusses the pros and cons of such employment-sharing policies in terms of efficiency and equity, and he indicates their feasibility as well as the policy changes that could facilitate their increased usage. While favouring such changes, he emphasizes that they 'should not be regarded as a substitute for aggregate policies designed to reduce deficient-demand policies' – a theme that is emphasized in many of the papers dealing with micro policies to reduce unemployment.

While there are some such common themes throughout the papers, there is also a diversity of opinions concerning the causes and consequences of unemployment and the appropriate policy responses. Hence the subtitle of the volume is not 'an international perspective' but rather 'international perspectives,' emphasizing the diversity of views.

OVERVIEW OF THE PROBLEM

JAMES TOBIN

Macroeconomic diagnosis and prescription

Unemployment in the 24 nations of the Organization for Economic Cooperation and Development (OECD) rose from 5.5 per cent of the labour force in 1979 to 10 per cent in 1983. The number of unemployed persons rose from 18 million to 32 million. This development was the second upward ratchet in unemployment in the decade following the first oil shock. (Table 1 summarizes the recent history of unemployment in the advanced economies of the non-communist world.)

The prospects of reducing unemployment to 1979 rates, let alone 1973 rates, are dismal for the remainder of the 1980s. For the government of the major locomotives of the world economy – the seven countries of the annual economic summit conference (Canada, France, West Germany, Italy, Japan, the United Kingdom, and the United States) – significant reduction of unemployment is not a high joint or individual priority. Nor is it apparently a big concern of the electorates of these democracies. The prevailing attitudes, among both governors and governed, are fatalism and complacency; not much can be done, not much needs to be done, about unemployment. The fiscal and financial plans of most governments contemplate adjustment to permanently higher unemployment rates.

Europeans seem more resigned to the intractability of unemployment than North Americans. In the United States, return to unemployment rates less than a point above those of 1978 and 1979 is considered possible and desirable. The strong economic recovery which began in mid-1982 buoyed optimism on this side of the Atlantic; unemployment has subsided from a cyclical peak of 10.7 per cent in December 1982 to 7.8 per cent in February 1984. Recovery in western Europe has been later and weaker; unemployment is still rising, and common projections envisage a 'recovery' that leaves joblessness on a new higher plateau. Japan is a special case. Overt

TABLE 1
Selected macroeconomic data for OECD economics

	Unemployment rates* (%) (average for year)			Capacity utilization indexes†		
	1973	1979	1983	1973	1979	1983
United States	4.8	5.8	9.5	88	86	75
Japan	1.3	2.1	2.7	100	90	83
West Germany	0.8	3.2	8.5	87	84	78
France	2.6	5.9	8.3	85	82	77
United Kingdom	3.3	5.6	11.5	43	42	32
Seven summit countries	3.4	5.0	8.3			
Fifteen OECD countries	3.3	5.1	9.0			

	Real growth (% per yr) GNP or GDP			Output gap: % shortfall of 1983 GNP/GDP below 1979, projected to 1983 by	
	1965–73	1973–9	1979–83	1973–9 trend	mean of 1973–9 and 1965–73 trends
United States	3.8	2.8	0.9	7.1	8.9
Japan	9.8	3.7	3.6	0	11.2
West Germany	4.1	2.4	0.5	7.5	10.4
French	5.2	3.1	1.1	7.7	11.3
United Kingdom	3.8	1.4	0	5.3	9.8
Seven summit countries					
Fifteen OECD countries					

	Money wage inflation‡ (%)			Unit labour costs§ (% Increase over prev yr)		
	1973	1979	1983	1973	1979	1983
United States	7.1	8.4	4.6	3.4	6.9	3.7
Japan	23.4	7.4	4.5	2.3	−2.5	1.2
West Germany	10.7	5.5	2.7	5.4	2.0	−1.2
France	14.6	13.0	11.0	7.2	6.1	8.0
United Kingdom	12.7	15.5	8.0	5.4	12.8	1.2
Total OECD	13.0	9.6	6.0			
Seven summit countries				4.6	5.3	3.5

(continued on next page)

	Price inflation, GNP/GDP deflator (% rise over prev yr)		
	1973	1979	1983
United States	5.8	8.6	4.2
Japan	11.9	2.6	1.0
West Germany	6.5	4.1	3.0
France	7.1	10.4	9.0
United Kingdom	7.1	15.1	5.2
Total OECD		8.4	4.7
Seven summit countries		7.4	5.2

NOTES: Except for the United States, figures for 1983 are OECD estimates from incomplete information. The seven summit countries include Italy and Canada. The fifteen OECD economies are the advanced countries, for which employment dates are meaningful.
*Unemployment rates are standardized by OECD to US definition.
†Estimates of utilization of manufacturing capacity. For Japan, the Ministry of International Trade and Industry index is normalized to 1973. For the United Kingdom, figures are percentages of firms reporting full utilization.
‡Hourly earnings in manufacturing for the United States and West Germany; monthly earnings for Japan; weekly earnings for the United Kingdom; hourly wage rates for France
§Labour costs per unit of manufacturing output, for Germany, includes mining
SOURCES: *Economic Outlook*, OECD, No. 27 (July 1980) and No. 34 (December 1983); *Main Economic Indicators*, OECD; *International Financial Statistics* (International Monetary Fund); and *Economic Report of the President*, 1984 US Governmnet Printing Office).

unemployment is always low, but the measured increases since 1973 and 1979 none the less are symptoms of large and growing margins of economic slack. Recent improvements in western Europe and Japan reflect mainly export demands due directly or indirectly to the American recovery.

Half a century ago, four years of precipitous decline in world economic activity generated mass unemployment. Most of this persisted through the six years of recovery prior to the Second World War, which brought with it shortages of labour and everything else. The depression of 1979–83 was much less severe, and now society treats the jobless more generously than in the 1930s. Yet there are disturbing parallels. Then as now, governments and central banks eschewed active measures to create jobs in favour of austere fiscal and financial policies designed to win the confidence of international bankers and bond-holders. Their efforts, individually and collectively, made depression and unemployment worse; and in the end they failed to balance budgets, protect currency parities, or prevent exposed banks from falling like dominoes.[1] Chancellor Heinrich Bruning adhered religiously to the canons of sound finance, and within a year after he left office, the Weimar Republic fell to Hitler. France, the leader of the gold bloc, eventually succumbed to the disasters it helped to inflict on its neighbours. Weakened by economic strife, political chaos, and class warfare throughout the 1930s, France was no match for Nazi Germany. Capitalism, democracy, and Western civilization barely survived.

Such momentous dangers seem remote today. But passive acceptance of prolonged high unemployment cannot be taken for granted either. Another decade of poor economic performance can undermine allegiance to the institutions of democratic capitalism, especially among successive cohorts of youth who fail to find jobs. Macroeconomic disappointments can also erode support for the international economic and political order on which the security and prosperity of the free world have been based since 1945. They have already triggered autarkic measures and proposals in nearly every nation, *sauve qui peut* expedients that protect some jobs and businesses at the expense of others and sacrifice the gains from efficient trade in the process. Stagnation in the developed 'North' is devastating to the less developed and debt-burdened 'South.' The austere prescriptions of the International Monetary Fund are politically risky in many countries friendly to the West. They may be inevitable when sick economies are treated one by one. But in aggregate the medicines, like the belt-tightening national policies of the Depression, make the world situation worse.[2] Moreover, neither the examples nor the effects of current performance and policies in the advanced countries are likely to win the contest for the hearts and minds of the Third World.

The Depression taught the world that mass unemployment in advanced capitalist economies was a *macroeconomic* problem. That revelation means several things. First, when millions of people become unemployed, it is not because of their individual characteristics. They have not suddenly become lazy or unruly or unproductive or untrainable. The jobs are just not there. When jobs reappeared in the late 1930s and the 1940s, as in all subsequent cyclical recoveries, the unemployed were willing and able to fill them.

Second, mass unemployment is not due to shortages of capital equipment, land, or other productive resources complementary to human labour. Indeed, industrial capacity is underused too. Table 1 shows for the most recent decade how measures of capacity use have fallen while unemployment has risen.

Third, unemployment and underuse of capacity both vary inversely with aggregate production and real income. This relation also is illustrated in

Table 1, where shortfalls of gross domestic product (GDP) from trend have risen parallel to unemployment.

Fourth, short-run fluctuations in production, employment, and capacity use are principally fluctuations in aggregate demand of goods and services. Potential aggregate supply, the productive capacity of a national economy or group of national economies, varies little from year to year. Of course, supply is the determinative constraint over horizons longer than business cycles. Growth of productive capacity is the source of secular progress in standards of living.

Fifth, mass unemployment is not technological in origin. New technologies do, of course, displace particular workers and work hardships upon them, and upon whole industries and regions. But human labour in general has never yet become obsolete. Despite the dire science fiction prophecies that accompany every period of high unemployment, revival of aggregate demand has always created jobs in numbers vastly beyond the imaginations of the pessimists – or to put the point the other way round, productivity has not spurted to the heights imagined by the optimists. Given a buoyant macroeconomic climate, market capitalism has repeatedly demonstrated its capacity to adapt to new technologies, new patterns of demand, and new structures of comparative advantage in inter-regional and international trade.

Sixth, governments' monetary and fiscal policies are powerful influences on aggregate demand. They can be used to reduce unemployment due to deficiences of demand. After the Second World War, every economically advanced democracy resolved not to allow unemployment to become again the scourge it had been in the 1930s. The next quarter-century was an era of prosperity, growth, and stability without parallel in economic history. Compared to pre-war experience, even excluding the Depression, unemployment rates were low and fluctuated in a narrow band. The use of monetary and fiscal policies contributed to the favourable macroeconomic climate. The perverse policies so disastrous in the early 1930s were not repeated. But they are being repeated now.

Aside from its macroeconomic instruments, a modern democracy governing a decentralized economy has almost no tools to cope with unemployment. So-called structural, manpower, or labour-market policies are by no means new. Almost every advanced country has pursued them for decades. They can, as their successful use in Sweden in particular suggests, smooth and speed movements of workers displaced by technological and industrial change to new jobs. They can, therefore, reduce the minimal frictional unemployment inevitable in a dynamic economy. But they cannot do so unless the jobs are there, and thus they are virtually helpless when the macroeconomic climate is inclement. They are a useful complement to, but no substitute for, macroeconomic policies that assure adequate effective demand.

To be sure, our governments have the responsibility to educate our youth, but one can scarcely argue that today's young people are more vulnerable to unemployment than their fathers and mothers were because they are less educated – the contrary is the truth. Government programs can train or retrain workers in skills relevant to contemporary technology and industrial practice. It is futile and even demoralizing if the graduates of those programs cannot be placed, or if they simply displace workers whom those programs passed by. In any case, evidence and common sense indicate that the best training is generally on-the-job experience itself. Governments can help to match job openings with available candidates by collecting and disseminating information on job specifications and workers' qualifications. But there is no reason to think that more than a tiny amount of unemployment is due to inefficiencies in these matchings at present. Nonetheless, there are vastly more unemployed than vacancies today. Governments can sharpen incentives for encouraging the unemployed to search for jobs and to accept less attractive offers by diminishing the compensation paid to them and by instituting other reforms. Several governments are currently doing just that. This may help, but the fact remains that low unemployment coexisted with generous unemployment compensation for a long time. Governments can spread more evenly the work opportunities available by encouraging or mandating shorter hours. This does not really reduce unemployment, except by the illusion of the statistical conventions that do not count persons involuntarily working short hours. A fairer distribution of the burdens may ease the pain to the affected workers, but it does not diminish the overall economic waste.

An all-too-common misconception about unemployment is that its social cost is negligible when the incomes of the unemployed themselves are substantially maintained by the welfare-state subventions to which they are entitled. For one thing, those payments are not compensation for the stigma and demoralization of enforced idleness in a society where achievement at work is a principal source of esteem and self-esteem. Economists are wrong to think that most people positively dislike work and engage in it only for the pay. In any case, the cost of unemployment and of excess capital capacity to the society is the shortfall of GDP. The lost output could have augmented private and public consumption or national wealth, either productive capital at home or net claims on the rest of the world. That loss is the burden; unemployment insurance and work-sharing redistribute but do not eliminate it. The substantial size of the burden is shown in Table 1, the percentage shortfalls of GDP from trend. Economists generally use the unemployment rate as a barometer of macroeconomic performance and of cyclical fluctuation. In this sense, reduction in unemployment is valued not just in itself but as the symptom of economy-wide gains of output and income.

Those who expect structural labour-market policies to make a significant dent in current unemployment are, I believe, whistling in the dark. Many who propose them are probably rationalizing conscious preferences for continued slack in labour markets. Macroeconomic stimulus is necessary to lower unemployment to rates comparable to those of the late 1970s. It is probably sufficient as well. Structural labour-market policies can make only marginal improvements.

A long-standing constraint in all advanced economies on the reduction of unemployment by expansion of aggregate demand for goods and services, whether from stimulative policies or from other internal or external sources, is the possible inflationary by-product of such expansion. The extents to which inflationary risks are, and can reasonably be, the basic reasons for the reluctance of major governments to employ their macroeconomic policy instruments to lower unemployment will be discussed below. Structural policies to diminish those risks and loosen the constraints they impose on macroeconomic policies will be discussed below as well. They are to be distinguished from direct labour-market policies.

The principal intellectual obstacle to the use of policies of demand stimulus, monetary or fiscal, to reduce unemployment is fear of inflation. Demand management was discredited in the 1970s by the surges of inflation that terminated two cyclical recoveries in 1973–4 and 1979–80, recoveries driven or accommodated in degrees varying among countries by expansionary macroeconomic policies. The lesson learned by many policy-makers influential citizens, and economists is that unemployment cannot be cured in this way without unacceptable risk of inflation. This view is more solidly entrenched in western Europe than in North America.

Reconciling high employment and price stability has been a chronic dilemma in advanced democratic economies for nearly four decades, most pronounced in the stagflationary decade of the 1970s. Economists generally recognize that the occurrence of price and wage acceleration at low rates of unemployment limits the possibility of reducing unemployment by management of aggregate demand. But to estimate where the limit is, to give a numerical value to the minimal inflation-safe unemployment rate for a specific economy at a specific time, is very difficult. The implicit consensus view of that threshold – often called the 'natural rate,' though there is not necessarily anything natural about it, sometimes called the 'non-accelerating-inflation-rate-of-unemployment' or NAIRU – has appeared to rise secularly, for example, in the United States from 4 per cent in the 1960s to 5 per cent in the mid-1970s to 6 per cent or higher now. (President Reagan's Council of Economic Advisers pronounces it to be 6.5 per cent for the 1980s.) Governments and central banks which consider stability of prices, or at least stability of low inflation rates, their paramount goals, to which employment and production objectives are subordinate, are inclined to take no risk of crossing the threshold. In this view they are supported by a new generation of anti-Keynesian economists who believe essentially that labour markets are always in equilibrium, so that actual unemployment is always natural.

The dismissal of expansionary macroeconomic policies is in my opinion a misreading of, at least an overreaction to, the events of the 1970s. The frightening inflation accompanied two external price shocks without parallel in modern peacetime history. The Yom Kippur War, the oil embargo, and the first Organization of Petroleum Exporting Countries price hike (OPEC I) were not endogenous consequences of the 1971–3 recovery or of the major policies that fostered it. The Ayatollah Khomeini, the Iran-Iraq War, and OPEC II were not endogenous results of the recovery of 1975–9 or of the policies that supported it. Those two shocks would have been seriously inflationary and stagflationary even if demand policies had been more restrictive and unemployment higher before, when, and immediately after they occurred. This is not to exonerate demand policies of all responsibility for the inflation of the 1970s. It is to say that those events tell us little about the natural rate of unemployment and the safe limits of demand expansion in the 1980s.

It is true that the growth of American oil demand after 1974, due both to macroeconomic expansion and to continued controls on domestic oil prices, helped to bring world oil demand into collision with limits on OPEC's willing supply. It increased the vulnerability of oil-importing economies to the political interruptions of supply that occurred and to the hoarding of oil in anticipation of them. But if the inflation at the end of the 1970s tells us about any 'natural' rate, it was not that of unemployment but of oil consumption at the time.

Today the oil and energy situation is much improved. Abundant new non-OPEC supplies are available. Oil producers both within and outside the cartel are pumping far below capacity and far below their desired rates of exploitation. Thanks to decontrol of prices by presidents Carter and Reagan and to other incentives for conservation and substitution, Americans have, like consumers elsewhere, substantially reduced consumption of energy in general, and oil in particular. These improvements continue as producers and consumers put into use energy-efficient machinery, structure, and appliances. We have found less costly ways to economize petroleum than economy-wide, world-wide recession and stagnation. It is estimated that recovery will restore only one-quarter of Americans' reduction in oil consumption since 1979. A third oil shock cannot be ruled out, but we are much better prepared. It cannot make sense to run our economies at low speed permanently just because another oil shock would be somewhat less inflationary in those circumstances than if the world economy were prospering.

In other respects, too, the inflation outlook is pleasant. Table 1 includes figures showing the impressive progress in disinflation of price and wages in the major economies. The hardships of the past four years did accomplish something. The considerable slack in all economies should continue to discipline wages and prices even while utilization rates improve. Growth of productivity is reviving and holding down unit labour costs.

In western Europe the restrictive stance of macroeconomic policy in the face of the highest unemployment and deepest depression in half a century is rationalized by a pessimistic diagnosis of the maladies. They are not the type, it is argued, that management of demand can cure; hence expansionary fiscal and monetary stimuli will just be dissipated in inflation. In effect, the inflation threshold rate of unemployment is close to the current rate.

Specifically, the argument goes like this: in the jargon of economics, the unemployment is classical, not Keynesian, i.e. the culprit is not low demand but rigidly high real wages. Wage rates, relative to the prices employers receive for their products, are too high to make expansion of employment profitable. Trade union power, exercised on behalf of senior employees, defends uneconomically high real wages against the potential competition of the less privileged workers whom they render involuntarily unemployed. Raising mark-ups and prices will not relieve the profit squeeze because money wage rates will promptly and fully follow prices up. The process may or may not be formalized by indexation; in either case, the convention that money wages should rise with the cost of living is strong. It is especially damaging to profit margins and employment when, as in the cases of oil price shocks or exchange depreciations, cost-of-living indexes are rising relative to the prices of local products. Unless the real wage impasse is broken, demand stimulus is impotent to raise employment and production. Misdiagnosing and treating unemployment as Keynesian will only release an inflationary wage-price spiral.

According to this theory, classical unemployment arose in western Europe after the first oil shock.[3] Organized labour was accustomed to the pre-OPEC growth of real wages and resisted departure from the trend. But employers could no longer afford to pay those wages, and the 'wage gap' grew as the growth of labour productivity slowed down. Countries like the United Kingdom, which none the less tried to restore high unemployment, suffered from inflation, while West Germany, the most important example, recognized the new situation and kept inflation under control. This scenario makes some sense through 1979 or even 1980 but strains credulity for the subsequent rise of unemployment. For the later period, structural disturbances due to new technology and foreign competition are said to have rendered much existing human and physical capital obsolete.

It is difficult to tell by inspection whether unemployment is Keynesian or classical, or in what proportions it is the one or the other. It is difficult to tell whether real wages are above those that would be consistent with a lower unemployment rate, and if they are, to say whether or not they would naturally fall during a demand-driven recovery. And even if all those doubts are resolved on the pessimistic, classical side, it is gratuitous to assume that governments can do nothing to modify the recalcitrant path of real wages.

Squeezed profit margins are characteristic of cyclical lows of business activity and sometimes but not always reflect high real wages. Recoveries generally restore profit margins, and not necessarily by lowering real wages (relative to trend).

In retrospect no one doubts that mass unemployment in the 1930s was Keynesian. But an observer of the world scene in 1933 would have noted a severe profit squeeze. Real wages had risen in terms of labour's product from 1929 to 1932 in West Germany, Sweden, and the United Kingdom; they had fallen in the United States. Labour's share of product had risen by 38 per cent, 9 per cent, and 16 per cent in the first three countries respectively, and also by 11 per cent in the United States.[4] It would have been easy to call unemployment in the Depression classical. Indeed most economists rejected monetary and fiscal solutions at the time.

Keynes pointed out how real wages could be high and profits squeezed because of the same deficiency of aggregate demand that caused the unemployment.[5] In recession and depression, businesses cut prices competitively but lay off workers and cut production until their (marginal) costs at existing wages are lowered as much as their prices. During reflations and recoveries they reverse the process, enjoying higher profit margins as prices rise relative to wages, while increasing employment and production. Workers gladly accept additional employment even though their real wages may be falling. The Keynesian mechanism envisages cyclical price movements around relatively stable money wages. Keynesian adaptations of real wages occurred in the recoveries of the three European countries in the 1930s. In the United States real wages gained as production, employment, and profits recovered.

Almost immediately after publication of the *General Theory*, empirical investigations challenged Keynes's unquestioning acceptance of the conventional view that real wages, because they must be equal to the marginal productivity of labour, will vary counter-cyclically.[6] Those and many subsequent studies concluded that both labour productivity and product-wages more usually rise than fall during cyclical upswings, as was true in the United states in the 1930s. The classical theory of marginal-cost pricing is not a reliable guide to the cyclical behaviour of prices and real wages. In an imperfectly competitive economy in disequilibrium, relief of profit squeeze is provided by higher volume, increasing returns to scale, and efficient use of both overhead labour and redundant employees. As aggregate-demand expansion shifts out firms' product-demand curves, employers with constant or declining marginal costs will raise employment without any reduction of product wages.

For these reasons, observations of high real wages and squeezed profit margins do not per se show that unemployment is classical and not susceptible to Keynesian remedies. Rigidly high real wages may be the effective constraint on expansion of output and employment in particular economies in particular circumstances. Credible recent examples are the United Kingdom and Sweden in the 1970s, where export industries unprofitable at internationally competitive prices could not be made competitive by devaluation because of wage indexation. The immediate question is the applicability of the classical unemployment thesis to the 'locomotive' economies today, discussed in the next section.

One other point of macroeconomic theory deserves emphasis. Even if real wage reduction is necessary for expansion of output and employment, it may not be sufficient. Suppose, for example, that workers economy-wide give up one annual cost-of-living increase of money wages to allow business profit margins to increase. The redistribution of purchasing power does not obviously increase aggregate demand and may indeed diminish consumption. A positive outcome can come from net exports; this will benefit any one open economy at the expense of others, but it is not a solution for all countries together. In a closed economy, or in the world as a whole, the hope would centre on business investment. Will it be encouraged enough by the improved outlook for profit margins to overcome the disincentives of current excess capacity and sales prospects? Maybe, if the profit improvement is expected to be permanent. Maybe not. The safest course would be to combine durable wage corrections with assurances of accommodative and, if necessary, stimulative demand policies.

By far the most formidable barrier to monetary and fiscal stimulus to recovery and jobs is the risk of reacceleration of wages and prices. The danger seems remote today, when OECD economies are performing so far below capacity. But any business cycle recovery raises some prices. The prices of raw materials and foodstuffs traded in world commodity markets, sensitive to demand and supply, fell precipitously in the recent depression. Flexible upwards too, they are bound to rise in recovery. Likewise, businesses will have to restore to normal profitable rates the mark-ups they shaved in hard times. These reversals are one-shot price increases, but they worsen month-to-month inflation statistics temporarily while they take place. Nervous policy-makers cannot know for sure that they do not presage a more stubborn escalation of inflation.

Central banks and governments are so sensitized to inflationary dangers that they will resolve on the side of caution and restriction their uncertainties about the location of the minimal inflation-safe unemployment rate. They will buy insurance against a new spurt of inflation at the cost of extra points of unemployment. For their economies and the world, this insurance is very expensive. It may well be increasingly expensive, and ultimately self-defeating, in the long run. Experience suggests that prolonged high unemployment becomes 'natural' and structural – a self-fulfilling prophecy. The mechanisms are obvious: unemployed workers lose, or never acquire, the skills and habits imbued by actual job experience. Businesses lack the profits and prospects that spur investments in new capacity and technology; the advance or producitivity falters, and bottlenecks loom at ever higher unemployment rates.

The obvious desiderata are policies to diminish the inflation risks of demand expansion and to lower the inflation-safe unemployment rate. The candidates fall into two somewhat overlapping categories: *institutional reforms* and *incomes policies*. The prospects and the particulars differ widely from country to country. Here is possible only to indicate general principles, with illustrative examples.

In most countries the institutions of wage- and price-setting are biased upward. That is, wages and prices – other than those commodity prices set continuously by supply and demand in auction markets – rise more readily than they fall. Consider government-supported floors on farm prices, minimum wages, and asymmetrical indexation. Consider the inexorable ascent of costs of health care, undisciplined by market forces when payments are by third-party insurers, governmental or private. Consider the limited sensitivity to excess capacity of 'administered' industrial prices and the stubbornness of negotiated wages in the face of unemployment. When government interventions are responsible for these biases, they are obvious, though politically elusive, targets of legislative reform. When governments grant private agents and groups – trade unions or trade associations – immunities from competition, the public has at the very least the right to insist that the privileges are not exercised in ways that inflict inflation or unemployment on the whole society. For example, if indexing is permitted at all, it should be symmetrical; and the price index used should exclude cost-of-living increases that are burdens to employers and to the whole society as well as to workers, like important price boosts and increased sales taxes.

In most countries, collective bargaining procedures are sanctioned, protected, and regulated by legislation. A general problem is that no one represents workers laid off or never hired. All too often the wages of senior employed workers take precedence over the number of jobs. Remedies are hard to find. Perhaps official recognition as bargaining agents could be denied to unions that restrict membership and deny voice to the unemployed. Perhaps employers who raise wages while curtailing employment, or while qualified workers are in excess supply in their industry or region, should have to pay penalty surcharges into unemployment insurance funds. Perhaps legislation should provide incentive subsidies for employers and workers to agree on compensation systems which, like the Japanese model, condition some payments to workers on the profits or revenues or productivity gains of the firm.

Incomes policies are an alternative more readily available. In one form or another, they have on occasion been practised by almost every country. They range from the full-blown detailed price and wage ceilings of wartime mobilization to advisory guideposts dependent on persuasive interventions by government leaders. In a sense, threats, promises, and conditions respecting monetary and fiscal policies are also incomes policies. Their recent use in the United States and the United Kingdom was not encouraging. They work better where wage bargains are synchronized in time and in significant degree centralized; where government officials, union leaders, and business representatives can annually discuss wage and price patterns in their macroeconomic contexts.

Explicit incomes policies have failed when they attempted to suppress inflation in overheated peacetime economies; when they were removed before inflation expectations were damped; when they lacked or lost the consensus of the parties; when they were overwhelmed by uncontrollable price shocks, as in the oil crises of the 1970s. Past failures have made incomes policies unfashionable, but *faute de mieux* they deserve to be reconsidered.

Today conditions are favourable in several major economies. There is plenty of economic slack; inflation and expectations of inflation have been receding; both workers and employers can see how much they have to gain from a sustained non-inflationary recovery. In similar circumstances from 1961 to 1965 the Kennedy-Johnson guideposts, though without the teeth of legal compulsion, helped to keep recovery free of inflation. Today they probably should be strengthened by incentives for compliance, either the stick of tax penalties or the carrot of tax rewards. Tax-based incomes policy (TIP) is designed for decentralized, unsynchonized institutions of wage- and price-setting and designed to avoid the rigidities and inefficiencies of absolute controls. It may not be necessary in economies with institutions for economy-wide bargaining. Whatever the institutions and the policy, the indispensable ingredient is the leadership of presidents and prime ministers to develop and sustain the underlying consensus. Unfortunately, this leadership will never come from governments whose laissez-faire ideologies tell them that market economies will on their own achieve full employment without inflation – unless they define 'full employment' tautologically as whatever unemployment occurs.

Ordinary citizens never believe economists and bankers who tell them unemployment is the only cure for inflation. They think there must be a better way, and they are right.

Among the seven summit countries, the United States, West Germany, and Japan are the decisive actors in the macroeconomic drama. They have the opportunity and responsibility to restore prosperity and growth for the whole world. Canada must willy-nilly follow in the footsteps of its large neighbour to the south, amplifying its world impact. In Europe, West Germany's is the key economy. Its macroeconomic performance and policy set the tone for the European Community and for the whole area. Of the three other large economies of western Europe, only the United Kingdom has much room for independent manoeuvre just now. France is still paying the penalties of deviating from the deflationist ranks of its trading partners in the first year of François Mitterrand's socialist governmment. The Italian economy is too unruly and uncontrollable to be a significant force in the world economy. The discussion here will focus on West Germany, the United Kingdom, and Japan.[7]

As recorded in Table 1, West German inflation is enviably low and still falling, despite the adverse effects of the Deutsche Mark depreciation against the dollar and in lesser degree against the yen and the pound sterling. Since 1980 unemployment has more than doubled and is still rising. Job vacancies have virtually vanished. In the late 1970s, with unemployment at 3.5 to 4 per cent, there were four unemployed for every vacancy. Now there are 40! Money-wage increases have slowed to 3.5 per cent per year. After allowance for productivity trends, labour costs per unit of output are stable or declining. Could anyone seriously contend that macroeconomic expansion is now barred by rigidly high real wage rates? Surely at least half of current unemployment is Keynesian, not classical.

The view that West Germany was afflicted by classical unemployment, that its 'natural rate' rose after 1973, gained currency during the post-OPEC stagflation. The onset of experience energy coincided with immigration restrictions that limited the role of potential *Gastarbeiter* as an uncounted reserve army of unemployed. One signal of structural deterioration is that during the last ten years unemployment of labour rose more than underutilization of capacity. Another signal was the rise in the 'wage gap,' a measure of unit labour costs relative to prices, compared to a base year, specifically one of normal pre-OPEC prosperity, 1969. An increase in the wage gap is a squeeze on profit margins. The gap rose significantly, perhaps as much as 10 per cent, in the early 1970s, but it has since declined to its 1969 norm. In any event, labour costs relative to after-tax net incomes to capital are low in West Germany compared to the United States. (In 1974 and 1982 the West German ratios were 3.1 and 3.0 respectively, while the American ratios were 3.6 and 3.4) The wage-gap theory of the post-OPEC West German slowdown through 1979 is plausible, though debatable. It is not a credible explanation of the rise of unemployment in the 1980s.

The trend of potential real output in West Germany, i.e. output at a constant unemployment rate, is lower than before 1973, but still appears to exceed 3 per cent per year. The bulk of it is productivity growth; the labour force is virtually stationary. A conservatively high estimate of the present inflation-safe rate of unemployment is 4.5 per cent. The 'Okun's law' coefficient, relating percentage shortfalls of real GDP to excess unemployment, seems to be 2 or 2.5. Thus the loss of GDP at 9.5 per cent unemployment is 10 to 12 per cent. Eliminating it would take five years of growth in real GDP averaging around 5 per cent per year. With so much room and time, the Bundesbank and government would have plenty of chance to apply the brakes on evidence of price acceleration before unemployment fell the full amount.

There is another reason why fatalistic acceptance of the classical unemployment thesis is especially puzzling for West Germany. The history of wage determination in the Federal Republic is by and large not one of confrontation but one of moderation and 'codetermination.'[8] Realities of international competitiveness, macroeconomic trade-offs, and monetary and fiscal policies have influenced collective bargaining more successfully than in most other countries, including the United States and the United Kingdom. This has been true even after 1977, when the unions withdrew from the annual summit sessions with representatives of employers, the central bank, the government, and the Council of Economic Experts. Rigidities are not built into the system. Contracts last only one year, and indexation is outlawed. Government, unions, and employers have recognized that wage-setting is a matter of national political economy and economic politics. The West German government has actively pursued income policies, using macroeconomic policies and the wage-employment trade-offs they imply as both threats and promises.

If, as the influential economist Herbert Giersch has argued,[9] West Germany needs a *Lohnpause* (pause in wage increases) to clear the road for macroeconomic expansion, the record does not suggest, at least to an outside observer, that it could not be negotiated in return for a promise that policy will assure the expansion. If, under its new conservative government, West Germany is in the process of reforming its system of labour relations in the direction of decentralization, non-intervention, and confrontation, the outsider may be excused for observing 'if it ain't broke, don't fix it.'

The situation of the United Kingdom is similar to that of West Germany, except that unemployment and inflation are both about three points higher. Both wages and unit labour costs have been decelerating, while a modest recovery – enough to raise capacity utilization and employment but not to stop the unemployment rate from rising – has been under way for two years. Of course, labour relations and wage behaviour have been throughout Great Britain's post-war history a much greater source of macroeconomic difficulty than in West Germany. Evidently a major objective of the Thatcher government has been to break the unions' grip on the economy. The question is whether, after five years of disinflationary policy and rising unemployment, the groundwork for expansion without wage and price acceleration is finally in place. And if not yet, when? Maybe by now even British trade union leaders would be ready to offer stability in exchange for jobs.

Japan absorbed the two OPEC shocks of the 1970s and the subsequent world slumps with remarkable success. Real growth was interrupted only mildly in 1974-5. But growth rates after OPEC I were less than half the double-digit annual rates common previously, and they fell still farther in the 1980s. These slowdowns have opened a wide GDP gap, suggested by declining indicators of capacity utilization but not easy to discern in unemployment statistics. The 1983 unemployment rate, though under 3 per cent, is twice the rate of 1972. In Japan, far more than in Western economies, slack demand is absorbed by keeping redundant workers on the payroll – in effect a system of private unemployment insurance. As a result, the Okun coefficient for Japan is estimated to be from 13 to 25.[10] The lower number indicates that an extra point of unemployment in Japan signifies the same degree of slack as an extra five points in the United Sates or West Germany. Today, therefore, Japanese production is far below potential trend.

Like West Germany's, Japan's inflation is low and declining. With the help of a one-shot reduction of real wages, Japan overcame the inflationary consequences of the first oil shock by 1978. The second one Japan took pretty much in stride. Wage pressure is a minor problem in a country where unions are weak and the bonus system makes labour costs move up and down with employers' ability to pay – the workers' quid pro quo for immunity from layoffs.

The severe decline in world economic activity after 1979 was the result of restrictive macroeconomic policies deliberately and concurrently adopted in almost all major countries. The common goal was to overcome the price acceleration accompanying the second oil crisis, when oil demands enhanced by the 1975-9 recovery confronted supplies interrupted by the Iranian revolution and the beginnings of the Iran-Iraq war.

The firm, unanimous, and single-minded dedication of macro policies to the conquest of inflation reflected experience after the first OPEC shock in 1973-4. Then, too, restrictive policies brought severe recession and disinflation throughout the world. But subsequent experience differed from country to country. The most striking differences were between the United States and the two other big locomotives, West Germany and Japan. In the United States, fiscal and monetary policies turned stimulative or accommodative in 1975, and the subsequent recovery lowered unemployment rates by more than three percentage points. In West Germany and Japan, the macro brakes were relaxed very little. Unemployment and economic slack in those countries, indeed throughout the OECD outside North America, remained much higher than before. But the more austere governments preserved more of the disinflationary gains of the mid-decade recession and were less vulnerable to inflation following the second oil price shock. The United States and Canada, together with those European countries (notably the United Kingdom, France, and Italy) with chronically high inflation, were also vulnerable to crises of confidence in foreign exchange markets. The lesson perceived by all central banks was applied as the second OPEC shock hit: tighten promptly, tighten hard, and stay tight.

In the United States, Federal Reserve Board Chairman Paul Volcker announced in October 1979 a policy of relentless gradual reductions in the growth rates of monetary aggregates to continue until monetary growth would accommodate only sustainable non-inflationary rates of increase in gross national product (GNP). The policy differed from the restrictive measures taken in mid-1974 by Chairman Arthur Burns and his Federal Reserve colleagues in Volcker's explicit disavowal of counter-cyclical monetary policy. This time the Federal Reserve would not rescue the economy from recession by accommodating continuing inflation, as the Burns régime was perceived to have done from 1975. In the United States, as in the United Kingdom and western Europe, many economists, financiers, and policymakers believed that the effectiveness of recession as therapy for inflation was diluted and rendered transitory by the expectations of workers, unions, and businesses that anti-recessionary policies would save them from hard times whether or not they gave way on nominal wages and prices. The same theory predicted that if the private sector were convinced that policy-makers would 'stay the course,' a disinflationary recession would be shorter and do less damage than past recessions to employment and production.[11] The theory has influenced fiscal as well as monetary policies in most major economies: the Thatcher and Reagan governments foreswear counter-cyclical macro policies as a matter of principle, and others act in the same spirit.

The Federal Reserve nevertheless relented in the late summer and fall of 1982. US inflation rates had by then fallen dramatically. But the side-effects, in unemployment, business failures, lost production, and low investment, were much more damaging to the American and world economies than had been intended. The advertised commitment to 'stay the course' had not noticeably speeded the disinflation or limited the damage. Third World debtor countries, notably Mexico and Brazil, could not earn enough hard currency in export markets to carry debts at the high interest rates resulting from restrictive monetary policies in the United States and elsewhere. Their difficulties threatened the solvency of their creditors in North America and Europe. A sharp decline in the velocity of money in the United States, partly because deregulation was making chequing accounts in banks more attractive vehicles for saving and partly because general pessimism increased preference for safe, government-insured liquid assets, was making the Federal Reserve's money supply targets even more restrictive of nominal GNP than had been expected. When those targets were suspended to allow higher money growth, interest rates of all maturities fell sharply, and interest-sensitive expenditures, for residential construction and consumer durable goods, revived. The economy turned up in November, assisted strongly by the usual cyclical rhythm of inventories as businesses stopped liquidating them and began restocking.

The strong recovery of final sales of goods and services (GNP less net inventory accumulation) throughout 1983 was powerfully assisted by consumers spending the proceeds of two 10-per cent cuts of personal income tax rates, one in July 1982 and one in July 1983. These were the second and final instalments of the three rate reductions scheduled in the Economic Recovery Tax Act of 1981. Likewise the build-up of defence spending, also planned in 1981, began to provide markets and jobs, more via the placement of orders than by actual outlays.

By pure serendipity the administration carried out a classic well-timed Keynesian anti-recession fiscal policy complementary to the counter-cyclical change in monetary policy in late 1982. Neither of the deficit-increasing measures was intended to be a demand stimulus. In 1981 no recession clouded the officially projected scenario, and the administration was on principle opposed to counter-cyclical demand management. The tax cuts were supply side incentives, intended to encourage saving, work, and risk-taking, not spending. The defence build-up was for national security and diplomatic strategy, not for any economic purpose.

Whatever their motivations, expansionary monetary and fiscal policies worked as traditionally expected in the United States in 1983. Three or four million new jobs[12] were created, and the unemployment rate came down from 10.7 per cent to 7.8 per cent. As recently as the summer of 1982, the air was full of pessimism about the intractability of unemployment: the feeling then was that even as business activity recovers it will not create jobs. Congress, in a desperate attempt to do something, raised gasoline taxes to fund additional public jobs. The program was to create at most 300,000 jobs, but at least an equal number were probably lost by diversion of private spending to tax payment. Also as recently as early 1983 the air was full of dire predictions that federal deficits would 'choke off recovery,' even while pragmatic business forecasters correctly knew they would do the opposite.

The 1979–82 episode achieved a substantial but incomplete victory over inflation in the United States. The 'core' inflation rate, which excludes patently nonrecurrent price changes, has fallen four or five points, from 9 to 10 per cent per year to 4 to 5 per cent per year. Wage inflation has fallen similarly; what this portends for price inflation depends on the productivity trend of the 1980s, which is not yet clear. In any event recovery has not reversed, or even arrested, gradual progress on inflation to date. This was to have been expected given the slack in utilization of labour and capacity still remaining. It was not to have been anticipated by those who expect price inflation to follow monetary growth regardless of the economic climate, because the Federal Reserve allowed double-digit growth of M-1 (currency in circulation plus demand deposits) from July 1982 to June 1983. (Since then M-1 growth has slowed to 4 per cent, leading some monetarists to predict an early recession.)

The Federal Reserve has by no means abandoned its anti-inflation objective. After the initial drop of interest rates in 1982, the Federal Reserve raised them about 100 basis points in June 1983 and has held them steady to date. Paul Volcker and his colleagues will probably be content so long as, on the one side, no new recession begins and, on the other side, the expansion is well-behaved. A well-behaved recovery in this context means that the pace is slowing and approaching sustainable growth; prices and wages are not accelerating; unemployment is safely above the 6 per cent rate of 1978–9; and monetary aggregates are within the target ranges for their growth, lower for 1984 than for 1983. In the absence of any one of those conditions, Chairman Volcker has made clear that the Federal Reserve is ready to apply the brakes and raise interest rates. Continued recovery will not receive the benefits of the doubt against the risk of accelerating inflation.

Interest rates in the United States are still by historical standards very high in relation to actual inflation and to reasonable expectations of future inflation. These rates are a formidable obstacle to accumulation of domestic capital – residential and non-residential, human and physical, private and public, fixed and working. They are even more devastating to US foreign investment; here indeed the nation is disinvesting, running large deficits on current account because of enormous merchandise trade deficits. How long the sheer momentum of the recovery, the general optimistic mood and the fiscal stimulus can prevail over these obstacles is the main near-term uncertainty about the strength and duration of the recovery.

The machanisms by which American interest rates crowd out the nation's exports is a striking illustration of textbook analysis of the workings of macroeconomic policies in today's international monetary environment, a world of floating exchange rates and closely connected financial markets. As differentially high interest rates have attracted funds into dollar-denominated assets, the dollar has appreciated against the yen, Deutsche Mark, franc, and other currencies – actually by 52 per cent on average since 1980, 45 per cent when account is also taken of differences in national inflations over the period. The appreciation handicaps American exports and encourages imports.

The unique strength of US recovery in 1983, and prospectively in 1984, also raises American imports while the sluggishness of foreign economies continues to depress their demands for American exports. Dollar appreciation since 1979 has, however, contributed to disinflation in the United States by making imported goods less expensive in dollars – US inflation is estimated to be one or two percentage points lower as a result.[13] But this effect is only a transitory contribution to disinflation. It cannot be repeated without further appreciation, and it is more likely to be reversed.

While interest-rate differentials are the major source of the dollar's strength in exchange markets, they are not the only factor. International political developments and longer-run assessments of economic prospects may have improved the dollar's standing as a safe haven. There is no assurance that continued interest differentials will maintain the dollar's exchange value. Portfolio adjustments to exploit the perceived advantages of dollar assets in risk and return are not endless; most of them may have already occurred. US current-account deficits shift wealth to foreigners who tend to prefer their home currencies. Those deficits also raise doubts about the long-run viability of heavy US reliance on foreign borrowing to finance budget deficits and domestic investments.

High American interest rates and high exchange value of the dollar have been and still are important determinants of the world macroeconomic environment in several respects. First, because of the weight of the United States in international financial markets, high interest rates in the United States make interest rates high everywhere. In this way they contributed to the universal world depression, and they are still an obstacle to world recovery. Second, they intensify Third World debt burdens, especially in a period of disinflation and depression. Third, the appreciation of the dollar has exacerbated trade frictions, particularly between the United States and Japan, and inspired protectionist measures and proposals in the United States. Fourth, American interest and exchange rates have constrained macroeconomic policy options in Europe and Japan, although not as tightly as those governments claim. This point will be discussed next.

The 1983 recovery was unique to North America, and so were the shifts to expansionary macroeconomic policies. Western Europe and Japan lag far behind, benefiting from the overspill of American demand into their economies but doing nothing else to stimulate domestic demand. Their certainties that active policies of expansion would be futile and inflationary should be reconsidered in light of the American example.

As stated above, monetary policies in those other countries are in some degree constrained by American interest rates. Major foreign central banks have lost some control of their own interest rates and exchange rate, but not all. The more expansionary their domestic monetary policy is, the lower their own interest rates will be, and the more their exchange rates will depreciate. Such depreciation is advantageous to exports and to domestic economic activity and employment. In effect, foreign central banks could capture for their own economies even more of the expansion of demand in North America than they already have. In particular, this is a realistic opportunity for Great Britain, whose international competitive position is still less favourable than in the 1970s.

There are several reasons western Europe and Japan do not exploit this opportunity. It would raise the local prices of imports invoiced in dollars, not just goods of American origin but other interntionally traded goods, notably oil. Inflation statistics would be temporarily worsened. Moreover, central banks impose on themselves monetarist targets and are determined to stick by them. A special reason applies to Japan, the fear of increased trade friction with the United States.

What about fiscal policy in the major economies outside North America? Demand stimulus by tax reductions or government spending would not lower interest rates and further depreciate currencies against the dollar but would have the reverse effects. Those effects, indeed, would create room for additional monetary expansion at existing interest and exchange rates, if monetary targets were adjusted accommodatively. In fact, however, fiscal policies outside North America are severely restrictive, not stimulative. All major governments are trying to reduce their budget deficits by fiscal economies and tax increases.

The depression itself has, of course, automatically increased actual budget deficits, both by drastically reducing revenues and by requiring increased outlays for unemployment compensation and for relief of economic distress. Those features of modern fiscal systems, which raise deficits in cyclical recessions and lower them in recoveries and prosperities, are 'built-in stabilizers.' They sustain incomes and spending during downturns and restrict them in booms. Cyclical deficits are passive consequences of bad times. They buffer the decline in demand but do not actively stimulate demand.

Measures to overcome cyclical deficits are actively contractionary, intensifying recession or retarding recovery. This lesson was supposedly learned long ago, for example in the early 1930s from the counter-productive efforts of presidents Herbert Hoover and Franklin D. Roosevelt to balance the US federal budget and from the disastrous consequences of Chancellor Bruning's sacrifice of German unemployed to fiscal orthodoxy. The fiscal policies of major European governments and Japan in the 1980s are similarly perverse, if less extreme.

Table 2 summarizes the effects on budget deficits of recent fiscal actions in the seven summit economies and the OECD as a whole and compares them with the passive cyclical components of recent deficits. The table shows remarkable 'success' in wiping out the built-in stabilizers. Another way to interpret these policies is to consider their effects on the 'structural' or 'high employment' budget deficits, i.e. those that would hypothetically occur if economic activity were on it normal growth trend. Those deficits are being significantly reduced, in some countries transformed into surpluses. The Thatcher government, for a notable example, had moved the budget into substantial structural surplus, a remarkable 'achievement' during a long and severe economic decline. Evidently the general objective is to raise the unemployment rate and lower the GDP level at which permanently acceptable budget outcomes will be achieved. In other words, these governments have lowered their sights and are adapting their budgets to macroeconomic performance chronically weaker than in the past.

Almost all these countries have higher national propensities to save than the United States. Even in prosperous times, when private investment demands are strong, they have less reason to worry about the 'crowding out' consequnces of government deficits. In these slack times, their saving is ample to finance both public and private borrowers and indeed to acquire dollar claims as well. Table 2 also shows deficits in various economies relative to national saving.

The tightening of fiscal policies in the locomotive economies of Europe and Japan has serious international ramifications. Fiscal stimulus would not only increase domestic demand and employment but raise imports, spilling badly needed demand into the rest of the world – the smaller countries of Europe and Asia, the Third World in general, and North America.

TABLE 2

Fiscal policies and outcomes in major OECD economies

	Increases in surplus (decreases (in deficit), % of GNP or GDP, cumulative 1981–4*			Budget deficits relative to GNP/GDP, and to net private saving (%)	
	Actual	Cyclical	Non-cyclical	1983	1984
United States	−2.5	−0.9	−1.6	3.8, 67.8	3.7, 58.3
Japan	+2.0	−0.9	+2.9	3.4, 28.3	2.5, 22.2
West Germany	+1.0	−3.7	+4.7	3.1, 37.3	2.1, 26.1
France	−4.1	−3.8	−0.3	3.4, 47.0	3.8, 52.9
United Kingdom	+1.2	−3.4	+4.6	2.7, 54.8	2.3, 46.1
Seven summit countries	−1.4	−2.0	+0.6	4.1, 56.1	3.8, 48.4

NOTES: OECD calculations and estimates for 1983 and 1984; figures cover both subordinate and central governments.

*The figures shown are sums of four annual figures. This approximation is not strictly accurate but is indicative. Non-cyclical changes are discretionary actions on taxes and outlays. Cyclical changes are passive responses to economic fluctuations, given the tax legislation and the budget program. Actual changes are the sum of the two.

SOURCE: *Economic Outlook*, OECD (December 1983), Tables 9, 10, and 13

By putting their fiscal engines into perverse gear, Europe and Japan are setting back recovery throughout the world.

Appropriately stimulative policies need not, by the way, commit any country to high budget deficits in times of prosperity because tax cuts or job-creating expenditures could be designed to terminate at a scheduled date or be contingent on economic circumstances. They need not favour consumption, public or private; they could take the form of tax incentives for investment or of public investment projects. They need not commit governments to larger public sectors than they desire in the long run. Whatever the national priorities of the country and its social philosophy with respect to the roles of public and private economic activity, they can be reconciled with fiscal policies appropriate to macroeconomic circumstances.

The contrast in macroeconomic policies between the United States and the other locomotives of the world economy is striking. The United States is pursuing a tight high-interest monetary policy, albeit one what was sufficiently relaxed a year and a half ago to avert economic and financial collapse and start recovery. American fiscal policy is easy and becoming looser every fiscal year. The combination has produced a vigorous recovery at home and arrested economic decline throughout the world. But the extreme policy mix portends serious problems for the United States in the future, and the contagious high interest rates retard recovery elsewhere. Other countries have a right to complain, though they should address their complaints to American monetary authorities as well as the fiscal policy-makers in the White House and Congress. With unchanged monetary policy, tightening of the US budget would worsen, not relieve, the economic predicaments of other nations. Europe and Japan, in contrast, are pursuing tight monetary and tight fiscal policies both. Their monetary policies are tight because of US interest rates and their own monetarist principles. Their fiscal policies are, for the most part, difficult to understand and justify.

Both West Germany and Japan have traditionally enjoyed and depended on export-driven growth of demand and have eschewed demand management for either domestic or international objectives. Both governments have plenty of room for expansionary fiscal policy and have high-saving citizens to whom to sell bonds. The continued series of budget austerities of these governments seem quite misguided. Both countries have domestic needs, individual and collective, to which their unused potential product could be devoted. Both could expand their assistance to the less developed countries. It is high time for these reluctant locomotives to pull their share of the weight of the world economic train.

Macroeconomic expansion is the key to progress against unemployment. It will not solve all the problems, to be sure. The pathology of urban neighbourhoods that condemns nearly half of black youth to unemployment cannot be cured by monetary and fiscal policy. The same is true of growing youth unemployment in Europe. Macro policies and general prosperity will not restore the old high-wage jobs in smoke-stack industries in the American Midwest or the Ruhr. There is plenty of room and need for intelligent public policies to treat these difficult cases. But they will be hopeless unless prosperity and growth are restored. That is the first and highest priority.

From an international standpoint, policy corrections are needed both in the United States and in the other locomotives of the world economy. These require international co-operation. Monetary stimulus by any single country acting alone expands home demand and at the same time depreciates its currency to the benefit of its exports and to the detriment of its trading partners. Internationally concerted monetary stimulus that lowers interest rates simultaneously everywhere can give the whole world economy a boost, expanding everybody's exports and imports and creating no trade imbalances. The United States is in the position to take the lead. Since our interest and exchange rates are too high, other countries could lower interest rates by smaller amounts, narrowing the differential and engineering an orderly decline in the exchange value of the dollar. Continuing on the present course may at any time provoke a disorderly decline of the dollar.

In fiscal policy, the United States would be shifting to a tighter budget while other countries would substitute for their fiscal restrictions expansionary measures appropriate to the economic situations in their own economies and in the world at large. These monetary and fiscal actions should be the major agenda of the next economic summit conference; no topics deserve higher priority.

Can the major economic powers effectively co-ordinate their macroeconomic policies? On the record, the prospects are not good. It is true that central banks agreed, after the second oil shock, on single-minded disinflationary policy. The heads of the seven economic summit governments affirmed the priority at their Venice and Ottawa meetings in 1980 and 1981 respectively. Since that was the disposition of each country individually, agreement and synchronization were not difficult to achieve. At Williamsburg in 1983 unemployment and stagnation were clearly the pressing macroeconomic problems of the day. The best the group could do was to commit its governments to attack their structural budget deficits. Fortunately, President Reagan, the target of this vote, did not take it seriously. Unfortunately, his peers did.

The nine annual economic summits[14] have usually concentrated on energy, trade and commerce with the Soviet bloc. At the Bonn summit of 1978, however, the United States succeeded – in return for pledging decontrol of its domestic oil prices, a long overdue reform – in persuading reluctant allies to fire up their locomotives. Several governments promised increased growth of output. West Germany and France agreed to specific amounts of extra fiscal stimulus, 1 per cent and 0.5 per cent respectively. Japan and the United Kingdom had already instituted expansionary budget measures – Japan in response to American diplomatic pressure prior to the summit. The United States, whose recovery had been running ahead of the others, promised modest fiscal contractions. Six months later the Shah of Iran was overthrown. The world was hit by the second oil shock, a new spurt of inflation, and international financial disarray. The locomotive theory of the Carter administration was discredited, along with demand management in general. That legacy stands in the way of any internationally co-ordinated recovery program, even though the locomotive theory seems quite correct in today's circumstances.

Perhaps our leaders could be inspired by an earlier example. As the 1960s began, the world economy had been beset by a slump, by an unpleasant history of inflation, and by international monetary disturbances. The United States had suffered two recessions in quick succession, designed to bring down an unacceptably high inflation rate and to protect the dollar. As recovery from the slump began, the Ministerial Council of the OECD announced that the member nations (which did not yet include Japan) had pledge themselves to aim for a 50 per cent growth of output by the end of the decade for the group as a whole. The council noted that this growth would not only increase the welfare and strength of the member countries but would also lead to an increased flow of resources to developing countries. [15] Though this declaration was a statement of hope and intent, it was taken seriously by member governments both individually and in their consultations with each other on specific macroeconomic issues. In the event, the growth target was fulfilled with room to spare.

The present situation is more serious and more difficult. It will take statesmanship and imaginative leadership to turn the 1980s from a decade of unemployment and stagnation to one of prosperity and progress, from a period of discord in the alliance over competition and trade to one of co-operation and mutual benefit. Alliances are strengthened not just by resolving conflicts of interest but by undertaking together enterprises that offer substantial benefits to all. Macroeconomic policy co-ordination is a good place to begin.

NOTES

I am greatly indebted to Gabriel de Kock for his capable research assistance and instruction, but the opinions and errors are my own responsibility. I have benefited greatly from the expertise of Sylvia Ostry, both from personal conversation and from her article, 'The World Economy: Marking Time,' *Foreign Affairs, America and the World* (1983).

This paper appeared originally in *Unemployment and Growth in the Western Economies*, ed Andrew J. Pierre (New York: Council on Foreign Relations Inc, 1984), 79–112.

1 For the tale well-told see Charles P. Kindleberger, *The World in Depression* (Berkeley: University of California Press, 1973), especially chapters 6 through 8 and 11. It should be required reading for the economic statespersons of the 1980s.

2 For analysis and projection of Third World debt problems, see William R. Cline, *International Debt and the Stability of the World Economy*, (Washington, DC: Institute for International Economics, 1983). Cline shows how solvency depends on export volume and terms of trade highly sensitive to OECD economies' real growth and on restoring a positive margin between debtor countries' export growth rates and the interest rates at which they borrow.

3 Herbert Giersch, 'Aspects of Growth, Structural Change, and Employment – A Schumpeterian Perspective,' and Michael Bruno and Jeffrey Sachs, 'Supply versus Demand Approaches to the Problem of Stagflation,' in *Macroeconomic Policies for Growth and Stability: A European Perspective*, ed Giersch, Symposium 1979 (Tübingen: Mohr, for the Institut für Weltwirtschaft an der Universität Kiel, 1981)

4 Jeffrey D. Sachs, 'Real Wages and Unemployment in the OECD Countries,' *Brookings Papers on Economic Activity, No. 1* (Washington, DC: Brookings Institution, 1983); Shelia Bonnell, 'Real Wages and Employment in the Great Depression,' *Economic Record*, September 1981, 227–81

5 J.M. Keynes, *The General Theory of Employment, Interest, and Money* (New York: Harcourt, Brace & Co., 1936)

6 J.T. Dunlop, 'The Movement of Real and Money Wages,' *Economic Journal*, No. 48 (September 1938), 413–34

7 The OECD Economic Outlook series and Economic Surveys of particular countries are indispensable sources. The Bruno-Sachs paper cited in note 3 and the Sachs paper cited in note 4 are important in advancing the argument that supply limits and the 'wage-gap' were the important constraints on output in OECD economies outside North America after OPEC I. However, in the second paper Sachs concludes that a large component of European unemployment in 1981 was Keynesian, and presumably an even larger proportion of 1983–4 unemployment is attributable to deficient demand. In a study for the Center for Economic Policy Studies of the European Community, R. Dornbusch, G. Basevi, O. Blanchard, W. Buiter, and R. Layard, 'Marcoeconomic Prospects and Policies for the European Community' (Brussels, April 1983), argue the case for a co-ordinated expansion. See Wolfgang Franz, 'German Unemployment and Stabilization Policy,' *European Economic Review*, No. 21 (1983), for a careful econometric analysis leading to the conclusion that the West German natural rate of unemployment is now around 4 per cent or 4.7 per cent, according to an amendment by R.J. Gordon in the same issue.

8 R.J. Flanagan, D.W. Soskice, and Lloyd Ulman, *Unionism, Economic Stabilization, and Income Policies: European Experience* (Washington, DC: Brookings Institution 1983), chapter 5

9 Cited and quoted in translation by Dornbusch et al, 'Macroeconomic Prospects.' Giersch's article is 'Kaufkraft und Löhne,' from Deutsche Bundesbank, *Auszüge aus Presseartikeln* (6 November 1982).

10 Koichi Hamada and Yoshio Kurosaka, 'The Relationship between Production and Unemployment in Japan: Okun's Law in Comparative Perspective,' paper presented at International Seminar on Macroeconomics, Paris, Maison des Sciences de l'Homme, June 1983

11 The theory is associated in the economics profession with the 'new classical macroeconomics' and the 'rational expectations' revolution. Independently the late William Fellner set forth the 'credible threat' policy in several papers and in his book *Towards a Reconstruction of Macroeconomics* (Washington, DC: American Enterprise Institute, 1976). For exposition and criticism of these ideas see the papers of McCallum, Fellner, Tobin, and Okun in *Journal of Money, Credit and Banking*, November 1980, part 2. For tests of the theory against the recent disinflationary recession, see papers by George Perry and by Fellner and Philip Cagan in *Bookings Papers on Economic Activity*, No. 2 (Washington, DC: Brookings Institution, 1983)

12 The ambiguity arises from an unusual discrepancy between the gains in employment reported in the household survey by workers and those reported in the establishment survey by employers. The former is the higher number; possibly the reduction of unemployment, remarkably large considering the growth of output, is an overstatement.

13 Otto Eckstein, 'Disinflation,' *Data Resources Economic Studies Series*, No. 114 (October 1983)

14 For a useful review of economic summitry, see George de Menil and Anthony M. Solomon, *Economic Summitry* (New York: Council on Foreign Relations, Inc.), 30–4 and 78–9.

15 Reported in *Economic Report of the President*, 1962 (Washington, DC: US Government Printing Office, 1962), 38

W. R. DYMOND

Prospects

The purpose of this paper is threefold: (1) to present an overview of employment and unemployment over the past recession and the current recovery and some medium-term forecasts of employment and unemployment; (2) to identify some significant inter-country differences in employment and labour supply trends; (3) to identify and describe several factors that may be said to underlie these trends.

An estimated[1] 20,000 net new jobs will have to be created every day in the five years 1984-9 if the level of unemployment in the OECD (Organization for Economic Cooperation and Development) area is to return to its 1979 level of 19 million from the 32.3 million of 1983. The distribution of the needed job growth would be 40 per cent for North America, roughly the same for western Europe, and 10 per cent for Japan. In terms of performance during 1984, North America exceeded this rate (primarily due to the United States), Japan came close to the target, but western European employment continued to decline.

While employment growth is expected to pick up in most OECD countries and to remain particularly strong in the United States, it is unlikely to result in significant declines in unemployment apart from the United States. Although the fall in employment in western Europe stopped in 1984, after having continued for over three years, the labour force will continue to expand. As a consequence, western European unemployment was expected to increase from a current level of over 18 million to nearly 20 million by the end of 1985.

During the 1979-82 recession, the OECD unemployment rate worsened dramatically, rising from 5.1 per cent in 1979, to peak at 9.1 per cent in the first half of 1983. The rate then declined to 8.8 per cent in the second half of

1983. This modest decline for the area as a whole, the first since 1973, has been confined to a few countries – Canada, Sweden, West Germany, Australia, and especially the United States, the latter because of a major expansion of employment.

In western Europe, however, employment continued to fall through the second half of 1983, with large variations among countries. Employment decreases were particularly large in Austria, France, Ireland, the Netherlands, Portugal, and Spain, while in the United Kingdom, after three and a half years of uninterrupted decline, employment growth resumed. With a continued rise in the labour force surpassing modest rates of employment growth in western Europe as a whole, unemployment continued to rise through the second half of 1983 and the first half of 1984, reaching an estimated 11 per cent in mid-1984. In Japan, over this period, employment growth was modest, and despite stronger output growth, given a parallel sharp acceleration in the growth of the labour force, the unemployment rate reached 2.7 per cent in the first half of 1984.

Employment should continue to increase in the United States and Canada, although the rate of growth is likely to weaken in line with an expected deceleration of economic growth. Although overall western Europe employment stopped declining in the first half of 1984, the prospects are for rather widespread but modest employment gains, with only Austria, Belgium, France, Greece, and Luxembourg possibly recording further employment losses next year. Employment in Japan should continue to increase modestly, while Australia and New Zealand may record employment increases during the forecast period. During 1985, these patterns should lend a stabilization of US unemployment at around 7 per cent and a peaking of western European unemployment rates at around 11 per cent, albeit with considerable variation across countries. For Japan, the unemployment rate is expected to decline to 2.5 per cent, with some decline in unemployment in Australia and some rise in New Zealand.

There is also a general trend for the female unemployment rate to increase faster than the male rate although during the last recession this was masked by the greater cyclical sensitivity of male employment and hence of male unemployment. The recession also increased the youth unemployment rate both absolutely and relative to the adult rate. In most OECD countries the youth unemployment rate is currently expected to decline slightly and then stabilize. However, in some European countries, youth unemployment rates will likely continue to rise and could reach as high as 44 per cent in Spain, 35 per cent it Italy, and 28 per cent in France. A slight increase in youth unemployment is also projected for Japan, but the rate may not reach as high as 5 per cent.

Long-term unemployment varies considerably between countries and is particularly high in many western European countries. By 1985 it could approach 45 per cent of the total in France and exceed 40 per cent in the United Kingdom and 30 per cent in Germany. Long-term unemployment is highest among the adult unemployed, especially those aged over fifty, and it is slow to respond to economic recovery.

This recent picture of OECD employment and unemployment, and the prospects for the future, reflect the accumulation of numerous labour-force developments since the first oil shock in 1973. In particular, new jobs created through employment growth have been much more pronounced in North America and Japan than in western Europe. The slower employment growth in Europe reflects the declining industrial and agricultural sectors that are important components of the European economy. In contrast, in North America and Japan the declining agricultural sector and the slow-growing industrial sector are not as important components of the economies, and the negative or slow growth of these sectors has been more than offset by the rapidly growing service sector, which is an important component of the North American and Japanese economies. In essence, the slower European growth in employment reflects, in part at least, a changing industrial structure from traditional agriculture and industry toward the service sector – a change toward which European economics have been slow to adapt. This retention of workers in the declining sectors may have exacerbated unemployment in western Europe relative to North America and Japan, where these declining or slow-growing sectors are less important and where employment has shifted to the expanding service sector.

The growing disparity in unemployment between western Europe and North America and Japan was moderated somewhat by the fact that the European economies did not have to absorb a labour force that was increasing as rapidly as in North America and Japan. In addition, hours worked declined more rapidly in Europe than in North America and Japan, possibly absorbing some potential unemployment. Were it not for their slower labour-force growth and more rapid decline in hours worked, European countries likely would have experienced an even greater deterioration in their unemployment relative to North America and Japan.

Over the past decade the positive employment performance in North

America, as compared to the negative performance of western Europe, has been associated with almost continuous increases in unemployment in western Europe, whereas in North America unemployment has fluctuated with the business cycle and exhibited an upward trend. During the 1960s and early 1970s the average unemployment rate in major OECD countries (except Italy and Canada) was at roughly half the US rate; by 1983 the unemployment rate in Europe approached or exceeded that of the United States. The differing employment performance as between western Europe and the United States over the years since the first oil shock up to 1982 cannot be explained in terms of differential gross domestic product (GDP) or output growth, as the patterns were nearly identical in the two areas. The differential employment performance is the subject of differing empirical analyses and theories, including neo-classical explanations (wage inflexibility), Keynesian explanations (inadequate demand), and structuralist adjustment theories (market rigidities). Some light on this debate may be shed by identifying some of the critical economic variables that affect the differential performance of employment as between western Europe and the United States.

Given the roughly comparable output performance over the period 1973–82, stagnant employment performance for western Europe means by definition that productivity increases for western Europe have been much greater than for the United States. (Calculations indicate that for the years 1973 to 1982 the averge annual productivity growth was 0.6 per cent in the United States and 2.8 per cent for the four major European economies.) Western European enterprises may have responded to the need to increase output by increasing productivity rather than by increasing employment, or their increased unemployment may have meant that only the most productive workers remained. In addition, western European economies are more oriented to the manufacturing sector (where productivity increases are technically more feasible than in the service sector).

Real labour costs over the years 1973–81 have risen much more in western Europe than in the United States, both absolutely and relative to the price of capital and energy. Also, non-wage labour costs in 1978 (the latest date for which figures are available) were 43.7 per cent of total labour costs in France, 40.8 per cent in Germany, and 43.0 per cent in the Netherlands, compared to only 26.0 per cent in the United States.[2] Lastly, in both Europe and the United States, in sectors (e.g. manufacturing) where labour costs grew substantially, employment grew slowly (in the United States) or fell (in Europe). In contrast, where labour costs grew slowly (e.g. services) employment expanded. While causality can be difficult to establish, the evidence does suggest that high labour costs can be a barrier to employment expansion and the reduction of unemployment.

North America's employment performance can largely be explained by cyclical developments, although undoubtedly structural factors play a role particularly from the large influx of youths and women. Western Europe's employment performance, influenced by the responses to the first two oil shocks, is largely conditioned by structural factors that have developed over a long period and are complicated by more restrictive fiscal and monetary policies in recent years. Comparative levels of unemployment substantially understate the degree of labour-market slack in western Europe because of higher rates of decline in participation rates for older workers, reductions in hours, and greater increases in part-time employment.

The evidence suggests that the western European response to rates of output growth comparable to that of North America in the decade prior to 1982 have been through much higher productivity growth as a consequence of the high price of labour in relation to capital and energy and the relative inflexibility of wages at both the macro and micro level. There are also other elements of greater labour-market rigidity in western Europe, including higher non-wage labour costs which discourage employers from hiring labour and reduce their capacity to adjust to market changes. All these factors act as a drag on employment growth and the capacity of labour markets to adjust to change.

The critical policy implications point in the direction of increasing the flexibility of wage determination through making collective bargaining more responsive to economic constraints, modifying social policy measures to reduce disincentives, reducing taxes on employment, and strengthening training and labour-market adjustment measures. Such measures should help to improve the efficiency and flexibility of labour markets so as to create a better basis for increasing economic and employment growth and to reduce the natural rate of unemployment.

The central problems of unemployment in most western European countries are high youth unemployment combined with continuing and growing long-term unemployed (over 1 year) which amounts to 40 per cent or more of total unemployment in many countries. While the problem of priority in access to employment between youth and prime-age or older long-term unemployed is a difficult political choice, the primary priority should go to youth. However, there is a secondary priority (particularly as employment expands again) to improve the competitive position of the long-term unemployed through retraining and other incentives and to assist the least competitive older workers to withdraw from the regular labour market through early retirement or community employment programs.

NOTES

The text is the sole responsibility of the author and is not the responsibility of the OECD or its member countries.

1 Much of the data and analyses contained in this paper is based on OECD *Economic Outlook No. 35* (Paris, July 1984) and OECD *Employment Outlook* (Paris, September 1984).
2 Swedish Employers Confederation, 'Wages and Total Labour Costs for Workers,' *International Survey* (Stockholm, 1980)

MICHAEL ELLMAN

Eurosclerosis?

The divergent experience with respect to unemployment of the United States on the one hand and western Europe on the other hand has moved to the centre of political debate in western Europe. Whereas in the current upswing US unemployment has fallen sharply and employment has grown significantly, in western Europe unemployment has continued to rise and employment has barely increased (Dymond, this volume). Not only is unemployment higher in western Europe than in the United States, but its average duration is much longer (six months versus one month) (Albert and Ball 1983, 12). In 1983, those unemployed for over a year accounted for 40 per cent of western European unemployment but only 13 per cent of North American unemployment (OECD, 1984, 9). Further, whereas in the ten years to 1983 there was a net loss of 1.5 million jobs in OECD Europe, there was a net gain of 15.8 million jobs in the United States.

This divergent experience has given rise to the diagnosis of 'Euro-sclerosis.' According to this view, which has become orthodox among policy-makers in a number of western European governments and central banks and also in some interntional agencies, the divergent experience results from the lesser freedom of the market mechanism to operate in western Europe. The downward inflexibility of real wages, the welfare state, restrictions on the right of employers to fire redundant workers, high minimum wages, and a political and cultural climate hostile to enterprise have prevented the price mechanism fulfilling its normal function of match-ing supply and demand. In the United States, in contrast, the flexibility of the economy, relatively unhindered by counter-productive government regulations, and stimulated by a positive attitude to entrepreneurship and profits, has enabled employment creation to flourish. Is there any evidence for the 'Eurosclerosis' diagnosis, or is it simply hypothesis based on tradi-tional neo-classical reasoning?

The view that current unemployment was not Keynesian, to be cured by increasing demand, but structural, to be cured by cutting real wages, emerged in the Netherlands in the mid-1970s. For example, den Hartog and Tjan (1976) argued that higher real wages lead to accelerated scrapping of old capacity and thus a decline in employment growth or employment. This kind of unemployment is structural rather than Keynesian in the sense that, given the level of value added per unit of output, there is no way in which the economically obsolescent equipment can be profitably used at the prevailing level of real wages, regardless of the level of demand. Hence variations in the level of effective demand are entirely ineffective in determining the level of employment, whereas changes in the level and rate of growth of real wages have a dominant importance in determining the level and rate of growth (or decline) of employment. The crucial behavioural assumption that distinguishes the den Hartog–Tjan world from the Keynesian world concerns price formation. In the former, firms are price-takers and (if employment is to be maintained in the medium and long run) the level of real wages has to adjust to the value added generated by production. In the latter, firms are price-makers and, given enough demand, can set prices on marginal output so as to ensure profitability.

Emphasis on labour costs as a cause of unemployment has been increased by the contrast between developments in western Europe and the United States. In the United States the expansion of employment in recent years has been largely in low-wage service jobs. In much of western Europe such jobs cannot come into existence in the legal sector (as opposed to the 'underground' economy) given the high level of labour costs resulting from minimum-wage legislation, the burden of taxes and social security contributions, and the activities of trade unions in the legal sector. Although in many western European countries there are many people (e.g. women, immigrants, young people) who would be prepared to accept low wages to enter the labour market, the labour aristocracy (mainly prime-age males) is well organized to repel them.

The structuralist diagnosis, of which the paper of den Hartog and Tjan (criticized sharply in de Klerk et al 1977) was one of the earliest expositions, gave rise to three kinds of work: empirical studies of the relative importance of different kinds of unemployment, theoretical studies of various kinds of unemployment, and empirical studies of the price formation process.

Driehuis (1978) distinguished between labour-market failures ('search structuralism'), demand, and cost factors as explanations of unemployment. His results indicate that in 1975, about two-thirds of the unemployment in the

United Kingdom, France, and Belgium was caused not by cost, demand, or cyclical factors but by problems internal to the operation of the labour market ('search structuralism'). Hence, neither real-wage cuts nor government anti-cyclical policies would have been the most effective means of tackling unemployment. Rather, appropriate remedial labour-market policies include:

a) improvement of on-the-job experience combined with the abolition of the minimum wage for young workers;
b) reduction of the sensitivity of employment to changes in demand;
c) raising the quality of jobs and reducing bad employment habits, physical disability, and psychological problem;
d) subsidizing firms and public employment for workers who are marginal or difficult to place;
e) abolition of the minimum wage;
f) elimination of the perverse effects of employment benefits;
g) improvement of inter-firm and inter-regional migration and/or the regional redistribution of production.

Driehuis professed agnosticism as to which of these policies, alone or in combination, would be most effective.

This paper was interesting for its stress on the mismatch between the demand and the supply of particular sorts of labour as a cause of unemployment and for its scepticism about both real-wage cutting and demand management as solutions to the unemployment problem. It was followed by a large number of empirical studies of the labour market (e.g. Hartog 1980; Wilkinson 1981).

The empirical rediscovery of non-Keynesian types of unemployment naturally led to theoretical studies about the relation between various types of unemployment (e.g. Malinvaud 1977; 1980a; 1980b; 1984). Malinvaud's distinction between classical unemployment, resulting from a shortage of capital, and Keynesian unemployment, resulting from a shortage of demand, and his conviction that both are important in contemporary Europe have been widely accepted. In his discussion of classical unemployment Malinvaud (1977, 108–9) refers to the 'convincing' paper of den Hartog and Tjan as providing a firm empirical basis for his analysis.

One aspect of European writing on unemployment theory is scepticism about 'modern classical macro-economics' (Buiter 1980). For example, the idea that the general labour market is always in equilibrium and that observed changes in employment simply represent intertemporal substitution (Lucas & Rapping 1970) strikes Malinvaud (1984, chapter 1) as implausible on both theoretical and empirical grounds. Andrews & Nickell (1982) examined unemployment in the United Kingdom since the Second World War, contrasting the equilibrium and disequilibrium approaches and concluded that the former did not fit the facts.

Given the key role of price formation in determining whether unemployment is classical or Keynesian, it is natural that the price formation process has received renewed attention. Coutts, Godley, and Nordhaus (1978) argued that British industrial prices are determined by normal costs and are independent of demand. This argument suffered from two weaknesses. First, it was unable to explain the observed post-war decline in the mark-up, as pointed out by the authors themselves. Second, their claims that there is no relation between British industrial prices and the prices of competitive imports cannot be sustained (Sylos-Labini 1979a; 1979b). Coutts, Godley, and Nordhaus did demonstrate that costs are of great importance in industrial price formation in Britian, but they certainly did not establish that classical unemployment there is impossible.

An important aspect of 'Eurosclerosis' concerns the impact on the economy of a rise in raw material prices (relative to output prices). If there is such a rise, then the maintenance of full employment requires a fall in real wages (assuming there is no Keynesian unemployment prior to the rise in raw material prices). Otherwise profits, and hence investment and economic activity in general, will be squeezed, so generating unemployment. If real wages are sticky downward (e.g. because of trade unions or Keynesian governments or both) then growing unemployment will result. Bruno and Sachs (1982), for example, provide evidence that such input-price shocks account for a significant part of the observed decline in economic growth and increase in unemployment in British manufacturing. The two energy shocks of the 1970s, in which energy prices suddenly rose very sharply and subsequently stayed well above their former levels, plus the food price shock of 1972–4 and the sharp rise in the US dollar in the 1980s rapidly became part of the conventional wisdom about the reasons for the end of the great post-war boom (1951–73).

According to some authors (e.g. Benjamin and Kochin 1979, 1982; Minford 1983; Minford and Peel 1981), an important factor explaining the high level of unemployment in the United Kingdom in the 1920s and throughout western Europe today is an excessively high level of unemployment benefits. For example, Minford and Peel (1981) have estimated that in the United Kingdom, 'allowing for benefits in kind and the cost of working, a man with a wife and two children would obtain *permanently* in benefits in living standard about three-quarters as good as he would on *average earnings*.' Such benefits can make unemployment more attractive than working and they can enable people to afford to be unemployed more often and for longer periods.

There are two problems with this thesis as an explanation of the current high and rising unemployment levels in western Europe. First, unemployment benefits in fact are not as high and do not last so long as is sometimes suggested (Atkinson 1982; Dilnot and Morris 1983; OECD 1984, chapter 6). Second, in the current recession rising unemployment is associated with falling income replacement rates of unemployment insurance. One would have to assume a very odd lag structure in order to explain the current rising unemployment by the improved replacement rates of the 1960s and 1970s.

Another widely accepted view is that the increased unemployment in western Europe is a result of the rapid growth of the state sector in the 1950s, 1960s, and 1970s. The share of public expenditure in GDP has grown rapidly throughout the OECD since the mid-1960s and currently in a number of western European countries significantly exceeds the level in countries such as Australia, Japan and the United States, with Canada in an intermediate position.

Bacon and Eltis (1976) argued that if workers defended their after-tax disposable income, then rising public expenditures would generate and sustain an inflationary process. Also (albeit with some exceptions), if firms were not prepared to accept a deterioration in their balance-sheet ratios, then rising public expenditure would cause a decline in private investment and reduce economic growth and hence generate unemployment. Since inflation and low investment (and hence low growth and high unemployment) were the chief economic problems in western Europe in the 1970s, and low investment is the main problem of the 1980s, the Bacon-Eltis argument provides a theoretical mechanism that could be of major importance in explaining the current lamentable economic position in western Europe.

A similar line of research concerned the balance budget multiplier, which, if positive, implies that an increase in government expenditure financed by increasing taxes will increase the national income. This proposition played an important role in the theory of the welfare state. Originally a radical and surprising result, for a whole generation of economists it was so obvious as not to need arguing. Commenting on Reaganomics, Cornwall (1983, 220) simply assumes that cutting expenditure and taxes by the same amount cannot increase output, because 'the balanced budget multiplier theorem tells us that by cutting taxes and Government spending by similar amounts, GNP falls by the size of the budget cuts, but disposable income is unchanged.'

The possibility that the balanced budget multiplier might be negative seems to have been first extensibly discussed in the Netherlands in the mid-1970s. This discussion reflected a situation in which the attempt, after the first oil shock, to use Keynesian demand management techniques failed to have the desired and expected results. A recent estimate of the value of the negative balanced budget multiplier for various countries (Knoester 1983) suggests that after five years an increase in public spending of 1 per cent of GDP financed by a simultaneous increase in direct taxes or social security contributions reduced output by 2 per cent in West Germany, 3 per cent in the Netherlands, 1 per cent in the United Kingdom, and 2 per cent in the United States. The multipliers, combined with the increase in public expenditure that took place in the 1970s, are able on their own to explain more than 100 per cent of the increase in unemployment in the Netherlands, West Germany, and the United States and most of the increase in unemployment in the United Kingdom (Knoester 1983, 573).

Although this phenomenon may well have been important for the 1970s (Knoester's model was estimated for the 1960s and 1970s), it does not seem able to explain the high and rising western European unemployment levels of the 1980s. In this recent period fiscal orthodoxy is on the offensive, the share of public expenditure is being stabilized or reduced, the burden of taxes and contributions is being stabilized or reduced, labour militancy on the wages front is greatly reduced compared with the 1960s and 1970s, and profits are reviving (because of cyclical factors, government subsidies, and a decline in real energy and raw material prices).

An interesting and important aspect of the general 'crisis of the welfare state' (OECD 1981) is the way the welfare state can function as a built-in destabilizer (Ellman 1984a; 1984b). As is well known, in the short run the welfare state is a built-in stabilizer. When the business cycle turns down, the decline is less than it would otherwise be since social insurance and welfare programs pump extra money into the economy. In the long run, however, the situation is different. The social insurance system may prevent employment from stabilizing, let alone recovering. This is because of its supply-side effect of increasing costs and squeezing profits and thereby reducing employment and output. When unemployment rises, the burden of taxes and social security contributions necessary to finance the increase in unemployment and welfare benefits rises. This increase in costs itself wipes out jobs. Firms that are price-takers (e.g. because of international competition) find their profit margins squeezed or are forced into bankruptcy. Firms that fix prices on a cost-plus basis lose overseas and domestic markets to foreign competition. Firms transfer economic activity to countries where labour costs are lower and profit margins higher; they engage in labour-saving investment, substituting relatively cheap capital goods for expensive labour. The rise in unemployment caused by the reaction of firms to higher costs leads to higher taxes and social security contributions to finance the increase in unemployment and welfare benefits. The higher taxes and social security contributions lead to higher unemployment, and so on in a vicious circle. This built-in destabilizer effect is particularly severe in countries where the welfare state is financed by payroll taxes that fall most heavily on labour-intensive businesses in the market sector. Naturally this built-in destabilizer effect will be biggest in a small economy where the price level is determined by foreign competition and the authorities successfully pursue a hard currency exchange rate policy.

The idea that an important cause of the high and rising unemployment in contemporary western Europe is the past excessive growth of the public sector has become widely accepted. Hence in most western European countries the 1980s have seen attempts to reduce this rate of growth, to reduce the importance of the budget mechanism and expand the role of the market mechanism. Although this has not so far been successful in significantly reducing unemployment, it is possible that this is a result of the long time lags involved. It is well known that demand management policies have significant time lags before they produce their full effects. One might expect that supply-side policies would have still longer lags.

Employment protection legislation which inhibits employers from firing redundant employees has been cited as explaining from zero to a quarter of the rise in unemployment in the United Kingdom between the mid-1950s and the mid-1970s (Andrews and Nickell 1982) and as having an adverse effect on the demand for labour in France (Malinvaud 1984, 109). While employment protection legislation may explain a part of the current unemployment, it can scarcely explain its size and rapid growth. In the Netherlands, for example, dismissal of an employee without the prior written permission of the local labour exchange has been illegal since 1945, but that did not prevent the great post-war increase in employment.

Another aspect of the 'Eurosclerosis' diagnosis is the idea that in western Europe the environment for entrepreneurship in general and for new business in particular is very poor, hence inhibiting the job creation that Birch (1979) argues comes primarily from the activities of small firms in the United States. Armington and Odle (1982) argued that Birch's conclusions are one-sided and partly misleading, and Huisman et al (1980) showed that the situation in western Europe differed sharply between countries. Partly as a result of this research there has been a flood of policy initiatives throughout western Europe in recent years to stimulate and encourage small firms. These include enterprise zones, state guarantees for bank loans to new firms, tax concessions to providers of equity capital to new or young firms, worsening of the pay and conditions of employment in the public sector, and reductions in corporation tax and employers' social security contributions. The entire social and political climate for small business has been radically improved. However, the severe recession of 1980–2 and low growth since then, combined with sharp international competition and high real interest rates, have caused numerous bankruptcies.

The large rents or income gains resulting from the sale of domestic energy at high world prices (e.g. in the Netherlands in the early 1970s and the United Kingdom in the late 1970s and early 1980s) could also have contributed to European unemployment. This can occur as income from domestic energy sales substitutes for other sources of income (Kaldor 1981), or as it leads to an appreciation of the countries currency, thereby reducing manufacturing sales (Bond and Knöbl 1982) or to domestic deflationary policies. The importance of such unemployment-generating responses eminating from energy riches (termed the *Dutch disease*) is the subject of considerable debate, as is its inevitability as evidenced by the fact that Norway has deliberately and successfully pursued a full employment policy despite energy discoveries much larger in relation to its income than either the United Kingdom or the Netherlands. Employment in Norway has been maintained by expanding public-sector employment, a cautious depletion policy, exchange rate management, employment subsidies, and incomes policy. In May 1984, when the standardized OECD unemployment rate for the Netherlands was 14.5 per cent and for the United Kingdom 13.4 per cent, for Norway it was 3.2 per cent. A major cause of the current high and rising unemployment levels in western Europe is the decline in investment growth during the 1970s. Further, during the 1970s, a decreasing proportion of investment was expansionary investment which would have led to an addition to output and employment, and an increasing proportion was defensive investment, concerned with cost cutting and labour saving. The 'Eurosclerosis' diagnosis suggests that the causes of the decline in investment growth in western Europe are to be found in the welfare state aspects of the European economic environment. However, the decline in the rate of growth of investment has also manifested itself in Japan and the United States, neither of which are welfare states in the European sense.

Another possible diagnosis is that the causes of the decline in investment growth are internal to the investment process and are a natural result of leaving investment to market forces, which inevitably lead to long cycles characterized by alternating phases of investment hunger and investment satiation. One variant is the Marxist over-investment theory (Mazier 1982), according to which periods of rapid investment under capitalism, by absorbing the reserve army of labour and hence strengthening the labour movement, and by creating the possibility of producing more goods than can be sold under capitalist social relations, inevitably lead to over-investment and hence to periodic recessions.

Various policy conclusions follow from this type of analysis. According to van Duijn (1979; 1981), although long cycles are a normal and natural phenomenon in a market economy, the down phase can be shortened and the up phase lengthened by suitable policies aimed at simulating investment and growth. According to Marxists, over-investment crises can be overcome only by the socialization of the means of production. This line of argument was an important reason for the nationalizations carried out in the first phase of the Mitterand government's economic policy. According to Keynesians, the obvious policy is to increase public-sector investment.

When one focuses on low investment growth and the spread of defensive investment as the key factors explaining mass unemployment, then the 'Eurosclerosis' diagnosis appears one-sided. Perhaps 'Eurosclerosis' as a cause of unemployment is like minimum wage legislation – undoubtedly a cause of unemployment but quantitatively not very significant (Hughes and Perlman 1984, 123). The 'Eurosclerosis' argument is based on the idea that the current high and rising level of unemployment in western Europe is structural or classical rather than cyclical or Keynesian. Is this really so?

Despite the dominance of structuralists among policy-makers in contemporary western Europe, some Keynesians survive in the academic world. According to Maddison (1983) an important cause of high unemployment in western Europe is the deflationary policy stance now everywhere orthodox. Malinvaud (1977, 109) also observed: 'There is no doubt that the main features of the 1975 unemployment are again Keynesian. 'Similarly, Buiter and Miller (1981) have argued that the sharp rise in unemployment under Margret Thatcher is largely a result of demand restraint.

The Keynesian model was originally worked out for a closed economy. In it, an increase in consumption or investment leads to an increase in output and employment. In an open economy, however, an increase in domestic demand also leads to a worsening of the balance of payments (Kaldor

1971; Eltis 1976). Since for many years the rate of growth of international trade has exceeded that of national income in most countries, deficit financing in one country has become less and less effective in generating increased employment and more and more effective in generating a balance of payments crisis (as the Mitterand administration recently learned). Because of the high volume of trade within western Europe, the Community multiplier is much higher than individual country multipliers, and therefore the Keynesian recipe for western Europe is not national deficit financing (doomed to be reversed after a balance of payments crisis) but a simultaneous fiscal simulus throughout the Community.

Although intra-Community trade is large and important for all the Community members, exports to non-Community states are also important. The poor economic situation in many of them (debt crisis, low commodity prices, low growth rates) reduces the export markets of western Europe and partly explains the low growth there.

According to Keynesians, the current sharp contrast between employment development in the United States and that in western Europe is largely to be explained by differences in fiscal policies. In the United States, the inflation-adjusted structural budget balance moved in an expansionary direction throughout the period 1982–5. This was quite the opposite of the increasingly conservative fiscal policy pursued in most western European countries (OECD 1984, 28). The US policy was possible because it is a large country for which foreign trade is relative less important than for the smaller western European countries and because the rest of the world was prepared to finance the growing US current account deficit with capital inflows.

Adherents of the 'Eurosclerosis' diagnosis tend to subscribe to the view that full employment is the normal state of a market economy and unemployment an exceptional state of affairs which must have been caused by impediments of one kind or another to the smooth working of market forces. Both historical and theoretical analyses (Kornai 1980, chapter 11; Weitzman 1982) show that this is an illusion. Open unemployment is a normal attribute of the market economy, just as 'unemployment on the job' is a normal attribute of the administrative economy.

The unemployment problem is not uniformly serious throughout western Europe. Unemployment (seasonally adjusted as of June 1984) is well below the US level of 7.0 per cent in Sweden (2.8 per cent), Norway (3.2 per cent), and Austria (4.3 per cent). All three countries have adhered to full employment policies and rejected the current orthodoxy in the rest of the OECD. In all three countries, traditional Keynesian/welfare state weapons, such as currency depreciation (in Norway and Sweden), public investment, public-sector job creation, and income policy, have been successfully used to maintain full employment.

At a time when much is being written about 'Eurosclerosis,' it is important to be aware of the existence of 'Eurodynamism.' The rate of labour productivity growth for a number of years have been significantly higher in western Europe than in the United States (OECD 1984, 27).

To some extent this is a purely statistical phenomenon (Darby 1984). The growth of low-paid service-sector jobs in the United States naturally leads to a decline in measured aggregate productivity growth. In many service sectors 'output' is measured by, or mainly determined by, wage costs. The increase in employment in the fast-food sector, for example, simultaneously increases employment and reduces measured productivity growth. To some extent, however, it may be a real phenomenon. For example, Eckstein et al (1984, 46) estimate that the lead of labour productivity in manufacturing is now marginally higher in West Germany, France, and Italy (but much lower in the United Kingdom) than in the United States.

Given this discrepancy in the rates of labour productivity growth, just to hold the level of employment constant requires a higher rate of economic growth in western Europe than in the United States. (The alternative would be Luddism or the development of a low-wage service sector. The former is unattractive to business, the latter to organized labour.) Similarly, given the current low rate of economic growth and the rising (potential) labour force, even to maintain the western European unemployment rate at its current level requires a reduction in average time worked per person. This is now official policy throughout the European Community (except the United Kingdom). As European trade unions have long argued, a reduction in average hours worked is a natural way of spreading the unemployment over the whole working-age population rather than concentrating it in particular vulnerable groups (e.g. the young, immigrants, women). A reduction in average hours worked (with a corresponding reduction in real wages per employee) could be avoided by a higher rate of economic growth. So far, in western Europe this has been conspicuous by its absence.

Critics of 'Eurosclerosis' argue that the inflexibilities resulting from such factors as social welfare benefits, protection from sudden dismissal, and guaranteed real wages have led to 'Eurodynamism' rather than 'Eurosclerosis.' Whereas in a pure market economy workers may have good reason to resist technical progress (it may make them destitute after they lose their jobs), in a welfare state, workers co-operate with innovation, since it is no threat to them and holds out the prospect of higher real wages in the future (Osberg 1984).

Further, at a time when the welfare state is under attack, it is worth remembering its major achievements: the abolition of the financial insecurity of a purely market economy; the provision of basic needs for the entire population; a reduction in poverty and inequality; and more humanization of work. In view of these achievements it is not surprising that some North American authors (Fry 1979; Cornwall 1983; Ginsburg 1983) consider that there is much to learn from Europe in these areas.

The 'Eurosclerosis' diagnosis has been seized by long-standing opponents of the welfare state to provide arguments for their long-standing wish to alter the institutions of the OECD countries in a more market-oriented direction. That is one possible institutional change, but far from being the only one that might reduce unemployment (Ellman 1979; Weitzman 1984).

A widespread current view is that unemployment in western Europe is structural, resulting from such factors as excessive real wages, energy shocks, too large a public sector, the welfare state, employment protection legislation, and a hostile environment for entrepreneurs. In other words, unemployment is a result of too many restrictions on the free operation of market forces. There is no doubt that all these factors have caused some unemployment. The food/energy/dollar price shocks combined with sticky real wages probably did reduce employment. Obviously employment protection legislation and minimum wage legislation reduce the demand for labour. Moreover, the past excessive growth of the public sector seems to have been an important source of job losses in the market sector. Similarly, the Netherlands suffers from a lack of dynamic job-creating small firms. Hence measures to deal with these problems are likely to reduce unemployment in the long run.

Nevertheless, the 'Eurosclerosis' diagnosis is one-sided and partial. To a considerable extent, unemployment results precisely from leaving things to market forces. This is the case with the consequences of energy development in the United Kingdom and the Netherlands and with respect to the long cyclical downturns in investment. Conservative fiscal policy and limited export markets also have led to a shortage of effective demand. More generally, open unemployment is a normal attribute of a market economy, just as 'unemployment on the job' is a normal attribute of the administrative economy. OECD European countries like Sweden, Norway, and Austria have pursued conscious macroeconomic and labour-market policies to achieve their low unemloyment rates. The level of labour productivity in

Europe relative to that in the United States has risen sharply in the post-war period ('Eurodynamism'). Ultimately, the 'Eurosclerosis' diagnosis is based on one particular vision – the classical liberal one – of the good society.

Hence, while policies based on the 'Eurosclerosis' diagnosis are likely to have a favourable effect on employment, policies exclusively based on this diagnosis are unlikely to achieve their professed aims. In view both of the other causal factors at work and of the time lags involved, rolling back the welfare state and increasing the flexibility of the economic system, on their own, are not likely to produce full employment in the short run.

NOTE

I am grateful to the participants in the conference, Andre Gunder Frank, Joop Hartog, Louis Nicolini, Andrew Sharpe, and Geert Reuten, for helpful discussion. I am also grateful to the Economic Council of Canada for the financial assistance that made my participation in the conference possible. An expanded version of this paper is available as Research Memorandum no. 8506, Department of Economics, University of Amsterdam, Jodenbreestraat 23, 1011 NH Amsterdam, Netherlands.

REFERENCES

Albert, M., and R.J. Ball. 1983. *Naar Het Herstel van de Europese Economie in de Jaren Tachtig*, Report submitted to the European Parliament

Andrews, M. and S. Nickell. 1982. 'Unemployment in the UK since the War,' *Review of Economic Studies* 49, No. 5

Armington, C. and Odle, M. 1982. 'Small Business – How Many Jobs?' *The Brookings Review* 1 (winter)

Atkinson, A.B. 1982. 'Unemployment, Wages and Government Policy,' *Economic Journal*, March

Bacon, R., and W. Eltis. 1976. *Britain's Economic Problem: Too Few Producers.* London

Benjamin, D., and L. Kochin. 1979. 'Searching for an Explanation of Unemployment in Interwar Britain,' *Journal of Political Economy* 87, No. 3

– 1982. 'Unemployment and Unemployment Benefits in Twentieth Century Britain: A Reply to Our Critics,' *Journal of Political Economy* 90 (April)

Birch, D.L. 1979. *The Job Generation Process.* Cambridge Mass: MIT Press

Bond, M.E., and A. Knöbl. 1982. 'Some Implications of North Sea Oil for the UK Economy,' *IMF Staff Papers* 29 (September)

Bruno, M. and J. Sachs. 1982. 'Input Price Shocks and the Slowdown in Economic Growth: The Case of UK Manufacturing,' *Review of Economic Studies* 49, No. 5

Buiter, W.H. 1980. 'The Macroeconomics of Dr. Pangloss: A Critical Survey of the New Classical Macroeconomics, *Economic Journal* 90 (March)

Buiter, W.H., and M. Miller. 1981. 'The Thatcher Experiment: The First Two Years,' *Brookings Papers on Economic Activity* No. 2

Cornwall, J. 1983. *The Conditions for Economic Recovery*. New York: M.E. Sharpe

Coutts, K., W. Godley, and W. Nordhaus. 1978. *Industrial Pricing in the United Kingdom*. Cambridge: Cambridge University Press

Darby, M.R. 1984. 'The U.S. Productivity Slowdown: A Case of Statistical Myopia,' *American Economic Review* 74 (June)

Dilnot, A.W., and C.N. Morris. 1983. 'Private Costs and Benefits of Unemployment: Measuring Replacement Rates,' *Oxford Economic Papers* 35, No. 4

Driehuis, W. 1978. 'Labour Market Imbalances and Structural Unemployment,' *Kyklos* 31, No. 4

van Duijn, J.J. 1979. *De Lange golf in de economie*. Assen: Van Gorcum

– 1981. 'Economic Policy during a Depression.' Paper presented to a conference at the Graduate School of Management, Delft, April

Eckstein, O., et al. 1984. *The DRI Report on US Manufacturing Industries*. McGraw-Hill

Ellman, M. 1979. 'Full Employment – Lessons from State Socialism,' reprinted in M. Ellman, *Collectivisation, Convergence and Capitalism*. London: Academic Press

– 1984a. 'The Crisis of the Welfare State – the Dutch Experience,' in K.E. Boulding (ed), *The Economics of Human Betterment*. London: Macmillan

– 1984b. 'Recent Dutch Macro-economic Experience.' Paper presented at a symposium on macroeconomics, Ottawa, Macdonald Commission, June

Eltis, W. 1976. 'The Failure of the Keynesian Conventional Wisdom,' *Lloyds Bank Review* 122 (October)

Fry, J.A. (ed). 1979. *Industrial Democracy and Labour Market Policy in Sweden*. Oxford: Pergamon Press

Ginsburg, H. 1983. *Full Employment and Public Policy: The United States and Sweden*. Lexington, Mass: D.C. Heath

den Hartog, H. and H.S. Tjan. 1976. 'Investments, Wages, Prices and the Demand for Labour,' *De Economist* 124, No. ½

Hartog, J. 1980. *Tussen Vraag en Aanbod*, Leiden: Stenfert Kroese

Hughes, J.J., and R. Perlman. 1984. *The Economics of Unemployment.* Brighton, England: Wheatsheaf

Huisman, D., de Boer, A., Ketelaars, A.A.C., and Bonnock, G. 1980. *New Economic Activities.* Amsterdam: Indivers & SKIM

Kaldor, N. 1971. 'Conflicts in National Economic Objectives,' in N. Kaldor (ed), *Conflicts in Policy Objectives.* Oxford: Blackwell

– 1981. 'The Energy Issues,' in T. Barker and V. Brailovsky (eds). *Oil or Industry?* London: Academic Press

de Klerk, R.A., H.B. van den Laan, and K.B.T. Thio. 1977. 'Unemployment in the Netherlands: A Criticism of the den Hartog–Tjan Vintage Model,' *Cambridge Journal of Economics* 1 (September)

Knoester, A. 1983. 'Stagnation and The Inverted Haavelmo Effect: Some International Evidence,' *De Economist* 131, No. 4

Korrai, J. 1980. *Economics of Shortage.* Amsterdam: North Holland

Lucas, R.E., and L.A. Rapping 1970. 'Real Wages, Employment and Inflation,' in E.S. Phelps (ed), *Microeconomic Foundations of Employment and Inflation Theory.* New York: W.W. Norton

Maddison, A. 1983. 'Economic Stagnation since 1973,' *De Economist* 131, No. 4

Malinvaud, E. 1977. *The Theory of Unemployment Reconsidered* Oxford: Blackwell

– 1980a. *Profitability and Unemployment.* Cambrdige: Cambridge University Press

– 1980b. *Unemployment in Western Societies.* London: Macmillan

– 1984. *Mass Unemployment.* Oxford: Blackwell

Mazier, J. 1982. 'Growth and Crisis – A Marxist Interpretation,' in A. Boltho (ed), *The European Economy: Growth and Crisis.* Oxford: Oxford University Press

Minford, P. 1983. 'Labour Market Equilibrium in an Open Economy,' *Oxford Economic Papers* 35, No. 4

Minford, P., and D. Peel. 1981. 'Is the Government's Economic Strategy on Course?' *Lloyds Bank Review*, April

OECD. 1981. *The Welfare State in Crisis.* Paris: Organization for Economic Cooperation and Development

– 1984. *Employment Outlook.* Paris: Organization for Economic Cooperation and Development

Osberg, L. 1984. 'Star Spangled Economies,' *Marxism Today* September

Sylos-Labini, P. 1979a. 'Industrial Pricing in the United Kingdom,' *Cambridge Journal of Economics* 3 (June)

– 1979b. 'Prices and Income Distribution in Manufacturing Industry,' *Journal of Post Keynesian Economics,* Fall

Weitzman, M.L. 1982. 'Increasing Returns and the Foundations of Unemployment Theory,' *Economic Journal* (December)

Weitzman, M.L. 1984. *The Share Economy.* Cambridge Mass: Harvard University Press

Wilkinson, F. 1981. *The Dynamics of Labour Market Segmentation.* London: Academic Press

MARTIN NEIL BAILY

Rising unemployment in the United States

The unemployment rate in the United States is expected to remain above or close to 7 per cent over the next year (1985). If this forecast is accurate, the unemployment rate through 1980–5 will average more than 8 per cent. This compares with an average of 6.2 per cent for the 1970s, 4.8 per cent for the 1960s, and 4.5 per cent in the 1950s. The purpose of this study is to analyse the reason for this rising unemployment rate. This requires a determination of how much, if any, of this increase is due to rising cyclical unemployment (which can be cured by aggregate economic policies), and how much is due to structural causes.

Milton Friedman believes that a free-market economy will always move toward a level of use of its resources of capital and labour that is economically efficient. At this efficient point there are frictional and structural sources of unemployment, and the amount of such unemployment determines what he calls the natural rate of unemployment. In the short run, he says, fluctuations in money growth induce variations in both the unemployment rate and the inflation rate that may generate an apparent trade-off between the two. This is not a stable relationship that can or should be exploited for policy purposes.

Other economists, including me, disagree with Friedman and believe that at any given moment there is a short-run trade-off between inflation and unemployment that is very relevant for policy choices. But despite the differences between Friedman's analysis and those who accept the trade-off view, there is a sense in which Friedman's idea of a natural rate of unemployment has won broad acceptance. The working through of the wage-price spiral can mean that attempts to reduce unemployment below some critical value will result in continuously increasing inflation. This critical value of unemployment is now usually called the natural rate of unemployment, following Friedman's terminology.

The term *natural rate of unemployment* will be used here to denote the minimum level of unemployment that can be reached by demand policies without generating rising inflation. The level of the natural rate of unemployment is determined by the structure of the labour market, so that increases or decreases in the natural rate can be considered to be changes in the amount of structural and frictional unemployment. Fluctuations in the unemployment rate above or below the natural rate will be considered cyclical changes.[1] Frictional unemployment resulting from normal job turnover is included as part of the natural rate, so it is important to remember that when unemployment is equal to the natural rate, not all of this unemployment represents waste or hardship. A certain amount of job search associated with choosing careers or entering the labour market is efficient and desirable. However, the word 'natural' goes much too far in this direction. It implies that if the economy were to operate at its natural rate there would be no hardship or problem unemployment. And that is not true either. If it were not for the problem of inflation, there would be a good case for operating the economy with less unemployment than the natural rate.

The hard task now is to decide how much change there has been in the natural rate of unemployment, and the obvious way to approach this problem is to work from the definition of the natural rate as an inflation constraint. Many economists have attempted this task, but unfortunately the results have not been conclusive. However, all the studies recognize that changes in the demographic composition of the labour force have increased the natural rate. The differences among the studies come in assessing how much increase has taken place beyond that. At least until 1980 inflation fluctuated around a rising trend, and this means either that the natural rate was rising or that the inflation increase was due to supply shocks (such as the increased price of energy and food and the slowdown in productivity growth), or both.

Gordon (1982) looked directly at the rate of price inflation, taking careful account of all the different variables that influence inflation, including the supply shocks. He found no clear evidence that the natural rate has risen, apart from the demographic changes.

Medoff (1983) looked at the rate of wage change rather than at prices. He assumed that the supply shocks had no direct impact on wages but caused increased wage inflation only through the working out of the wage-price spiral. He concluded that after 1973 there was an increase in the natural rate of unemployment.

The basic reason for the different findings in the two studies is that they make very different estimates of the impact of the supply shocks on inflation. Medoff's results indicate that even though the supply shocks may have had a major immediate effect on inflation, their longer-run effect through the wage-price spiral was attenuated, because price increases feed back only partially into wage increases. In other words, when Gordon and Medoff divide the blame for high inflation in the 1970s between the effect of supply shocks and increases in the natural rate, they do it in rather different proportions. And it is not obvious who is correct; the data allow different interpretations.

Perry (1983) did not focus directly on whether or not the natural rate had risen. Rather, he was interested in understanding the decline in inflation that took place between 1981 and 1983. He found that by the middle of 1983 wage inflation had declined by more than could have been expected, suggesting that there has been no increase in the natural rate.[2]

The direct estimates of the natural rate have narrowed the possibilities, even though they are not in agreement. Once the supply shocks are accounted for and once the experience of 1981–3 is included, it is clear that there has been at most a small increase in the natural rate of unemployment in the United States, over and above the impact of demographic changes. Given that the studies of unemployment and inflation still leave room for doubt as to the relative importance of cyclical and structural/frictional factors in explaining the unemployment trends, it is important to examine other evidence in particular the dispersion of unemployment rates and the relation between unemployment and vacancies.

Suppose that the amount of rigidity in the labour market were diminishing, so that workers moved more quickly to the jobs, jobs moved more quickly to the workers, and training and retraining were taking place quickly and easily. Then the unemployment rates that are measured for different cities or for different types of workers would tend to equalize. This equalization would not be complete, but the decrease in structural rigidity in the labour market would be associated with a decrease in unemployment differentials. Conversely, more dispersion in unemployment rates across different labour markets would be a sign of greater labour market rigidity and structural unemployment. Solow (1964), for example, found that the dispersion of unemployment had not increased between the 1950s and early 1960s and thereby concluded that structural unemployment had not increased over that earlier period.

To provide a current analysis, I looked at unemployment rates broken down in three ways; by demographic group; by city (the thirty largest urban areas); and by industry. The dispersion of unemployment for each year is computed as the average absolute deviation of, for example, the different city unemployment rates from the overall rate of all the cities together. For each of the three categories comparisons of the dispersion of unemployment over time were made for a given level of the adult male unemployment rate to control for short-run or cyclical fluctuation that otherwise may have led to increased dispersion simply because the level of unemployment was increasing. This was done by plotting the dispersions against the adult male unemployment rate and observing whether these were upward shifts in the dispersion of unemployment (interpreted as increase in structural unemployment), for a given level of male unemployment, over time.

The evidence indicated a clear upward shift in the dispersion of unemployment rates by different demographic groups, providing empirical support for the demographic adjustments used in the inflation studies. During the 1960s and 1970s the composition of the labour force changed and the labour market was not able to absorb fully the group of relatively disadvantaged workers whose size increased. Similarly, a graph of the dispersion of unemployment across the major urban areas showed that there has been some increase in the geographic dispersion of unemployment, albeit the shifts are not as large as in the demographic case. The dispersion of unemployment rates across industries does not appear to have increased, suggesting that changes in industrial structure have not caused an increase in structural unemployment.

The basic conclusion from this examination of dispersions is that, in contrast to Solow's findings for the early 1960s, there is now some clear evidence of increased structural unemployment. But the evidence supports the idea that the problem has to do with people and, to some extent, regions. It is not a problem associated with declining industries. The results indicate that workers displaced by a declining industry do not have a major problem in finding re-employment, provided the area they live in is not depressed and provided they do not have the disadvantages associated with certain groups, including discrimination and lack of skills. Independent work by Bendick (1981), who has studied the post-layoff work/unemployment experience of displaced workers, confirms the importance of the status of the local labour market and the qualifications of the individual. He finds that the industry of previous employment plays a rather minor role in the experience of displaced workers.

Unemployment and vacancies can coexist for a number of reasons. The unemployed may lack the skills required for a job or may be unwilling to accept an available wage offer. It may take time for the worker and employer to find each other even in a well-functioning labour market. In general, there is an inverse relation, or Beveridge curve, between unemployment and vacancies that shows up over the course of the business cycle. In a boom the economy will move down the curve, with a falling unemployment rate and rising vacancies; in a recession the economy will move up the curve, with high unemployment and few vacancies. A shift of the entire curve away from the origin indicates that the natural rate of unemployment has risen; that is, there is a higher level of unemployment for every given level of job vacancies, and vice versa.

Except for a brief experiment in the 1960s the United States has not collected data on the vacancy rate. The only way to draw a Beveridge curve for the United States is to use the help-wanted index (HWI), reported by the Conference Board as a proxy for the vacancy rate. This can be plotted against the unemployment rate as adjusted by Perry (1970) to remove the effect of demographic change from the diagram.

For the period 1951–82 this proxy for the Beveridge curve clearly has moved out, indicating increased structural unemployment over and above the demographic changes. This evidence somewhat conflicts with the previous evidence suggesting that the increased structural unemployment eminated mainly from demographic changes. However, there are reasons to be cautious in accepting this new evidence, mainly because the HWI is a rather weak proxy for the true vacancy rate. First, it is constructed from a survey of the number of advertisements in the leading newspapers in the major cities. But most blue-collar jobs are not advertised. Production workers usually find their jobs through personal contacts. Second, there have been factors that may have caused an upward trend in the HWI that do not necessarily indicate an increasing mismatch between the unemployed and vacancies. In particular, more jobs may be advertised today than in earlier years because of equal opportunity laws. Also, more advertising may be done in the leading newspapers in the survey because rival newspapers have closed as the newspaper industry has become increasingly concentrated.

Because of the rather mixed findings so far, we turn now to consider alternative reasons why the natural rate of unemployment may have risen.

One important reason for increases in the natural rate of unemployment in the past twenty or thirty years has been the change in the composition of the labour force and of the unemployed. In 1955 white men over 24 accounted for 54 per cent of the labour force and 37 per cent of the unemployed. In 1979, this group was only 40 per cent of the labour force and only 20 per cent of the unemployed. In contrast, women, blacks, and especially young people have been increasing their shares of both the labour force and unemployment.

The impact of such demographic change can be illustrated by contrasting the official aggregate unemployment rate with the unemployment rate, adjusted for demographic changes, constructed by George Perry (1970). The differences between the two unemployment rates should indicate how much the natural rate has risen as a result of the demographic changes. The two unemployment rates are virtually identical in the early 1960s, but the gap between them then widens to 2 percentage points by the late 1970s, suggesting that the demographic changes pushed up the natural rate by 2 percentage points over this period. The gap is reduced slightly to 1.5 percentage points in the period 1980–2, reflecting the fact that the trends have begun to move more favourably for the natural rate, as the 'baby boom' generation gets older. The decline also reflects the fact that the 1980 and 1982 recesions hit the heavy industrial sectors of the economy especially hard, and adult men make up the bulk of employment in this sector.

Unemployment insurance (UI) is the main program designed to sustain the incomes of the jobless. UI may increase the unemployment rate both by encouraging individuals to prolong their spells of unemployment and by encouraging businesses to increase the number of layoffs they make.[3] There is empirical evidence to support the existence of both of these incentive effects, with the later being somewhat greater than the former. For example, Clark and Summers (1982) estimated that if the UI program did not exist in 1978 this would reduce the number of layoffs into unemployment by between one-fifth and one-quarter. The overall effect of the program on the natural rate of unemployment is substantially less than that, however, because only about one-half of the unemployed receive UI benefits.

Clark and Summers (1982) and Hamermesh (1981) indicate that the natural rate would be reduced by between one-half and one percentage point if there were no UI programs. This does not necessarily mean that the program has contributed to the upward trend in unemployment. After all, the program has existed since the 1930s. Examination of the two important measures of the generosity of the UI program reveals that while there has been an upward trend in the ratio of the average weekly benefit to average take-home pay, there has also been a downward trend in the fraction of the unemployed receiving benefits. If the two measures are combined to give an estimate of the fraction of lost wage earnings that are being replaced by UI, there is virtually no trend at all. The evidence does not support the hypothesis that the unemployment insurance program has caused an increased in unemployment in the United States in the past 25 years. The program does make the natural rate of unemployment a little higher than it would otherwise be. But that has been true for a long time. Moreover the program also brings substantial advantages. It reduces the risk of income loss and helps sustain demand during recessions.

Multiple-earner families are becoming more prominent, and hence may be more choosy about accepting jobs, given the alternative source of family income. In 1980, 49 per cent of unemployed husbands had working wives, and another 10 per cent had wives looking for work. In the same years, 81 per cent of unemployed wives had working husbands. We do not know the exact circumstances of all the unmarried unemployed. But we do know that nearly half of the unemployed teenagers (aged 16–19) were enrolled in school as their primary activity. It can be expected that most of those teenagers were being supported by their families. Teenagers were 26 per cent of the unemployed in 1979.

The increase in female employment could lead to an increase in the number of multiple-earner families and this could cause the natural rate of unemployment to rise. The evidence does not support this, however, because there have been countervailing trends (Klein 1983). Certainly there has been a rise in the employment rate in the economy (the fraction of the population employed), even though unemployment has been rising. The rise is more modest than one might have thought, however, because the labour-force participation of men over 50 has been declining.

The other trend that has offset the impact of increased female participation is the decreased stability of the family. Family groupings are smaller, and there are fewer husband-wife families, relative to the population. More women work now, partly because they are the only source of wage income for their families.

Transfer payments from governments to individuals also have been rising as a percentage of disposable income. Households were receiving 17 per cent of their disposable income from the government during the 1980–2 period. And most of the revenue for these transfer payments came from taxes paid out of wage income. The government now takes a substantial slice of the income that households receive from employment and returns it to the household sector again in forms that usually do not require employment and frequently discourage employment.

By far the biggest component of the transfers, however, consists of payments to the retired and the disabled. There is some evidence that these payments discourage employment, but no evidence that they result in higher measured unemployment. On the contrary, in the absence of these programs, many elderly and disabled persons would have had difficulty finding employment. Because of social security, such persons can drop out of the labour force and collect benefits. If anything, the growth of social security has probably lowered the natural rate. In a review of the overall effects of the growth of transfer payments on the natural rate, Hamermesh (1981) concludes that while transfer payments may increase joblessness, they are unlikely to have increased measured unemployment and have had no effect on the natural rate.

Structural change in the economy (i.e. changes in the mix of jobs that are available) can have an impact on the amount of structural unemployment. Employment in certain occupations or industries may decline, even though the level of demand in the economy as a whole is adequate. There were major shifts in employment shares between 1955 and 1979. Services, the government, and trade have substantially expanded their shares of employment, while agriculture, manufacturing, and self-employment have all contracted. The declining employment share in manufacturing has been taken as evidence that there are many displaced workers who are unemployed. Foreign trade, and Japanese competition in particular, are given as the causes of the decline in manufacturing.

The shifts of employment among industries, however, do not tell us whether or not there are fewer good jobs. To answer this we need to look at the distribution of employment by occupation. The reported distribution of employment by occupation gives almost no support to the view that the number of good jobs has been declining. This distribution has changed only moderately over the period 1959–79.[4] At the top of the occupational distribution, the number of managers and administrators has declined because the number of managers and administrators has declined because the number of small farmers has declined. There has been an offsetting rise in the number of professional and technical workers. The skilled and semiskilled blue-collar occupations, craft workers and operatives, have declined a little. However, all of the decline has been among operatives, the lower-skilled category. Suppose, for the sake of argument, that labourers, and sales, clerical, and service workers, are all assumed to be holding bad jobs; then the share of employment in bad jobs increased from 42 per cent in 1959 to 44 per cent in 1979, hardly a dramatic change.

If we examine the distribution of jobs by earnings rather than by occupation, there is more evidence to support the idea of a declining middle. The share of employment in jobs where the earnings are less than 80 per cent of average earnings has been increasing over time. To a considerable extent this changing pattern of incomes reflects the trends that have already been described. The bulge of young people and women has occurred at the same time as a change in the overall distribution of earnings. These demographic groups unfortunately have always had low wages. And a large number of them work only part time.

The declining share of employment in the middle range also reflects the decline in the number of well-paid unionized jobs. This is due in part to the declining share of employment in manufacturing, mining, and construction. It is also true that the specific industries where blue-collar wages are very high have had difficulty in keeping their costs and prices competitive with imports.

As a result of demographic changes, the natural rate had risen by 2 per cent from 4–4½ per cent in the 1950s to 6–6½ per cent by the late 1970s. The evidence for any increase in the natural rate beyond this is mixed. The shift in the relation between unemployment and vacancies, even after demographic adjustment, is the most compelling reason to suggest a further increase. But to set against this there are the implications of the effects of transfer programs and occupational shifts, the absence of any increase in industry unemployment dispersion, and the fact that after balancing the different findings there was not much evidence of more than a demographic change in the natural rate from the inflation studies.

However, if we underestimate the natural rate, there is the danger of starting up the inflation problem over again. Yet each percentage point added to a target unemployment rate adds over a million to the total number of jobless in the economy and cuts 2 to 3 per cent from GNP.

Based upon actual demographic trends since 1979 and projected trends through the rest of the 1980s the natural rate will likely decline to 5½ per cent by 1989.[5] This means that monetary and fiscal policies could be set to target about a 6 per cent unemployment rate by 1985 and a 5½ per cent unemployment rate by 1989, without causing an acceleration in inflation and without any special programs to reduce the natural rate. Of course it is possible that food and energy price increases, or other inflationary problems, will strike during the 1980s. In this case, the choices will be: to accept the higher inflation, to allow unemployment to rise above the natural rate to offset the shocks, or to use some other anti-inflation policy, such as a tax-based incomes policy.

The estimates of the natural rate also allow the caluclation of a bottom line on the relative importance of cyclical and structural factors in explaining the rising trend of unemployment. Comparing the 1970s to the 1960s, there was an increase in average unemployment of 1.5 percentage points. This was split 40 per cent to an increase in the amount of cyclical unemployment and 60 per cent to an increase in the natural rate. Comparing 1980-2 to the 1970s, there was an increase in average unemployment of 1.9 percentage points, all of which was cyclical.[6]

NOTES

1 This definition means that when the unemployment is below the natural rate, then cyclical unemployment is 'negative.' This simply means that strong aggregate demand is cutting into structural and frictional unemployment.
2 There is an alternative explanation of the period 1981-3. The hard-line combination of Volcker and Reagan may have reduced inflationary expectations more rapidly than one would predict from the past.
3 The UI program is experience-rated in an attempt to offset the incentive to make layoffs. In practice the experience-rating provisions are not very effective.
4 The year 1959 is used rather than the earlier year 1955 because of the availability of data.
5 The sharp episodes or recession since 1979 make it hard to follow the trends year by year. If anything, it looks as if the surprisingly slow labour-force growth is reducing the natural rate somewhat faster than expected.
6 Since the natural rate is now falling, more than 100 per cent of the change is unemployment from the 1970s to 1980-2 was cyclical.

REFERENCES

Bendick, M., jr. 1981. 'Workers Displaced by Economic Change: Do They Need Federal Employment and Training Assistance?' *7th Annual Report of the National Commission for Employment Policy*. Washington, DC

Clark, K., and L. Summers. 1982. 'Unemployment Insurance and Labor Market Transitions,' in M.N. Baily (ed), *Workers, Jobs and Inflation*. Washington, DC: Brookings Institution

Gordon, R.J. 1982. 'Inflation, Flexible Exchange Rates, and the Natural Rate of Unemployment,' in M.N. Baily (ed), *Workers, Jobs and Inflation*. Washington, DC: Brookings Institution

Hamermesh, D. 1981. 'Transfers, Taxes and the NAIRU,' in L. Meyer (ed), *The Supply Side Effects of Economic Policy*. Boston: Kluwer

Klein, D.P. 1983. 'Trends in Employment and Unemployment in Families,' *Monthly Labour Review*, 106 (December) 21-5

Medoff, J. 1983. 'U.S. Labour Markets: Imbalance, Wage Growth and Productivity in the 1970's,' *Brookings Papers on Economic Activity*, No. 1, 87-120

Perry, G. 1970. 'Changing Labor Markets and Inflation,' *Brookings Papers on Economic Activity*, No. 3, 411-41

– 1983. 'What Have We Learned about Disinflation?' *Brookings Papers on Economic Activity*, No. 2, 587-602

Solow, R. 1964. *The Nature and Sources of Unemployment in the United States*. Stockholm: Almquist

PIERRE FORTIN

Unemployment in Canada: macroeconomic disease, macroeconomic cure

In Canada each percentage point increase in the national unemployment rate caused by demand deficiency over a year is accompanied by a decrease of two percentage points in annual national income. For instance, if, as I shall argue below, the shortfall of aggregate demand gives rise to at least 5 points of excess unemployment in 1984, then according to that rule of thumb – Okun's Law – the country as a whole is losing this year over $40 billion, or $5,000 per Canadian household. That loss is huge by any standard. Moreover, even if a substantial fraction of the financial cost is offset through our unemployment insurance and welfare systems, the economic burden and human cost fall disproportinately on the unskilled and the poor.

With these cost considerations in the background, my purpose here is to provide broad answers to two questions: why has the unemployment rate risen so much in Canada over the last 20 years; and what can be done to lower it effectively?

On the first question, I see no 'mystery of the rising unemployment rate' in Canada. Reasonable people can argue about the details of the explanation, but the broad picture would seem quite robust under closer scrutiny. In Table 1, I present new evidence that structural factors – demographic, labour-market policy, and other factors – did raise the unemployment rate by almost two percentage points between 1966 and 1977. These included the entry of the 'baby boom' into their working lives, the sharp rise in women's participation in the labour force, the sweeping 1971 redrafting of the Unemployment Insurance Act, the increase in the real minimum wages across provinces, and other factors like the upward trend in the public/private compensation ratio, increased regulation of the labour market, and shifts in the structure of demand.

TABLE 1
Sources of change in the aggregate unemployment rate, Canada, 1966–90*

	1966–77	1977–83	1983–90†
Initial unemployment rate	3.4	8.1	11.9
Sources of change			
Structural change	1.9	−1.2	−2.6
Labour force weights‡	0.3	−0.1	−0.3
Trend in youth population share§	0.8	−1.6	−3.3
Unemployment insurance	0.6	0.0	−0.1
Minimum wages	0.1	−0.6	−0.2
Other‖	0.0	1.1	1.3
Macroeconomic change**	2.8	5.0	n.a.
Total change	4.7	3.8	
Final unemployment rate	8.1	11.9	n.a.

SOURCES: Statistics Canada and author's calculations
*An appendix explaining the methodology is available from the author on request.
†Forecast
‡Effect of changing labour force weights in the calculation of the national average unemployment rate as a weighted average of age-sex-specific unemployment rates
§Effects of the changing weight of youths 15 to 24 in the total working age population on age-sex-specific unemployment rates
‖Effect of trend factors not otherwise accounted (e.g. demand structure, fertility trends, school attendance, public-sector wage policy, regulation trends, sociological factors)
**Equals total change minus structural change

However, since 1977 the structural factors have mostly worked in the opposite direction. Owing to more cautious labour-market policy, but mainly to the demographic recession in the younger age groups, structural unemployment declined by about one point between 1977 and 1983. It is now projected to decline by at least two more points by 1990. The number of young people aged 15 to 24 will fall 2.5 per cent per year on average, and their structural unemployment is bound to fall dramatically. The decline of their unemployment rate from 27 per cent to 19 per cent over the last two years in Quebec, where the demographic tide is receding earlier and more strongly than elsewhere, is a leading indicator of things to come in the rest of the country.

An immediate corollary of these findings is that, since the net increase in structural unemployment between 1966 and 1983 was only about one percentage point, the cumulative increase of more than eight points in the national unemployment rate over that period must be largely due to the shift of world and domestic aggregate demand management from sharp expansion in the mid-1960s to sharp contraction in the early 1980s.

Macroeconomic stimulus from tax reductions, public expenditure growth, the Vietnam War, and monetary accommodation was very strong in the 1960s. Concern about the inflationary consequences of excess demand arose in the late 1960s, but it became really serious only after the world expansion of 1972–4 and the accompanying food, materials, and oil price shocks. The 'Saskatoon monetarist manifesto' and the Anti-Inflation Program of 1975 signalled the gradual turn of macro policy to demand restraint. Between 1966 and 1977 the unemployment rate rose about five points, from 3.4 per cent to 8.1 per cent. In Table 1 three of the five points are estimated to have arisen from the shift of aggregate demand and the reorientation of macro policy toward inflation control. Then, the second food and oil price shocks in 1978–80 and the new resolve at the US Federal Reserve after 1979 convinced the Canadian authorities to deal inflation its final blow. The ensuing macroeconomic contraction brought us the great recession of 1981–2. Comparing 1983 to 1977 reveals that this contraction pushed the unemployment rate up by five more points. Fortunately, structural factors helped keep the increase down to four points, and the unemployment rate actually rose from 8.1 per cent to 11.9 per cent over the period.

So, again, there is no puzzle of rising unemployment. Demographic, labour-market policy, and other structural factors raised the unemployment rate by about two points between 1966 and 1977. But these structural factors are now working in the opposite direction and will have reduced unemployment by over three points between 1977 and 1990. The switch in macroeconomic management from expansion in the 1960s to gradual restriction in the 1970s and to sharp contraction in the 1980s is the source of most of the increase in unemployment in the last two decades. Current unemployment is not mainly structural, but caused by demand deficiency.[1]

This causal view naturally provides the clue to answering the second broad question I raised earlier: what can be done to lower unemployment quickly and substantially? My claim is that in dealing with our high unemployment rate effectively there is no good substitute for macroeconomic expansion. Demand restraint brought us high unemployment, and only demand expansion can bring back low unemployment.

I do not want to minimize the importance of structural and microeconomic policies, such as direct job creation programs, manpower policy, deregulation, public-sector wage policy, and other labour-market policies. These should be evaluated and actively pursued for their own sake as far as they can help the labour market and the whole economy become more productive, more adaptable, and more competitive. Unemployment is already being reduced by structural policies such as the 1975 restrictions on the generosity of unemployment insurance, and the decline, in real terms, of the average provincial minimum wage by over 30 per cent since 1975. However, the impact on the unemployment rate of even the most effective structural policies is of the order of a few tenths of a percentage point spread over several years. Only macroeconomic expansion can lower the unemployment rate by several percentage points over a few years. The implicit premises behind this statement are that the non-inflationary rate of unemployment is substantially lower than 11 per cent and declining and that the spontaneous forces of recovery in a modern, decentralized economy operate slowly by themselves.

To my best estimation, the current non-inflationary rate of unemployment in Canada is approximately 6 per cent. This order of magnitude is consistent with the average findings of several previous studies when they are adjusted for the recent decline in structural unemployment.[2] The time invariance of the slope of the Canadian Phillips curve through recent years also constitutes strong evidence that the inflationary content of our structurally adjusted measures of unemployment has not changed much in recent years.

The immediate implication of the 6 per cent equilibrium bench-mark is that the current unemployment rate of 11.5 per cent in Canada includes at least five points of non-inflationary disequilibrium unemployment. What establishes the case for macroeconomic expansion is that the automatic market forces drawing the unemployment rate back to equilibrium seem weak. Forecasts of unemployment for the short to medium term are gloomy.

We should do well to remember that this is not a new phenomenon in modern economic history. It took nine years after the trough of 1933, and six years after the trough of 1958 for the Canadian and US economies to recovery fully from the preceding recessions. Each time the return to normal employment levels were spurred by long-delayed fiscal or monetary expansion. Moreover, the swift recoveries of the post-1945 era were all aided by macroeconomic policy stimulus. In other words, it is hardly exaggerated to claim that expansionary demand management has been both a necessary and a sufficient condition for full recovery from recession. This essentially reflects the fact that our Phillips curves are very flat at high unemployment rates. It is, of course, this phenomenon that was a central motivation behind Keynes's (1936) *General Theory* and, more recently, in Professor Tobin's (1972) presidential address to the American Economic Association, in Professor Lipsey's (1981) presidential address to the Canadian Economic Association, and in Professor Malinvaud's (1984) address to the French Canadian Association for the Advancement of Science.

This lesson extends to other industrial countries as well. So far, the paths followed by the large industrial economies since the bottom of the recession of 1981–2 are consistent with the thrust of my argument. Outside the United States, monetary and fiscal politices are broadly restrictive, and real growth can barely prevent unemployment rates from rising further. In constrast, the strong output and employment recovery in the United States largely stems from the very expansionary fiscal policy pursued there since 1981. The Canadian recovery is weaker than the US recovery for four reasons: fiscal policy has been less expansionary; any given level of the interest rate structure hurts the Canadian consumer more than the American consumer because consumer and mortgage interest payments are not tax-deductible in Canada as they are in the United States; business debt ratios are much less favourable in Canada; and Canadian terms of trade have sharply deteriorated since 1979, and resource industries are generally depressed.

The statement that Keynesian unemployment in Canada will not be reduced by much in the next few years without macroeconomic expansion is most often confronted with two objectives. Demand stimulus would run the danger of rekindling inflation, and it would let government deficits get out of control.

The first objection is wrong. One robust implication of empirical research on Canadian wage behaviour over the last 15 years is that labour-market slack is disinflationary as long as the unemployment rate remains above the equilibrium level, now of 6 per cent or so. As long as the unemployment rate falls, but remains above equilibrium, what we observe is not wage acceleration, but a slowdown in the pace of wage deceleration. The dire predictions that US wages and prices would accelerate as soon as the recovery began have now been heard for two years, but they have not materialized, even if labour-market slack there is much smaller than in Canada. A fortiori, demand-led inflation will not return to Canada for quite a while.

Monetary expansion would, however, lead to exchange rate depreciation. That would raise the price level directly and would feed back onto wages. The practical question here is whether the inflationary consequnces of exchange rate depreciation are quantitatively important in Canada. The currently available evidence from six macroeconomic models of the Canadian economy indicates that the response of inflation to a depreciation of the Canadian-US exchange rate is small and disappears over time. A 10 per cent depreciation would leave our inflation rate 2.2 percentage points higher in the first year and 1.5 points higher in the second and third years. One key element in this consensus result is the strength of the Keynesian labour standard in Canada, where wage-wage imitation and emulation are prominent, as opposed to wage-price indexation. Whatever the widely publicized experience of a few European countries with very different labout market institutions, the price-exchange rate circle in Canada does seem quite virtuous.

The second objection to macroeconomic expansion is the fear of runaway deficits. I am firmly convinced like many others that deficits matter and that the public sector debt/GNP ratio must be brought under control in the medium term lest it become a serious threat to capital formation, international indebtedness, and future national income growth in Canada. However, the objection to macroeconomic expansion on that basis confuses overall expansion with fiscal expansion. There is one and only one logical means of reducing government deficits and unemployment simultaneously: tigher budgets coupled with easier money. The fiscal plan should aim at stabilizing the debt/GNP ratio over a number of years, while monetary expansion should set itself the double objective of offsetting the unemployment consequences of the fiscal restriction and of injecting a sufficient amount of additional net simulus to lift the economy out of the current stagnation of output and employment.

The current and prospective levels of the public debt in Canada are a legitimate cause for concern, but not for panic. The federal debt/GNP ratio rose almost 14 points, from 19 per cent to 33 per cent, in the three years between 1981 and 1984, but it was already expected to increase only four more points in the next three years under the previous government's fiscal plan. That plan aimed at stabilizing the debt/GNP ratio and was referred to as Operation Tilt. It called for tax reductions in 1982 and 1983 followed by tax increases in 1984 and later. This stood in sharp contrast with the lack of any serious plan in the United States to deal with its own deficit problem. Michael Wilson was obviously not tied by the details of Marc Lalonde's fiscal plan, but he was likely to implement at least the macroeconomic equivalent of his predecessor's debt control strategy, as the manuracturers' tax move and economic statement indicate.

The new minister had first to bring the vastly underestimated federal deficit back to the previously targeted path and then decide whether and at what pace he should go into further deficit-cutting. This is of immediate importance given the greater likelihood that the politically unpalatable decisions be made in the first two years after the last election than in the last two years before the next election. At one extreme, there are hawks to suggest that the debt/GNP ratio be fully stabilized over three years. At the other extreme, there are doves to argue essentially in favour of benign neglect.

I find that neither option is acceptable, because they are both too risky. The hawkish stance would increase the unemployment rate by at least another two points by 1987. The dovish approach would destroy the gains made so far in the area of debt stabilization and would steer the economy on a dangerous long-term course. The middle-of-the-road view is perhaps not as glamorous as the two extremes, but it had the distinct advantage of not sacrificing either employment in the short term or income growth in the longer term. As long as the unemployment rate shows no sign of falling, it would be imprudent to indulge in harsh deficit-cutting beyond the path projected in the February 1984 budget. We do need a determined, but small-step strategy for medium-term debt stabilization. I hasten to add that in my view expenditure reduction and loophole closing should pay a greater role in that strategy relative to tax rate increases than Operation Tilt suggested.

Monetary expansion has to offset the unemployment consequences of deficit-cutting and provide net overall stimulus. However, in an open economy like ours monetary expansion will inevitably lead to currency depreciation unless there is a parallel monetary expansion in the United States. It is this fear of depreciation that leads many to argue that Canada should not adopt an easier money course until the United States does so.[3] However, the logical implication of that view is that Canada should forgo even the slightest opportunity offered by the flexible exchange rate system to pursue domestic objectives. Unemployment in Canada cannot fall unless the Canadian dollar falls. We should be ready to go it alone if, as is likely for quite a while, the US authorities persist in their dangerous easy budget–tight money orientation.

But how big a currency depreciation should we aim for? Although there is no infallible way for out central bank to select the most appropriate value for the Canadian dollar, it is at least suggestive to measure the extent of the deterioration of our competitive position vis-à-vis our trade partners since 1979 – the last year before the current period of instability. According to recent OECD figures (1984), between 1979 and 1984 our unit labour costs in manufacturing increased 23 per cent more than those of our partners when expressed in a common currency. Re-establishing the same average degree of competitiveness as in 1979 for Canadian industry would roughly entail a one-time 15 per cent depreciation of our dollar, down to 64 US cents from its current level of 76 cents. The strength of our Keynesian labour standard would ensure that the depreciation would not simply lead to inflation smoke. The nominal depreciation would translate into a commensurate real depreciation.

Our net exports and business investment would rise, and we would share more equally in the North American recovery. The temporarily lower interest rates and the more competitive Canadian dollar would, according to conventional macroeconometric wisdom, expand real national income by over 2 per cent and reduce the aggregate unemployment rate by 1.5 percentage points over two years (O'Reilly, Paulin, and Smith 1983). That would at least represent a modest beginning on the road to higher employment.

Those who find the idea of a 65-cent dollar shocking should at least ponder the logic of the argument carefully. If we want to lower the unemployment rate, we need macroeconomic expansion. But if we want also to bring the public debt under control, expansion must come from the monetary side, leading to a cheaper Canadian dollar. Within the short horizon over which a social consensus on the appropriate incomes policy and on reform of our wage- and price-setting institutions is beyond reach, the only options currently available to Canada are either depreciating its currency or accepting high unemployment for quite a few more years to come. We do not have the choice between good or bad, but only between bad or worse.

The main obstacle to the return of high employment in Canada does not lie in our ignorance of the true causes of unemployment or in our inability to prescribe effective remedies. The problem is not structural but originates in a shortfall of aggregate demand. We know from historical experience that it will not go away by itself; macroeconomic stimulus is required. We have hard empirical evidence that demand expansion or exchange rate depreciation will not reignite inflation. And we know what policy mix will reduce unemployment and stabilize the public debt altogether: tighter budgets and easier money. There is a broad consensus on these matters across the spectrum of Canadian labour-market and macroeconomic analysts outside the extreme right or the extreme left, just as there is a broad consensus in Canadian public opinion that unemployment is the most pressing issue confronting the Conservative government.

This leads me to conclude that, if Canadian macroeconomic policy does nothing serious to lift the economy out of the current stagnation of employment, as would be the case if government deficits were cut but monetary policy did not more than offset its unemployment consequences, then it will be proof that something is wrong not with the Canadian economy, but with our ideologies, our vested interests, and our political process.

NOTES

1 There are of course other complementary analyses of the sources of the current unemployment than that offered by the rough calculations of Table 1 (e.g., Helliwell, 1984). Artus (1984) dismisses the excess real wage conjecture, which is so popular in Europe, as a valid explanation of the high unemployment rate in Canada. Another potential factor is the possible permanent shift in the structure of employment demand across industries, included here in the 'other factors' of Table 1.
2 An appendix summarizing these studies is available from the author on request.
3 Another objection is that you do not depreciate your currency when your current account balance is in surplus as is currently the case in Canada. This argument is totally misleading since the main source of the current surplus now is precisely the slow growth rate of the economy.

REFERENCES

Artus, J. 1984. 'An Empirical Evaluation of the Disequilibrium Real Wage Rate Hypotheses.' National Bureau of Economic Research Working Paper 1404
Fortin, P. 1984. 'Unemployment Insurance Meets the Classical Labour Supply Model,' *Economic Letters* 14:275–81
Helliwell, J. 1984. 'Stagflation and Productivity Decline in Canada, 1974–1982,' *Canadian Journal of Economics* 17 (May) 191–216
Keynes, J.M. 1936. *The General Theory of Employment Interest and Money*. London: Macmillan
Lipsey, R.G. 1981. 'The Understanding and Control of Inflation: Is There a Crisis in Macroeconomics?' *Canadian Journal of Economics* 14 (November) 545–76
Malinvaud, E. 1984. 'L'état actuel de la théorie macroéconomique de chomage.' Address to the French Canadian Association for the Advancement of Science (May); forthcoming in *L'Actualité économique*

OECD. 1984. *OECD Economic Outlook* 35 (July) Table 50
O'Reilly, B., Paulin, G., and Smith, P. 1983. 'Responses of Various Econometric
  Models to Selected Policy Shocks.' Technical Report 38. Ottawa: Bank of
  Canada
Tobin, J. 1972. 'Inflation and Unemployment,' *American Economic Review* 62
  (March) 1–8.

Comments

R. G. GREGORY

The key question raised in the Dymond paper is: why has labour productivity growth been relatively sluggish in the United States relative to western Europe? Dymond suggests that US labour markets are more flexible in their adjustment to unemployment, as evidenced by greater flexibility of real wages. The conjecture is that the greater increase in real wages in Europe (despite record unemployment) is generating faster labour productivity growth because of the greater incentive for employers to use less labour, for example, by substituting capital for labour. The model postulates that if real wage increases in Europe could have been confined to the increases in the United States, then labour productivity growth would have fallen dramatically in Europe and employment increased.

An alternative view is to regard labour productivity growth as being largely exogenous with respect to real wage changes and to argue that labour productivity growth determines real wages, through the translation of nominal wage increases into price increases. This view, that labour productivity growth is not primarily determined by factor substitution in response to relative factor prices, was the prevailing result from the technical-change literature of Solow, Denison, and others during the 1960s and 1970s. That literature found that capital labour substitution, presumably in response to relative factor price changes, was a very small part of the economy-wide labour productivity story.

It is also somewhat of a puzzle why a more flexible labour market does not generate more rather than less productivity growth. The important macro objective is to generate faster real output growth rather than to suggest that slower rates of labour productivity growth are desirable. Once this is realized, it leads to a different method of analysis in which output growth may be affected by a wide range of non-labour-market factors, including government expenditure, deficits, and trade restrictions.

In contrast to Dymond's paper, Lindbeck (1983) shows that between 1960 and 1973, when western Europe unemployment was the envy of the United States, labour productivity growth was also faster in Europe than in the United States. In those days, fast labour productivity growth was obviously associated with good things and not bad things as might be suggested by the Dymond paper, albeit Dymond is only suggesting that the productivity increase is an indirect by-product of the excessive real wage growth.

While labour productivity has recently been lower in the United States than in western Europe, the labour productivity relationship between the two geographic areas does not appear to have changed. Both Europe and the United States have been subject to a productivity slowdown of similar magnitudes. It seems inappropriate, therefore, to pin an explanation of the different unemployment records of Europe and the United States upon a labour productivity relationship between the two areas that has not changed. With respect to a labour productivity growth, both areas seem to have been affected by a common factor or set of factors. It is perhaps the similarity in the productivity slowdown that should be stressed.

Ellman makes the important point that although there are large differences between the US economy and the western European aggregate, not all European countries behave in the same way. Some economies such as Norway and Austria have low unemployment rates. Others such as the Netherlands, Switzerland, and West Germany have low inflation rates. Once the focus is shifted to inter-country differences *within* Europe, the labour market flexibility argument has less intuitive appeal and the analysis of the problem is seen to be more difficult. It is not obvious that West Germany, with high unemployment but low inflation has an inflexible labour market or that Norway, with low unemployment but relatively high inflation, has a flexible labour market.

There are other differences between Europe and the United States, apart from real wage and labour productivity growth, which are perhaps more important and that have not been directly addressed in any of the papers. These differences lie in the changing relationships between prices, nominal wage responsiveness, and variations in aggregate demand.

It is widely believed in Europe and Australia that the Phillips curve (if it exists!) has shifted considerably to the right and that over the last decade an increasing proportion of demand expansion has been dissipated in price increases rather than leading to increases in real output. This has led to 'policy pessimism' in Europe and Australia and a general weakening of the belief that expanding demand by increasing government expenditure or reducing taxes will expand real output and employment.

There is also evidence to suggest, at least since 1960, that a given amount of nominal demand expansion had had a greater effect on real output and a smaller effect on prices in the United States than in western Europe. Further, the responsiveness of real output to demand expansion has steadily deteriorated in Europe but improved in the United states.

In the United States and Canada it appears that the unemployment-vacancy relationship (Beveridge curve) has marginally shifted outward, and the unemployment-inflation trade-off (Phillips curve) is alive and well and has also shifted marginally.

On the basis of these two relationships it appears that the US and Canadian economies have not changed significantly. There is a presumption, therefore, that wherever there is an undue amount of unused capacity the economy can be expanded by conventional Keynesian policies without an unusual degree of dissipation of the expansion into price inflation. It appears that high levels of unemployment stem primarily from a deficiency in aggregate demand rather than an upsurge in structural imbalances in the labour market and the economy.

These results are supported by the current Keynesian experiment in the United States – the Reagan pump-priming by federal deficits. This Keynesian experiment is working in the way many of us believed during the 1960s and early 1970s. It seems odd that the United States has so many economists who believe that the US economy has changed with respect to the effect of government policy upon the economy when the evidence for this position appears not to be very great.

REFERENCE

Lindbeck, A. 1983. 'The recent slowdowns of productivity growth,' *Economic Journal* 93:369 (March) 13–34

RICHARD G. LIPSEY

Pierre Fortin has measured structural plus frictional unemployment (hereafter SU) by assessing the influence on unemployment of the following factors: changes in labour-force weights in respect to age and sex, unemployment insurance, minimum wage laws, and trend variables which are meant to catch some of the influences of other factors.

This gives us an estimate of SU that arises from the supply side of the labour market. All the rest of the unemployment is assumed to be due to deficient aggregate demand (hereafter DDU). Fortin argues that DDU requires aggregate demand policies for its removal, and he calls for a massive increase in aggregate demand induced by an expansive monetary policy. In what follows, I will concentrate on two questions. First, is Fortin's residual really all DDU? Second, is a massive dose of monetary expansion a sensible policy?

Ellman's western European overview should make us wonder if Fortin's classification is detailed enough. Ellman seems to come down with Malinvaud in believing that DDU, SU, and classical unemployment all coexist in western Europe, a judgment with which I concur. Of the forces taken seriously by Ellman (in addition to those isolated by Fortin), there are two that could be applicable to Canada: classical unemployment and demand-side SU.

Classical unemployment occurs when the real wages – which includes the total cost to an employer of hiring a unit of labour – is raised above its equilibrium level. Many studies suggest that such unemployment may well exist in western Europe, but that it is probably not a great problem in the United States. I know of no major Canadian studies of the problem. The strongest prima facie case for its existence in Canada would be in the primary export industries, where prices are set on international markets, where international demand exists, but where many Canadian mines and forest-product firms are shut down because they cannot cover their variable costs.

How could we see such unemployment if it exists? It is not always realized that if classical, or real-wage unemployment exists, it looks like DDU rather than SU. This important point can be in either of two ways.

First, if the real wage is pushed above its equilibrium level, the number of people wanting to work at the going wage rate rises while the number of jobs declines. As a result, vacancies fall while unplaced applicants rise. The economy is thus observed to move outward along a given U-V curve. This is just what happens when DDU develops. (In contrst a rise in SU shifts the U-V curve outward.)

Second, start from an equilibrium in which supply and demand for labour are equal at the going real wage rate. First, let the demand for labour fall off but wages be sticky. The new situation has the demand curve lying to the left of the supply curve for labour at the existing wage rate. Second, starting again from equilibrium, let the real wage be froced upward. The new situation has the demand curve for labour lying to the left of the supply curve at the existing real wage rate. Thus we see the two situations – unemployment due to a disequilibrium real wage that has been raised too high, and unemployment due to a declining demand for labour – are indistinguishable.

The important point is that if real wage unemployment does exist in Canada, it will not be included in Fortin's estimates of SU but instead will be measured by him as DDU.

As for demand-side SU, Martin Bailey refers to some evidence for increased structural unemployment due to the need to move labour from declining to expanding firms and industries, particularly where a region is heavily specialized in the declining industry. If this is also the case in Canada, there will be some structural employment arising fom the demand rather than the supply side of the labour market and this will not turn up in Fortin's measured SU.

So my first point is to call for further work in Canada, inspired by what has been learned in western Europe, to measure the possible contribution to unemployment of forces other than deficient demand and the demographic factors isolated by Fortin.

It is important to know the magnitude of DDU so as to know the possible effectiveness of aggregate demand measures. But why not find out by trial and error? As I put it twenty years ago (Lipsey 1965) in the context of the debate over the Kennedy-Johnson tax cuts:

The pursuit of correct lines of policy does not require further information on the dispute between structuralists and deficient-demand theorists. Since few, if any, structuralists deny that an increase in aggregate demand would reduce unemployment somewhat, the rational policy in the present situation would clearly be to increase aggregate demand progressively until unacceptable degrees of inflation were encountered. Once this deficient-demand unemployment had been eliminated, we could see how much structural unemployment remained and take steps to remove it.

With what we now know about lags we would have to temper this advice with the caution that if one were proceeding without any idea of where the NAIRU was, one should expand the economy cautiously and be fully prepared to halt the expansion as soon as signs of overheating occured. A further reason for the cautious approach is the evidence that the speed of the recovery can itself affect inflation, since wage and price inflation may in the short run be as responsive to the rates at which output grows and unemployment falls as it is to the levels of output and unemployment.

This discussion gets us to Fortin's policy recommendation which is to use monetary policy to expand the economy fairly quickly back to somewhere close to 6 per cent unemployment. Notice that this policy calls for an increase in the rate of monetary expansion during the recovery phase; it does not call for a permanent increase in the rate of monetary expansion, which all economists agree would be inflationary.

In so far as this is a call for a change in the policy mix to a less expansionary fiscal policy (as a medium-term strategy to get the deficit under control) combined with the more expansionary monetary policy (which would take the form of a once-and-for-all easing of credit conditions), this seems eminently sensible advice. Professor Tobin called for it in his keynote address to this conference, the C.D. Howe Institute has been calling for it, and a joint press release from the Institute for Policy Analysis at the University of Toronto and the C.D. Howe Institute urged the same policy on the minister of finance.

Although the advice sounds eminently sensible, I can assure Fortin that it will meet with strong resistance, particularly from members of the financial community and from many policy advisers. Many argue that micro policies will produce the expansion of aggregate demand that Fortin feels must come from macro policies. They look to micro policy incentives to increase investment incentives and create a more favourable business climate.

It is generally agreed that some tax measures introduced by the Reagan administration, particularly accelerated depreciation, encouraged investment in the United States. We may see some Canadian initiatives in this direction from the Conservative government. This is the macro change, more investment expenditure, that Fortin calls for, but it is brought about by micro changes in tax policy rather than changes in monetary policy.

Most people seem to agree that a favourable climate for business in general and for risk-taking in particular has helped the US recovery. This is another micro policy with potential macro effects that we will see tried in Canada and that may have some effect. (The European productivity 'miracle' mentioned several times in this session is partly the result of scrapping older plants and leaving the displaced workers unemployed. As a result, average productivity goes up without any employed workers's productivity going up. This is a major reason for the increases in measured productivity particularly in the United Kingdom, it can hardly commend itself to us as a way of achieving real gains.)

Many worry that expansive monetary policy will rekindle inflation. Correctly operated, it should not rekindle demand inflation. The object is to expand the economy somewhere back to the vicinity of the natural rate of unemployment and then hold it there. Of course errors could cause the expansion to overshoot into the inflationary range. This is a worry with any expansion, but it seems clear to me that, errors of execution aside, this is not a policy for causing a resurgence of demand inflation.

A further worry is that an expansionary monetary policy will rekindle expectations of inflation and the self-realizing effect of expectations will cause an outburst of inflation. Two considerations are important here.

First, we are not emerging from an ordinary recession but from one that was policy induced, and induced for the express purpose of breaking an entrenched inflation. If the central bank announces that the war on inflation is at least temporarily over, and that the war on unemployment requires a temporary burst of expansive monetary policy, the two 'temporaries' may pass unnoticed while the private sector concludes that we are in for a burst of inflation once the economy has been expanded rapidly back to full employment.

Second, Friedman's monetarism has been so oversold that any departure from a stable rate of monetary growth raises fears of a new outbreak of inflation. This may well be, but, if it is so, economists must try to educate people out of this view, which is destructive of rational macro policy. A fixed percentage rule for monetary expansion may make sense when the economy is on its long-run growth path (and the demand for money is stable), but it makes no sense when the path is being approached from below. If the central bank does not accommodate the temporary rapid growth of the economy, the recovery will be slowed and could be halted altogether.

In 1983, when the US economy was recovering rapidly, Milton Friedman opposed the Federal Reserve's efforts to accommodate that recovery with increases in the money supply and warned that the Federal Reserve was creating inflationary pressures. Evidently he was not believed, and the expansion was accommodated with increases in the money supply that met the increased demands for money balances following from higher income transactions and lower interest rates. A year or so later, it became clear that Friedman's worries were unfounded. We can be sure however, that Friedman's objections will be raised in Canada. Indeed, there is some worry that the Bank of Canada is not being quite as accommodating as it should be of the present gradual recovery in Canada.

Most middle-of-the-road Canadian economists would agree to the following. The Bank of Canada should expand the money supply to accommodate any expansion that emanates from the private sector to stop it from being cut off by a credit squeeze well before it gets within hailing distance of full unemployment. The contractionary effects of deficit reduction should be offset by a once-and-for-all easing of monetary conditions so as to ensure that the net effect on aggregate demand is not contractionary.

In both cases the interest rate is not driven below world rates; the monetary expansion merely stops it from rising above them. But Fortin would go further. He would have monetary police force an expansion. In this case, a burst of monetary expansion would put downward pressure on Canadian interest rates, and the outflow of short-term capital would depreciate the Canadian dollar against the US dollar.

If the monetary expansion embarked on for the two reasons listed above meets strong resistance from the financial community, monetary expansion that is sufficient to seriously depreciate the Canadian dollar evokes screams of pain. Let us look at some of the reasons why.

1. 'You can't play fast and loose with the exchange rate,' Fortin will be told. But Fortin is not arguing for direct Bank of Canada intervention into the foreign exchange market to drive down the Canadian dollar. All he wants is a more expansive monetary policy, and he is willing to take the consequences on the exchange rates.

2. 'You should not,' he will be told, 'drive the exchange rate below the purchasing power rate, and if anything, the Canadian dollar is currently a bit undervalued against the US dollar.' My own feeling is that the financial community is mesmerized over the exchange rate with the US dollar. In so far as there is an exchange rate target, it should be set by the trade-weighted exchange, and there is no doubt that the Canadian dollar is overvalued against the currencies of all of its trading partners except the United States.

But even allowing for this point, there seems to be some difference in perception. Most people seem to feel that, looking at prices, the Canadian dollar's purchasing power parity rate against the US dollar is probably about 77 cents US. Yet Fortin feels that, looking at costs, a competitive rate is around 65 cents. Possibly he feels that 75 cents is about the purchasing power parity rate, but that a predatory devaluation of 10 cents below that rate is justified. In this case, one must worry about possible American retaliatory action, particularly when more serious negotiations for freer trade between the two countries are a distinct possibility.

3. Some feel that a fall in the Canadian dollar would set off a speculative panic to which there would be no obvious end. I know that such panics do occasionally occur, but I have heard this worry advanced for thirty years in

several countries as an argument against doing anything about a fundamental imbalance in exchange rates, and I have concluded that it almost always reflects an unfounded fear.

4. An argument strongly advanced by the business community is that we should not use the exchange rate to compensate for our past excesses in wage settlements, as this will remove the discipline on further excesses. I have some sympathy with this argument.

There is a problem, however, in sticking to the above advice after a bout of excessive wage settlements. There are only two ways of restoring competitiveness; first, to wait for a lower domestic inflation rate to get our prices and costs back into line and, second, to allow the exchange rate to adjust. Given low rates of inflation around the world, the first adjustment could take 5–10 years, while the second can be accomplished in a matter of months. It is hard to stick to the path of virtue in the face of these differences.

5. The easy monetary policy would lead to an overshooting. The Canadian dollar would fall until everyone expected it to rise in value over the next year. The expected gain from its appreciation would then compensate for the lower interest rates to be earned in Canada. This is a serious worry.

6. If financial markets are seriously upset by this policy, whether or not the fears are reasonable, the resulting disrupting effect on employment-creating flows of international capital could be serious.

While I feel that some of these worries about an expansionary monetary policy are misguided, others are serious. In the end, therefore, I come to the following position:

1. The Bank of Canada should offset any deflationary impact of deficit reduction with a once-and-for-all easing of credit conditions.

2. The Bank of Canada should accommodate any expansion that emanates from the private sector by providing sufficient new money to eliminate pressure for Canadian interest rates to rise above the world rate.

3. Debate should now be joined on the advisability of a mild impetus to expansion being given by monetary policy. I say 'mild' because I think there is more chance of getting rational debate on this advice than on Fortin's policy of rapid expansion. If the outcome of the debate is that a mild expansion would be worth trying, debate could then be joined on the issue 'how mild is mild?' I see good reason for attempting a mild monetary stimulus and then feeling our way beyong that. I reject a rapidly expansive monetary policy as being far to risky for all the reasons outlined above and for several that are not relevant to the topics under consideration at this conference.

WESTERN EUROPE

EZIO TARANTELLI

Monetary policy and the regulation of inflation and unemployment

Over the last fifteen years, industrialized countries have witnessed to a varying extent three major sources of inflation. 1) There has been a wage push from industrial conflict which in a conflictual system of industrial relations, has the effect of shifting the short-run Phillips curve upward and to the right. This wage push effect has been particularly evident since the end of the 1960s, at least for the three 'cranky cases' (France, Italy, and the United Kingdom). 2) There has been a price push from an increase in imported goods and services (for instance, an OPEC oil stock). 3) There has been a labour productivity 'slowdown' due to slow adjustment of employment to a decline in productive activity following the wage and/or price push discussed above.

A basic argument of this paper is that the magnitude of the outward shift in the Phillips curve due to industrial conflict is a negative function of the degree of neocorporatism. Also, in so far as this induced shift, and/or any shift due to import price increases, are embedded into inflationary expectations, a more centralized system of industrial relations (possibly with a shorter average duration of contracts and with largely non-overlapping contract renewals) can lower inflationary expectations and reduce inflation with a lower cost in terms of unemployment. This, in addition to political exchange in the political arena, is a basic pay-off of a higher degree of neocorporatism.

It is therefore important to clarify what we mean by a high degree of centralization of the system of industrial relations which we shall henceforth, for brevity, call a high degree of neocorporatism.

As indicated in my forthcoming *The Political Economy of Labor and Com-*

parative Industrial Relations, the three main dimensions of the degree of neocorporatism can be summarized as:

1. *The neo-co-option of trade unions and employers' representatives*: A centralized system of industrial relations is one where the main unions and employers' representatives are willing to accept, and strong enough to implement, a 'fine-tuning' of economic policy, through the variable of the money wage for any given target rate of inflation. They can, thus, regulate the money and real wage in view of certain specified economic targets (e.g. inflation, internal demand, balance of payments equilibrium) shared by the other main partners and of economic and/or institutional reforms. In this sense, the money wage is the unit of measurement of an exchange that is transferred from the market to the so-called political arena. This arena must therefore be, to a large extent, ideologically consensual. Each of the main actors (e.g. trade unions, employers, and government) independently (hence neo-co-option) recognizes and accepts the role played by the other two main actors.

In this dimension of centralization, a certain degree of consensus is per se a necessary, but not sufficient, condition. What is needed, in addition to some degree of ideological and political consensus, is a degree of institutional or at least informal integration of trade unions within the political and economic machinery of government. This integration and, thus, co-responsibility in economic policy are quite high, though informal, in Japan and quite low in the United States. Yet, from a purely consensual point of view, it would be rather difficult to decipher which is the more 'consensual' of these two countries.

2. *The centralization of collective bargaining*: A centralized system of industrial relations is a system where contract renewals mainly take place at the national and/or industrial or regional level, rather than at the company and plant level. In addition, the hierarchical relation of unions to each other allows for a high degree of centralization of the organizational structure of trade unions. Further, a few contract renewals influence directly (through the so-called negative coalition right) or indirectly (through pattern bargaining) a high percentage of the labour force. Also, contract renewals tend to take place at close (e.g. one-year) and non-overlapping or synchronous intervals.

This condition of relatively close (and, especially in periods of economic crisis, possibly flexible) intervals between one contract and the next guarantees the possibility of fine-tuning wage agreements in the presence of changing economic circumstances. The other condition, that of non-overlapping intervals, means that contract renewals in different sectors tend to take place at the same time. It thus facilitates the synchronous observance by workers of 'fair relativities,' in contrast to a non-synchronous contract schedule which could benefit some groups of workers to the exclusion of the non-bargaining groups. In addition, the existence of a few key contracts that can influence a number of other contracts clearly reinforces the degree of centralization of a system of industrial relations.

3. *The neo-regulation of industrial conflict*: A centralized system of industrial relations is a system where labour dispute settlement laws and procedures render credible the contract renewal once the latter is signed. This must be true for the settlement of both disputes of right (relating to the application of the rules of an already agreed-upon contract) and disputes of interest (in the occasion of a contract renewal). In a sense, this third dimension of centralization is a corollary of the first dimension, which is partly based on the degree of consensus among the independent actors of the system of industrial relations. Consensus and co-responsibility with the government in decision-making often go together with a clearly defined set of procedures and laws that guarantee the stability and consequently the credibility of a labour contract once the latter is signed. These procedures also specify the channels through which a contract may be reached and its rules applied.

But this in no way implies a one-to-one correspondence between the first and third dimensions. This third dimension greatly varies according to the legal and jurisprudential system of each single country and the actual acceptance and respect of this system by the main actors involved, including the rank and file. This third dimension also stresses the degree to which the rank and file and single firms are willing to respect and follow the contract agreement reached at a higher level. This makes the agreement credible, so to say, from below rather than from above only.

The United States and Canada have systems of industrial relations where the third condition, but not the first and second, is satisfied. Their systems are highly decentralized with contracts of long duration (often three years) and overlapping renewals. The system exhibits a largely unstable and complex network of pattern bargaining, and the main US confederation, the AFL-CIO, does not bargain for its affiliated unions and therefore has never signed a wage contract.

Austria, Sweden, Norway, and Denmark, in contrast have more centralized systems of industrial relations where all three previous dimensions are, to a widely varying extent, satisfied. The same is true for West Germany and Japan. In the latter country, as is well known, bargaining takes place mainly at plant level, but it is heavily and yearly co-ordinated during the so-called spring offensive by all three major trade unions and the government. There is, in addition, a high degree of pattern bargaining.

The process of deceleration of inflation has been less difficult in the more centralized countries. The increase in US and Canadian unemployment in the 1970s and early 1980s, with respect to the average levels preceding the oil crisis (despite the higher growth rate of these two countries from the last quarter of 1975 to the end of the 1970s), has not allowed for a return of the rate of inflation to its previous lower average. In the six more centralized countries this has been possible, despite widely different costs in terms of unemployment and output lost. These costs have however been much lower than those paid by the more decentralized countries.

The fundamental reason for this difference, in my view, occurs because a sufficiently centralized system of industrial relations can lower inflationary expectations through a combined 'announcement effect' of both monetary and trade union policy. The central bank announces a monetary restriction, which is made concrete and credible by a contemporaneous announcement of a moderate wage policy on the part of trade unions.

When this happens, a restriction of the money supply has no effect, or has lesser effects, on employment and income. The monetary crunch does not have a severe impact on the goods and labour market, leading to unemployment. It largely affects nominal quantities, that is, money wages and price, by decelerating their speed. This makes an increase in unemployment less necessary.

An 'only money matters' (without trade unions) announcement effect is also considered in a second (and more recent) version of monetarist orthodoxy. According to this version, the simple announcement of a more restrictive monetary policy would by itself lower inflationary expectations and, thus, inflation, without recourse to higher unemployment. But the above discussion suggests that the announcement of a restrictive monetary stand is less credible, and thus, less concrete, if it is not accompanied by a contemporaneous announcement of trade union wage policy. This latter announcement implies, in turn, a level of centralization that has to be similar to the one traditionally enjoyed by the central bank (which suggests that the monetarist orthodoxy might be even less credible in a truly decentralized banking system).

In the presence of a decentralized system of industrial relations, a monetary crunch can, thus, reduce the rate of inflation only through much higher costs in terms of unemployment and output lost. This was the case in the 1970s and early 1980s in countries such as Belgium, the Netherlands, and (until the end of the 1970s) Finland, where the traditionally high industrial and regional level of centralization was lowered by divisions of language, religion, and politics. The same happened in Australia and New Zealand because of their partly fragmented system of collective bargaining, and in spite of the historical heritage of the system of arbitration (which in New Zealand collapsed in 1971). Similarly, unemployment and output losses were substantial in Britain, where the centralization of the system of industrial relations is quite low in all three dimensions discussed above (in addition to having the lowest velocity of adjustment of employment to changes in output), France (including the Mitterand government), and Italy, where the same has been true for both the first and third dimensions. Thatcherism and Reaganism provide similar important examples for the second oil crisis.

As argued above, a successful neo-Keynesian incomes policy, or a social contract, could in principle negate any inflationary effect of industrial conflict and can in fact even prevent industrial conflict from taking place at all. This depends on the degree of neocorporatism being high enough (e.g. of the Austrian rather than Italian type) to avoid, through political exchange, wage cost–push and poltical pressures. Likewise, the initial increase in the price of oil may be a one-shot increase in the presence of a successful neo-Keynesian policy which can, in principle, bring down inflationary expectations to where they were before the initial shift in the price of oil occurred.

One can, thus, distinguish three stylized cases:

1. In the presence of a high degree of neocorporatism, inflationary expectations can be lowered, following an initial increase in industrial conflict or import price increases, through a joint and consistent announcement of trade unions and the central bank. Such announcements have to be strengthened with a series of consistent policy decisions – including a consistent fiscal policy and political exchange – shared by the social partners (this is where the neo-co-option dimension comes in). In any actual situation the system may have to accept temporarily a (slightly) higher unemployment rate to make up for the initial wage or price push. This has been the path followed in the aftermath of the first and second oil crises by centralized and relatively consensual systems of industrial relations such as Austria, Sweden, Norway, and, partly, Denmark. To a lesser extent, this path was also followed by West Germany during the first oil crisis (but less so in the second) and, more informally, by Japan (both in the first and, especially, in the second oil crisis). Finland, in the aftermath of the second oil crisis, could also be added to this first group of countries.

A rapid cancellation of inflationary expectations is possible only in a sufficiently centralized system of industrial relations. If the degree of neocorporatism is not high enough (as is usually the case in a system with industrial conflict), inflationary expectations cannot be lowered without some cost in terms of unemployment since the monetary announcement alone is less credible and, thus, efficient.

2. This also implies that, in order to return to zero inflation, the economic system, if unable to lower inflationary expectations, would have to experience substantial unemployment. I submit that this, to a highly varying degree, has been the experience in the 1970s and early 1980s of some countries with a lower degree of neocorporatism such as Belgium, the Netherlands, Australia, New Zealand, and, at least till the end of the 1970s, Finland.

3. Given their incapacity to reduce inflationary expectations, because of their very low degree of neocorporatism, the United States and Canada (and especially the United States during the Reagan administration) had to experience considerable unemployment once they chose (albeit Canada had no real choice) to drastically lower inflationary expectations and the rate of inflation in the early 1980s. And so did the United Kingdom even before then as an effect of the deflationary monetarist stance chosen by the Thatcher government.

There are, in addition, two countries, Italy and France, with a highly centralized system of collective bargaining, which experienced both high inflation and unemployment in the first and second oil crises. There are two reasons for this. Both countries experienced between the end of the 1960s and the early 1970s a higher wage push from industrial conflict than any of the previous countries. In addition, they had a very low (and for the Italian case even a 'perverse') speed of adjustment of employment to changes in output that reflected itself in lower than trend increases in labour productivity.

This (political) rigidity of employment, and the fact that a more severe monetary restraint would have probably implied a politically unacceptable rate of unemployment, made it difficult for Italy and France to follow an economic policy to reduce inflation. The lower gains of productivity due to the recession and the concomitant rigidity in employment levels might have meant, especially in Italy, more rather than less inflation. Because of its high industrial level of conflict, the United Kingdom belongs to this same third group of countries in the above figure, until the monetarist stance chosen by the Thatcher government in the early 1980s.

In these three 'cranky cases' (Italy, France, and Britain), perhaps more than in all previous cases, one major reason for conflict was income distribution. This was also reflected, since the end of the 1960s, in the wage-push rounds mentioned above. But conflict also reflected itself in a lower speed of adjustment of employment to the decline in production through strong trade union resistance against layoffs following the 1973 crisis. This dramatically lowered turnover rates (e.g. the flow of dismissals and, as a consequence, the flow of hires) especially in Italy.

No country in the 1970s and early 1980s was able to immediately reduce its inflation. Even for neocorporatist countries with centralized bargaining, a substantial degree of stabilization of the rate of inflation, without a concomitant large increase in unemployment was achieved only after two years (on average) following the 1973 crisis. For countries with a lower degree of neocorporatism, the same or an even higher time horizon was needed together with a higher cost of unemployment to pursue the anti-inflation target. Countries with the lowest degree of neocorporatism (e.g. the United States, Canada, and Britain) experienced stagflation (i.e., a simultaneous increase in both inflation and unemployment).

One observation that emerges from the previous analysis is that, especially in countries like Italy, France, and the United Kingdom, restrictive monetarist policies and neo-Keynesian incomes policies were both present, at different points in time, in the same country during the 1970s and early 1980s in an attempt to cure the inflation disease. This apparent schizophrenia can be understood as the result of the changing degree to which unions were able and willing to be neo-co-opted with the economic and political machinery of the government, depending on the existing political alliances and economic environment.

In Italy a weak form of (implicit) incomes policy was successful during the 1976–9 government of national solidarity, which received fundamental support from the Communist party. At the opposite extreme, no incomes policy could even be thought of during the conflictual wave of the Italian hot fall of 1969 and until 1976 or in the early 1980s. During this entire period, cost-push inflation from both trade union action and the oil crisis of 1973 was the rule. Nor was there any agreement among the different components of the labour movement as to the instruments needed in order to lower inflationary expectations and the rate of inflation or to increase the neo-co-option and regulation dimensions and, thus, the degree of neocorporatism.

In conflictual cases of very low neocorporatism such as Italy, France, and the United Kingdom in the course of the 1970s, a number of conclusions can be drawn. In the presence of a cost push from trade union action (or the oil crisis), the relation between inflation and unemployment may become inverted with respect to the short-run Phillips curve (and, yet, the Phillips curve may still be a valid tool of short-run analysis), if the cost push is accompanied by a restrictive monetary policy attempting to enforce any given target rate of inflation. In the presence of a conflictual cost push, the relation between output and changes in the distribution of income may also become indeterminate. This occurs because, in the short run, price increases cannot fully compensate for the increase in labour costs; the resulting decline in the share of profits has two opposing effects on output. The fall in profit tends to induce a fall in investment, which is part of output. In contrast a decline in profits increases total consumption since, at least in the short run, the margainal propensity to consume out of profits, and of the self-employed, is lower than out of wages (both in a life cycle or permanent income model and in a Kaldorian model). Thus, the total effect of a change in the distribution of income is a priori indeterminate.

It follows that the lack in any one country of an institutional 'neocorporatist filter' capable of overriding or, at least, of diluting the economic effects of a wage-cost push may imply the indeterminacy of the post-Keynesian model both on the inflation-unemployment trade-off and on the income–relative shares relationship. This is an important conclusion in view of the complete disregard of economic orthodoxy (both monetarist and neo-Keynesian) for structural institutional differences from one country to another (and, more generally, for the degree to which the neocorporatist filter can be effective). These two effects can be regarded as an application of a more basic inversion of the traditional Keynesian paradigm that underlies the economics of neocorporatism.

In this paper I have argued that the degree of neocorporatism is a key concept in order to compare and contrast the regulation of economic policies in the sixteen major industrialized countries, from the first oil crisis to date. A high degree of neocorporatism is not only a shelter and an insurance against wage-cost push and industrial conflict but also an economic policy instrument that allows for a higher degree of credibility of an economic policy announcement concerning a lower target rate of inflation. This shifts downward the short-run-wage-unemployment trade-off. Any given target rate of inflation can, as a consequence, be achieved with lower costs in terms of unemployment.

Credibility is the name of the game. If the degree of neocorporatism is low, any monetary announcement of a lower target rate of inflation is also less credible. As a consequence, inflationary expectations remain high. A lower rate of inflation can then be achieved only through a higher rate of unemployment, sliding downward and to the right onto a higher short-run wage-unemployment trade-off.

I conclude that a monetarist policy of demand restraint, unaccompanied by a high degree of neocorporatism, is a second-best policy both in terms of inflation and unemployment. A first-best policy involves a neo-Keynesian incomes policy in the presence of a high degree of neocorporatism. Institutions matter most for the credibility of economic (monetary and fiscal) expectations.

DAVID GRUBB

Wage behaviour and macroeconomic policy

Econometric estimates of aggregate wage equations generally indicate that aggregate wage increases are larger when lagged inflation is high, with the response being greatest in western Europe and less in Canada and especially the United States, presumably reflecting the rigidity that results from long-term contracts in North America. In all situations aggregate wage changes were reduced by fairly similar amounts when unemployment increased.

Econometric estimates also indicate that in western Europe the NAIRU (non-accelerating inflation rate of unemployment, or the unemployment rate associated with a level of aggregate demand that leads to a stable inflation rate) generally increased because of the oil shocks of 1973–4 and 1979–80 and the labour productivity decline after 1975. In addition, the unexpected rapid growth of wages during the 1970s (possibly emanating from the increased labour militancy as evidenced by high strike rates) increased the NAIRU by slightly over three percentage points. However, that effect has been moderated in countries like Sweden, Norway, and Austria, which have powerful, centralized collective bargaining institutions that can agree to restrain wage demands and co-operate with government-imposed incomes policies.

This paper discusses estimates of aggregate wage equations, indicating that Canadian wage behaviour is intermediate between the United States and western Europe in the responsiveness of wages to inflation and unemployment. Based upon plausible views about the behaviour of inflation, unemployment will be minimized if macroeconomic policy aims to keep inflation low, perhaps at 3 to 5 per cent. In all countries macroeconomic policy faces similar constraints arising from the national and international relationships between inflation, unemployment, and the NAIRU.

Other things being equal, lower demand causes lower inflation, so there is some level of demand that would lead to a stable inflation rate. The unemployment associated with this level of demand is called the NAIRU.

A reduction in real wage growth $w' - p'$ is an increase in $p' - w'$. In the equations estimated here, an increase in $p' - w'$ causes an increase in $w' - w'_{-1}$, i.e. it causes inflation to accelerate. To prevent this acceleration, U has to increase. Real wage growth in the 1970s and 1980s has been reduced by two factors. The oil price shocks of 1973–4 and 1979–80 caused deterioration in the terms of trade for OECD countries, especially in relation to favourable trends during the 1960s; and many countries experienced marked declines in the trend growth rate of labour productivity after 1975. Increases in the NAIRU were analysed in terms of these variables by Grubb, Jackman, and Layard (1982).

Shifts in wage pressure due to other factors also affect the NAIRU. With a coefficient on unemployment of -1, the average 3.1 per cent increase in wage pressures in the European Community (EC) made a 3.1 per cent increase in unemployment inevitable if inflation were not to accelerate. Unfortunately, econometric analysis using a few decades of data cannot reliably determine the cause of such long-term shifts. Probably no simple economic explanation exists. Experience in European countries suggests the importance of labour militancy, labour-market institutions, and incomes policies. Therefore, two probable determinants of wage pressure are militancy and incomes policies.

There has been a decade of high rates, approximately from 1965 to 1977 in North America (the fall from 1978 is dramatic in the United States but not in Canada), from 1969 to 1979 in the EC, and from 1970 to 1980 in non-EC Europe. The first countries to experience the fall in strike rates were also the first countries to experience the fall in strikerates. Increases in wage inflation, starting between 1965 in the United States and 1970 in EC countries, correlate with the increases in strike rates, which suggests that 'militancy' was the cause of increases in wage pressure in Europe. Subsequent falls in strike rates were not accompanied by any immediate fall in inflation, and in most countries there is no estimated fall in wage pressure. But it may be significant that a fall in wage pressure has occurred in the United States, which has in the past been the leading country. Other countries may follow a similar pattern in the future.

The relatively favourable movements in wage pressue in some countries (after the initial wage explosion of 1970) may be due to consensus in favour of restraint in wage bargaining. For example, in Sweden, Norway, and Austria there are powerful and centralized collective bargaining institutions. In most other countries, where there is no evidence of favourable shifts in wage pressure, centralized employee and employer organizations have not been able to maintain any influence over the behaviour of the average employer or employee bargaining unit, and periods of incomes policy seem to have had no long-term impact.

The NAIRU probably increases when actual unemployment rates are high. Some individuals unemployed for a long time lose work skills, drop out of the labour market, and have no effect on wages. However, unless actual unemployment increases the NAIRU with a coefficient of one, this does not fundamentally alter the analysis, and it multiplies the long-term effects of any exogenous shifts.

Conventional wisdom suggests that a high 'natural rate' of unemployment needs to be tackled by microeconomic measures, such as measures to improve labour-market mobility, to retrain unemployed people, or (controversially) to reduce unemployment benefits. It is difficult or impossible to determine the role of these variables using macroeconomic data. But changes in these factors could hardly account for the size and the international nature of the increases in the NAIRU experienced by European countries in the last 15 years. The idea that there is a 'natural' rate of unemployment, determined by microeconomic factors in the labour market and changing only slowly, is completely unrealistic for western Europe, and probably not accurate in Canada and the United States.

Little can be done about a shift in the NAIRU due to changes in real wages, but there are some possible strategies to reduce other elements of wage pressure. In some countries, incomes policies negotiated with centralized union and employer organizations seem to have been effective. Tax-based incomes policy might reduce the NAIRU by increasing the incentives for wage restraint at the level of the individual bargaining unit. Governments may be able to reduce labour militancy by defeating strikes in the public sector, so that employees considering strike actions gradually come to regard them at futile.

The price level does not change immediately in response to a change in demand, and consequently the government can influence the level of unemployment at least in the short run. Total nominal spending in the economy can be increased by cutting taxes, increasing public expenditures, or increasing the money supply. As long as the price level does not increase, other factors in the economy (such as high real wages or adverse expectational effects) do not make demand management ineffective. An increase in nominal spending will give an increase in total real spending, with an increase in real GDP and a fall in unemployment.

Even if the price level does change in response to a government-induced demand stimulus, the NAIRU can be reduced by such a stimulus, depending upon such factors as the response of wages to inflation and unemployment. In other circumstances, however, any demand stimulus that leads to a reduction of unemployment above the NAIRU implies that a subsequent increase in unemployment above the NAIRU will be necessary to avoid a permanent increase in inflation. Based on plausible views about the behaviour of inflation, the empirical evidence suggests the unemployment will be minimized if macroeconomic policy aims to keep inflation low, perhaps in the 3 to 5 per cent range.

Policy based on an unemployment target can give quite different results from policy based on an inflation target. In the early 1970s, due to the adverse shift in wage pressure, the NAIRU in western Europe after 1969–70 was probably nearly twice the level of the 1960s. Actual unemployment in the early 1970s was slightly higher than during the 1960s, but inflation was also higher. OECD economies behaved as if they were following an unemployment target, keeping unemployment well below the NAIRU. There was an explosion of inflation in 1973–5 due both to internal demand pressures and to the tightness of world commodity markets. Subsequently, unemployment increased dramatically, in 1975–6 and in 1980–3, before inflation was restored to the level of the 1960s.

If policy had been based upon an inflation target, the early 1970s would have been a period of recession, induced to restrain inflation; but with no increase in inflation, unemployment would have been lower after 1975. In retrospect, expansions of demand in 1972–3 and 1978–9 probably increased unemployment, because they ignored inflation or were based on over-optimistic and out-of-date views about the NAIRU.

In reaction to the failures of the past, many governments in the 1980s, believe the demand policy should not be used at all, and they used tax and expenditure policy with no regard to macroeconomic effects. Now there is a danger that any favourable shift in the NAIRU, due to reductions in wage pressure similar to that which has occurred in the United States, perhaps combined with continuing weakness in the price of oil and other commodities, will not be exploited.

An inflation-target policy avoids mistakes due to misguided pessimism, or misguided optimism, about the level of the NAIRU. In countries where the

NAIRU falls, or where unemployment is above the current NAIRU, inflation is (or will fall) below 3 to 5 per cent, and under an inflation-target policy this will be followed by a reduction in unemployment. In countries where inflation remains continually above 5 per cent, current levels of unemployment, even where they are historically high, must be close to the current NAIRU, so fiscal or monetary reflation would bring no long-term benefit.

When inflation rates differ, countries following an inflation target will follow different demand policies, some reflating and some deflating. Our empirical evidence does not support the contention that reflations are a more successful policy when they are 'concerted,' i.e. when a number of countries take action to reduce their unemployment rates together. Therefore there is no rational reason for one country to press another to reflate. Also, co-ordinated action of any kind tends to cause greater fluctuations in world commodity prices, and all countries will benefit, through more stable commodity prices, if OECD countries follow sensible demand policies independently of each other and allow their business cycles to become desychronized.

NOTE

I would like to thank the Economic and Social Research Council for financial support. This is a non-technical summary of a larger paper, available from the author on request, which provides econometric estimates of aggregate wage equations for Canada, the United States, and western Europe. Details on the econometric procedures are also given in Grubb (1984) and Grubb, Jackman, and Layard (1982).

REFERENCES

Grubb, D. 1984. 'Wage Inflation and Unemployment: A Multi-country Empirical Investigation.' London School of Economics, Centre for Labour Economics, Working Paper 681
Grubb, D., R. Jackman, and R. Layard. 1982. 'Causes of the Current Stagflation,' *Review of Economic Studies* 44:707–30

Comments

KLAUS WEIERMAIR

The papers of Grubb and Tarantelli have in common their quest to more fully account for the long- and short-run instability of Phillips curves throughout time and across different jurisdictions. Although the two papers share this common objectives, they differ greatly in their basic approach and methodology. Grubb, following his own earlier work on wage inflation, proceeds as an ultra-empiricist, while Tarantelli appears to fall more into the mainstream traditions of logical positivism, developing and testing hypotheses of structural changes and/or states in labour market behaviour based on his own earlier theoretical work.

Grubb's analysis of alternate Phillips curve specifications can be considered an opus magnum in econometric experimentation without too much theoretical guidance or adherence to particular labour-market paradigms. The originality and probably greatest usefulness of his work lies in its probing for new variables (and/or proxies thereof) and in the specification of different relationships underlying the inflation-unemployment trade-off. His disection of the unemployment rate into a proxy for the natural rate and the cyclical component represents a novel and innovative way to probe further the instability of the unemployment coefficient. Such a formulation, if it were directly applicable to inter-country comparisons of wage and unemployment behaviour, should help reveal the relative magnitude and importance of long-term versus short-term determinants of labour-market behaviour. The investigation of the role of commodity prices and exchange rates upon the inflation-unemployment trade-off, similarily, reveals interesting results, in that it points at the sluggish if not perverse character of the exchange rate response to low demand/unemployment. Realizing the large unexplained international factor in wage inflation, the author subsequently experiments with a variety of more or less plausible surrogate variables responsible for the transmission of instability through the international financial system. Not surprisingly, Grubb reaches the conclusion that 'sociological' rather than 'monetary' changes must have been responsible for the spread of inflation across the OECD and later constructs a wage-pressure trend variable shown to correlate appreciably with levels of unemployment.

Interestingly, there appears to exist statistical evidence about large inter-temporal and inter-country variations in these wage-pressure shifts and in the associated levels of non-accelerating inflationary rates of unemployment which leaves us speculating on the determinants of the natural rate of unemployment and its variability across countries and time. At this point, the author himself recognizes the limits of his 'empirical tour de force' and suggests a more thorough examination of exogenous country-specific variables in future work. I would agree, if that meant a more thorough examination of differing and country-specific labour-market institutions and arrangements, as emphasized in the Tarantelli paper.

The major point raised in Tarantelli's paper centres on the effectiveness of monetary policy in restraining inflationary expectations under alternate systems of industrial relations. His main contention is that a more highly centralized, 'neocorporatist' system of industrial relations allows for the combined 'announcement effect' of both monetary and trade union policy, thus curbing free-rider problems associated with more fragmented and decentralized systems of industrial relations. He emphasizes that the pure technical aspects of non-overlapping short-term contracts combined with high-level bargaining can facilitate macroeconomic stability. However, what is crucial is a degree of political or ideological consensus, 'a certain degree of institutional or at least informal integration of trade unions within the political and economic machinery of government.'

Quite apart from the difficulty of measuring such varying degrees of consensus, there is a further problem of validating consensus formation processes in different economic circumstances. One might argue that an industrial relations system is put to a much harder test when coping with secular declines in productivity, rising technological changes, or massive reduction in unemployment through work-sharing schemes are compared to coping with an externally imposed oil price shock. Put differently, the free-rider, prisoner-dilemma problems of distributional compulsion may themselves be dependent upon the particular economic events.

This suggests the relevance of all the factors that determine the long-term efficiency of industrial relations (e.g. factors making for the perception of a just income distribution and associated low-cost modes of resolution of conflicts over income shares). Viewed this way, neocorporatism may simply be a 'façade' for the numerous and difficult-to-evaluate social, cultural, and economic factors determining the overall efficiency of labour-market institutions in different jurisdictions, just as contract theory proved to be a 'façade' in explaining institutional variations. A useful avenue for future research might be to assess relative transaction-cost differences of alternate labour-market arrangements vis-à-vis certain goals of macroeconomic efficiency along the market-versus-hierarchy or exit-versus-voice paradigm. In this way, we could assess the economic value of alternate labour-market arrangements. For the time being, we probably can only conjecture the instrumental role of neocorporatism on the basis of ex post and coarse empirical evidence.

THE UNITED STATES

DAVID E. BLOOM and
STEVEN M. BLOOM

Institutional change and labour-market adjustment

Professional economists have advanced a wide range of theories to explain different aspects of the problem of unemployment. These theories may be grouped according to whether they represent equilibrium or disequilibrium explanations. On the equilibrium side, we have theories involving implicit contracts, worker search behaviour, inter-temporal substitution, and efficiency wages. On the disequilibrium side, we have theories involving wage and other labour-market rigidities. Although debates over the relative merits of the alternative theories have been numerous, a consensus has yet to emerge on the suitability of any of these models as an explanation of the contemporary problem of unemployment in Western economies. This situation is particularly distressing since the difference theories suggest widely different policy approaches to the problem.

In this paper we examine the problem by adopting a new equilibrium approach to the analysis of labour-market rigidities. We view unemployment as one indicator of the efficiency (or inefficiency) of an economy's set of labour institutions and analyse the nature of institutional changes now under way in relation to the exogenous economic changes to which they are a response. By researching the extent to which American labour institutions have responded to changes in economic environments, we attempt to conduct a preliminary test of the hypothesis that the unemployment problem in the United States is at least partly due to the operation of a rigid set of outmoded labour institutions.

In a companion paper ('The Economics of Institutional Change and Market Adjustments'), we have set out a theory of institutional change in labour markets. We take a broad view of labour institutions, thinking of them as ranging from work rules and grievance procedures on up to unions, collective bargaining, and federal labour legislation in both union and non-union settings. Likewise, we construe institutional change broadly to encompass both the adoption of genuine institutional innovations as well as the increased or decreased prevalence of existing institutional forms in actual practice.

Changes in labour institutions primarily reflect medium-run and long-run changes in exogenous labour-market conditions. Because economic systems are perpetually in flux, a given set of institutional arrangements is likely to grow inefficient over time. The types of economic changes most likely to give rise to this inefficiency fall into three categories: changes in tastes and preferences of members of the labour force (as reflected by changes in the demographic composition of the labour force), in the technology of the work-place, and in the degree of competitiveness in product markets. Any of these changes may render a given set of institutional arrangements sub-optimal and therefore create incentives for institutional change.

Institutional change also is an inherently sluggish process reflecting the direct costs of institutional change; the indirect costs imposed on risk-averse economic agents by the uncertainty associated with the benefits of institutional change; the political problems associated with the fact that institutional changes must be agreed to by the people who are affected by the institutions; and the requirements that all of society's institutions mesh with each other, at least to some degree.

In general, then, we may think of economic agents in the short run as adjusting to disequilibrium subject to a given, stable institutional setting. In addition, in the medium and long run, the institutional arrangements themselves become subject to change, largely through collective action. However, because of their inertia, institutions simply may not be able to keep pace with labour-market conditions when those conditions are undergoing rapid change. Under these circumstances, high unemployment may reflect the short-run incompatibility of labour-market conditions and institutions. To illustrate this, we summarize the main recent changes in labour-market conditions and the associated institutional responses, as outlined in more detail in our companion paper.

In recent years the North American labour market has been dramatically affected by changes in demography, technology, and product markets. On the demographic side, the increased number of women and younger workers and the increased educational attainment of the labour force suggest that the tastes and preferences of workers are changing on average and are also becoming more diverse about the average. Technological change continues to displace labour in some industries but leads to growth and labour absorption in other industries. Productivity growth has slowed, although the degree of variability in productivity growth across industries has increased over time. Also key US industries are becoming more competitive, largely because of deregulation and increasing foreign penetration of American product markets.

Partly in response to changing labour-market conditions, a number of major institutional developments related to labour markets have occured. These include a decline of private-sector unionism in the United States, the advent of more sophisticated personnel practices and increased resource allocated to union avoidance in the non-union sector, and the erosion of national labour policy (i.e. the nation's policy toward organized labour) in favour of a long list of more piecemeal public policy changes. A central tenet of our analysis is that almost all these institutional developments have their roots in the economic changes discussed previously.

First, the decline of private-sector unions is partly attributable to the growing number of female, young, and educated workers, all of whom have traditionally expressed only moderately favourable union sentiment. Second, increasing international competition has led to the permanent contraction of several key US industries in which unions are heavily represented. For example, the United Steelworkers and the United Autoworkers unions, two of the nation's largest internationals, experienced membership declines of 51 per cent and 32 per cent, respectively, between 1970 and 1982. Increased product competition in the United States has also made it more difficult for unions to sustain themselves: for example, deregulation of key transportation industries has stimulated the entry of small non-union firms which, in many cases, are effectively competing for segments of markets previously served by union firms.

Third, the improvement of wages and working conditions in the non-union sector and the devotion of increased resources and attention to anti-union campaigns appear, to some extent, to reflect employers' desires to keep free of union constraints in increasingly competitive economic environments. These developments may also be examples of managers' inventing or adopting what are essentially new methods of keeping unions out of their firms in order to enhance the profitability and flexibility of their operations.

Fourth, the erosion of national labour policy and the nature of many of the piecemeal policy developments that are filling the resultant void appear to reflect the federal government's tacit acceptance of management's view that unions have a negative impact on profits, investment, technological modernization, and growth, and the increasingly unfavourable view of the public toward the trade union movement. Related to the government's acceptance of these views is the fact that many segments of the unionized sector have experienced substantial employment declines and little productivity growth over the past five to ten years. For example, productivity in the steel and automobile industries declined at average annual rates of 1.3 per cent and 0.5 per cent, respectively, between 1977 and 1982.

In addition to the major institutional developments a number of innovative institutional changes have occured at the level of the firm, also in response to the rapidly changing demographic and market conditions. For example, the growing number of two-earner families and the increasingly heterogeneous benefit preferences of the labour force have stimulated the development and implementation of 'cafeteria' plans under which workers have some degree of freedom to determine the form of their compensation. These same factors have also led to the growth of flexible work-scheduling and new child-care benefits and tax credits as employers and the government seek new ways to increase the compatibility of child-bearing, child-rearing, and labour-force participation. The changing nature of work – away from continuous-process shift work and toward service-sector employment which seems less demanding in terms of rigid time requirements – has also spurred the expansion of flexible hours by making this arrangement more feasible.

Changing product market conditions in general and the recession of 1979–83 in particular have led labour and management to seek new ways to increase productivity and profitability. Hence, the growing use of suggestion plans, profit-sharing and stock-ownership plans, quality-of-work-life programs, two-tier labour contracts, and early retirements plans. Technological change also has given rise to more extensive use of labour-management committees as well as a variety of innovative job-security arrangements. For example, in its landmark agreement with the United Autoworkers in 1984, General Motors established a one-billion-dollar job-security fund to compensate workers who are laid off because of technological change, the transfer of work to an outside supplier, or negotiated changes in the work process.

While inducing this myriad of institutional responses, changing labour-market conditions are pressing the American labour system to the limits of its ability to function efficiently. The original intent and prior application of the National Labour Relations Act is being increasingly circumvented by employers who are being aided by administrative decisions and by court rulings. Moreover, the void created by the decline of national labour policy is not being filled by comprehensive new labour legislation. Rather, the principal features of recent public policy developments in the labour area are their piecemeal nature and their lack of orientation toward the union setting. Thus, the void is being filled essentially by institutions that are being privately adopted by workers and employers. Indeed, whereas unions have been on the forefront of institutional innovation for much of the period since passage of the Wagner Act in 1935, the changing labour practices in the growing non-union sector of the economy are now becoming an increasingly important determinant of changes in the American labour system. These practices are becoming increasingly diverse in response to the growing diversity of the characteristics of the labour force and the increasingly uneven nature of productivity growth, technological change, and employment changes across industries.

American labour institutions are adjusting to changing labour-market conditions at an extremely slow pace and in an incomplete fashion. For example, concession bargaining, two-tier contracts, early retirement incentives, and job-security agreements are all mechanisms for smoothing the transition from one equilibrium to another. But in smoothing this transition, essentially be shielding incumbent workers from bearing the bulk of economic adjustment costs, the time period over which the transition takes place is substantially lengthened. Our analysis therefore suggests that persistent unemployment is attributable in part to sluggish institutional responsiveness to changing long-run labour-market conditions.

The institutional features of the American labour market in the future will reflect both a contemporaneous response to future labour-market changes and the continued evolutionary response to events of the recent past. Future institutional responses are likely to be induced by two expected labour-market changes of particular importance – technological changes and aging of the work-force.

Technological changes in many industries are likely to result in an accelerated use of increasingly expensive and complex equipment. This development is significant because of the growing belief that complex machinery tends to be used most productively when the individuals who operate it are encouraged to identify changes that need to be made and to modify their work behaviour accordingly. This type of flexibility is fundamentally incompatible with the philosophy of scientific management that pervaded the American labour system since the turn of the century and is further constrained by the nature of associated wage systems based on rigid work rules that restrict employees by carefully detailing their duties and responsibilities. Current responses to these problems include the growing use of suggestion plans, labour-management committees, and quality-of-work-life programs. Likely future responses include compensation systems that encourage workers to exercise independent judgment (e.g. wages tied to individuals and not to their jobs) and mechanisms that facilitate co-operation between workers and managers, especially on the shop floor. As the 'baby boom' population (which gave rise to problems of the transition from school to work and the associated youth unemployment) ages, a new set of labour-market problems are likely to ensue, putting new pressure on labour-market institutions. Relative to younger workers, older workers are likely to be more risk-averse and to experience greater non-pecuniary costs of mobility and losses of seniority and location-specific skills if they change employers. Also, older workers are less likely to be rehired elsewhere and have a shorter horizon than younger workers for the recoupment of training and relocation costs. Given these key differences, the aging work-force will probably show a declining propensity to respond to exogenous economic changes through market adjustments such as mobility. Instead, institutional change will be the preferred form of response, especially in so far as it lowers the likelihood of geographic mobility and provides job security. Indeed, legislation promoting worker buyouts of failing companies is an excellent example of just this type of response, and we would expect to see its relative frequency increase as the work-force ages.

Although workers' skills may grow obsolete and their capacity for physical labour diminish as they age, their judgment and maturity tend to increase. Thus, the capabilities of an older work-force may be quite complementary with the requirements of existing and new technologies in which worker judgment plays a more central role in the production process.

Employees with longer period of company service have traditionally been awarded preferential treatment in a broad range of decisions affecting the work-force, and seniority has served as an effective mechanism for performing that function. But, as the work-force ages, the distribution of workers will become increasingly concentrated at greater levels of service. This implies, for example, that seniority will provide less of a buffer against layoffs for workers with a given amount of service. In such circumstances it may be necessary to rely on alternative mechanisms (e.g. work-sharing, retraining) to shield older workers from the adverse employment consequences of business-cycle downturns.

Our perception, then, is that the American labour system, while accommodating considerable institutional change, simply has not been able to keep pace with the changing composition of the American work-force, changing technology, and the increased competitiveness of product markets. In part at least, this accounts for some of the general worsening of unemployment that has taken place over the past fifteen years. Given the inertia of institutional change, it is not likely, however, that the labour system operating in the United States by the turn of the century will be fundamentally different from that in operation today.

Given the importance of labour institutions, our perception is also that macroeconomists should focus more closely on labour institutions when formulating economic policy. In fact, we feel that the colossal challenge facing macroeconomists today is to design macroeconomic policies that both promote vigorous growth and are compatible with existing labour institutions. The pulse of the American labour system has weakened somewhat, and a co-ordianted effort on the part of labour economists, macroeconomists, and business, labour, and public policy officials may well be the best way to strengthen it.

LINDA BELL and RICHARD FREEMAN

Flexible wage structures and employment

In contrast to the employment experience of most OECD countries, the United States experienced a substantial increase in employment in the 1970s. While unemployment rates were historically high in the 1970s, so too were employment/population ratios. Some have argued that the great growth of jobs in the United States is attributable to wage flexibility in terms of aggregate wages, or in terms of relative adjustments across sectors. The extent to which US aggregate wage flexibility contributes to job creation has been much debated in the literature (see Sachs 1979; Branson and Rotemberg 1980; Gordon 1982).

This paper examines wage flexibility across industries and its connection to the growth of employment. We find little evidence linking the US employment record to flexible wages across industries. While industry wages vary with industry conditions to a greater extent in the United States than in other OECD countries, this does not enhance employment. In the 1970s it created greater dispersion of earnings across industry lines and shifts of labour across industries in a fashion inconsistent with standard models of how competitive markets determine wages and allocate employment among industries. Consistent with our rejection of the link between industry wage flexibility and employment growth is the fact that the other major OECD country with a sizeable expansion of employment over this period, Japan, has had a very different wage-setting pattern, with little or no flexibility of relative wages among industries.

The paper is divided into three sections. The first documents the fact that industry wages in the United States are flexible, in the sense of responding to industry-specific conditions. The second argues that flexibility in the industry wage structure is neither inherently good nor bad for employment. It lays out two polar cases: the 'competitive flexibility case,' in which a flexible industry wage structure is employment-enhancing, and the 'industry-productivity-wage case,' in which flexibility of wages may reduce employment. The third seeks to determine whether the observed flexibility of the US industrial wage structure is closer to the former or to the latter case.

Do wages in the United States respond to industry-level conditions, so that the pattern of wage differentials among industries varies over time? Our answer is yes. Alone among the major OECD countries, the United States has experienced substantial changes in the industry wage structure. Our calculations (given in the larger paper) indicate that the variation of log wages among industries increased dramatically during the 1970s. This pattern of increased inequality in the industrial wage structure since 1970 runs counter to the long-term trend toward lower dispersion of wages among industries (Cullen 1956; Reynolds and Taft 1956). This increased dispersion of the wage structure across industries was not simply a reflection of the growth of the service sector with its low-paying jobs; wage dispersion increased within both the service and manufacturing sectors over the 1970s. As illustrated in Table 1, the pattern of increasing dispersion in the 1970s is unique to the United States.[1] In western Europe and Japan wage structures remained relatively stable or narrowed in the 1970s, at least in manufacturing.

We estimate next equations linking changes in industry wages over an extended period of time to various potential wage-determining characteristics, using variants of the following equation:

(1) $\quad \Delta\ln W_i = a + b\Delta\ln(VA/L_i) + c\Delta F + d\Delta\ln\text{Skill} + e\text{Union}_i + \mu_i$

where W_i = wage in industry i; VA/L = value productivity per worker; F = proportion of workers who are women; Skill = a variable wage-weighted index of the occupations in an industry $(\Sigma W_S \alpha_{s,i})$ where W_s is the national wage in the occupation and α_s = share of occupation in employment; and union$_i$ = proportion unionized.

The key 'industry-specific' variable in this equation is the level of value productivity per worker, which we will later decompose into physical productivity per worker and output price. The notion that industrial productivity trends affect industry wages has a long history in economic thought, with some early post–Second World War studies of industrial wages finding evidence of a weak positive link between changes in wages and productivity at the industrial level (see Dunlop 1948; Garbino 1950). The prevailing view, however, favours the competitve model, in which wages and productivity

TABLE 1
Wage dispersion in other countries

	Japan $N=30$	France $N=29$	West Germany $N=31$	Spain $N=14$	Switzer-land $N=16$	UK $N=31$	Italy $N=31$
1975	0.269	0.164	0.164	0.210	0.167	0.169	0.192
1982	0.288	0.156	0.173	0.202*	0.167	0.179	0.122

SOURCE: US Department of Labour, Bureau of Labor Statistics, Office of Productivity and Technology
Numbers are standard deviations of ℓn hourly compensation costs for production workers based on US equivalents.
*1977 and 1981 figures respectively; no figures available for 1975, 1976 or 1982

are uncorrelated across sectors and where wages depend on aggregate, rather than sectoral, conditions (see Salter 1960; Meyers and Bowlby 1953; and most recently Kendrick 1983).

The increasing proportion of female employment in some sectors, is likely to have increased the dispersion of wages in the 1970s, since women tend to be clustered at the low end of the wage spectrum. Similarly, the widening of the inter-industry wage differential may reflect the widening of the wage differential between skilled and unskilled workers that has occurred over the 1970s in response to generally slack labour-market conditions (Hamermesh and Rees 1984). The union variable is introduced to take account of the well-known growth of the union premium in the 1970s (see Johnson 1981; Freeman and Medoff 1979).

Our econometric estimates (based on two different data sets) indicate that changes in wages are indeed positively related to changes in value productivity by industry over the 1970s. Also, when the changes in value productivity are decomposed into changes in prices and in output per worker, both terms matter; however, the price term has a somewhat greater effect on wages. While changes in the percentage female, in the skill mix, and in the percentage covered by collective bargaining affect changes in industry wages in the expected manner, they do not substantially reduce the coefficient on changes in value productivity. The positive response of industry wages to industry price and productivity changes is also confirmed when we use data from Kendrick (1983) over the period 1948–79.

Overall, our results show that industry wage differentials in the United States responded to industry-level conditions in the 1970s, a finding that contrasts sharply with the conclusions of most earlier studies that found wage and productivity movements were not correlated at the sectoral level (see Salter 1960 for the United Kingdom; Meyers and Bowlby 1953). While our results may be due to the omission of some aspect of labour quality that has diverged greatly across industries, the general consistency of our finding across data sets makes this possibility highly unlikely. The imperviousness of the findings to the addition of labour quality controls and unionization variables, together with the observed increased disperions of sectoral wages, suggests that industry wages are indeed responsive to industry conditions. On the basis of the constancy of the relative wage structure in other major OECD countries as shown in Table 1, and a brief examination of the relation between changes in value productivity and wages across two-digit industries in Japan which produced essentially a zero wage-productivity correlation, we conclude that this pattern of wage behaviour is unique to the US economy. A possible explanation for the singular US industrial experience is that the American industrial relations system is highly decentralized, with thousands of different firms and unions determining wages, in contrast to the more centralized wage-setting mechanisms found in most other countries (Bruno and Sachs 1984).

When does industry wage flexibility enhance employment and when does it reduce employment? It is common to hear the claim that 'wage flexibility' is inherently good for employment. After all, don't wage concessions save jobs in declining industries? While concessions in declining industries may indeed enhance employment, economists have long recognized that wage flexibility across industries is not uniformly good for employment. In particular, when industry wages respond to industry-specific productivity patterns with sectors experiencing rapid productivity growth raising wages more than other sectors, 'flexibility' can reduce employment in the technologically advancing sectors and possibly in the economy overall. In this section we sketch out briefly the circumstances in which flexible wages among industries may be employment-enhancing (the competitive flexibility case) and those in which flexible wages among industries can reduce employment (the industry productivity-wage-flexibility case). Whether flexibility of wages among US industries helps or hinders the growth of employment and the reduction of unemployment depends on which circumstances best fit US industrial wage developments.

When industry wages are responsive to shifts in demand and supply for workers in particular industries, employment will be greater than if wages are inflexible. Consider, for example, wage responses to upward and downward shifts in demand. If short-run labour-supply schedules are upward sloping, as seems reasonable, wage increases are necessary to increase employment when demand rises, while wage decreases will ameliorate the employment loss due to demand declines. In such a setting, dynamic shifts in demand for labour across industries will produce wage dispersion for similar workers among industries and a positive relation between changes in wages and changes in employment in the short run. The extent of wage flexibility necessary to produce a given employment change within a sector will depend on the labour demand and supply elasticities governing behaviour within the sector and on conditions external to the industry, such as the total number of unemployed workers.

According to the competitive model, however, differentials in pay of equivalent workers across industries should be short-lived, as mobility of workers produces roughly equal pay for equal work. Workers will move to industries that have had positive demand 'shocks,' thereby reducing the measured average wage and expanding employment even more. In equilibrium, industrial wage differentials will result exclusively from skill differences among workers and/or compensating differentials due to the nature of work. While changing demand for labour may influence wages in the short run, as adjustment takes place along upward-sloping labour supply curves, in the long run it is mostly through employment, not wages, that adjustment takes place. Mobility of workers ultimately links industrial wages to aggregate, rather than sectoral, conditions and assures the long-run elimination of wage differentials created by demand 'shocks.' A competitive industry wage structure should therefore be responsive to industry-specific factors in the short run but not in the long run.

While short-run wage flexibility due to competitive forces is employment-enhancing, flexibility due to industry-specific conditions independent of shifts in the demand or supply of labour need not have beneficial employment consequences. Consider, for example, a labour market in which wages respond to industry-specific changes in value productivity per worker that do not reflect shifts in labour demand. While downward flexibility of wages in response to declines in value productivity per worker can still 'save' jobs, upward flexibility of wages in response to increases in value productivity per worker will, in the same sense, 'cost' jobs, with industries experiencing rapid value-productivity growth hiring too few workers.

Whether or not wage flexibility of this type is good or bad for aggregate employment in comparison with the employment consequences of an inflexible industry wage system will depend both on the mix of positive and negative productivity shocks among industries and on the extent of downward and upward flexibility in wages. With equal-sized positive and negative 'shocks' to demand in equal-sized sectors with equal elasticities of labour demand and labour supply, a flexible relative wage system will not necessarily lead to greater employment. If there is asymmetry in response patterns, with wages declining more in industries doing poorly than rising in booming sectors, a flexible wage system will produce more employment than an inflexible system. If, instead, wages fall less with relative productivity declines than wages rise with relative productivity increases, the system of flexible wages will on net result in less employment than would otherwise have been observed.

In principle, then, there are two possible situations in which wage flexibility among industries has positive employment consequences: when the wages reflect 'competitive' market forces, and when wages are more flexible downward than upward to industry-specific productivity (or other) developments.

Our previous finding of a positive response of wages to productivity growth would fit the competitive model and thus be employment-increasing if industries with relatively rapid productivity growth also experienced relatively rapid growth of labour demand. In this case, productivity growth would be correlated positively with employment growth, as the associated wage increases attract more labour to the high-productivity growth sectors. Salter (1960) found such a strong positive correlation between productivity growth and employment in the United Kingdom. However, we find exactly the opposite pattern among US industries in the 1970s. Industries with rapid productivity growth tended to have lower rather than higher employment growth, making it difficult to interpret the industry patterns in competitive terms as demand shifts along upward-sloping supply curves. We also find evidence of a positive correlation between the growth of wages and the level of wages across industries, which is inconsistent with the competitive wage flexibility interpretation. It is difficult to argue that industries that already pay above-average wages 'need' wage increases to attract more labour, especially in the decade of generally slack labour markets. But, as indicated by the increase in wage dispersion since 1970, this is precisely what occurred: large wage increases in high-wage sectors.

The suggestion here is that the industry wage and employment figures reflect not the competitive flexibility model but rather the industry-productivity-wage model, in which increases in wages may reduce employment along demand schedules. To examine this point further we estimate the following simple labour demand relation across industries:

(2) $\Delta lE_i = \alpha + \beta \Delta \ln W_i/P_i + g\Delta \ln O_i$

where $\Delta \ln E_i$ = change in log of employment in industry i; $\Delta \ln W_i/P_i$ = change in log of product wage in industry i; and $\Delta \ln O_i$ = change in real output in industry i.

The patterns of change in employment, wages, and output by industry fit such a demand relation quite well. Industries with relative product wage increases had relative employment decreases, output held fixed. While equations (1) and (2) are not independent of one another and can be analysed with a simultaneous model in which both wages and employment are endogenous,[3] each shows wage-employment behaviour inconsistent with the standard competitive model of industry labour markets.

It is, of course, still possible that the flexibility of wages across industries is employment-enhancing. If wages respond more to relative declines in productivity than to relative increases in productivity, flexibility of wages will still lead to greater employment. To see if such asymmetries hold for the United States, we have re-estimated the wage equations allowing for asymmetric responses of wages to productivity changes, with separate variables for value productivity increases above and below the average. The results suggest, if anything, that wages are more flexible upward than downward. This same pattern emerges far more strikingly in regressions linking annual movements in wages to annual movements in productivity.[4]

Finally, to see if we can generate any evidence that industry wage flexibility contributes to employment growth in the United States, we have taken a more aggregate approach to examine the possibility of a link between the growth of employment to population by year and a crude indicator of the change in the industry wage structure over time, namely, the level of dispersion in wages by year. To test this we estimated, using aggregate data from 1950 to 1982, the following regression equation:

(3) $\ln(E/P) = 1.83 + 0.35\ln\text{GNP} - 0.06\sigma_w + 0.01T - 0.01T70,$

$\qquad\qquad\quad (0.06) \qquad\quad (0.33) \qquad (0.002) \quad (0.002)$

$\quad R^2 = 0.853,$

where E/P = employment/population ratio; GNP = GNP measured in constant 1972 dollars; σ_w = dispersion of industry wages in NIPA data; T = trend; and $T70$ = trend term for 1970. Holding the level of GNP and time, constant, there is a slight negative correlation between the dispersion of industry wages and employment/population which would suggest that industry wage flexibility has little or no relation to aggregate employment.[5]

In sum, our analysis suggests that the flexibility of wages across industries that we find in the United States diverges too much from the competitive flexibility case to contribute to the growth of employment. If anything, the disaggregate data suggest that the flexibility of industry wages to industry value productivity has been harmful to employment.

In this paper we have examined the flexibility of wages across industries in the United States using various data sets for the entire economy and for manufacturing industries and examined the impact of the changing industry wage structure on employment. Our findings can be summarized briefly.

1. Contrary to historic patterns, the industrial wage structure has become more disperse, with the dispersion of wages measured across sectors in the United States increasing in every year since 1970, leading to an overall rise of 35 per cent from 1970 to 1982. This trend has occurred in both manufacturing and service sectors and has produced an overall widening of the US wage structure, with the differential between top-wage and bottom-wage quartiles rising from an average of 80 per cent 1945–70 to over 90 per cent since 1970.

2. This pattern of dispersion is unique to the United States as a developed economy, as wage dispersion in both western Europe and Japan has either remained constant or declined.

3. Industrial wages at both two-digit and four-digit levels are positively correlated with productivity and price movements over the post-war period in ways.

4. The flexibility of the US industry wage structure has not contributed to employment growth; if anything, it has been inimical to employment and the competitive allocation of labour across sectors.

Let us return to the question with which we began, 'Does a flexible industry wage structure increase employment?' In theory, under certain circumstances, flexible wage across industries will increase employment, while in other circumstances they will not. In practice, as far as we can tell for the United States in the 1970s, flexible wages by industry did not contribute to employment.

NOTES

This is a condensed version of a larger paper of the same title (available from the authors on request) which provides the detailed econometric estimates.

1 International comparisons of hourly compensation costs for production workers in manufacturing industries in selected countries are prepared by the US Department of Labor, Bureau of Labor Statistics, Office of Productivity and Technology, annually since 1975. Since the calculation of labour compensation does not include the same items in each country, caution should be exercised in cross-country analysis. Hourly compensation is converted to US dollars using averge daily exchange rates for the reference period.

2 Though not reported, in our analysis of industry wages we experiment with several different time periods. The results are not sensitive to the time period of analysis. Regressions for both the pre-1970s period (1948–70) and the entire post–Second World War period (1948–82) yielded qualitatively similar wage-productivity relationships.

3 The simultaneous two-equation model is explored in thesis work currently in progress by Linda A. Bell.

4 In the short term, movements in productivity may be wage-dependent and therefore not truly exogenous in a wage equation. The technical issue of productivity exogeneity in the short and long term is explored in thesis work currently in progress by Linda A. Bell.

5 We have also estimated variants of equation (3) with current rather than constant dollars, and obtained a -0.09 (0.82) coefficient (standard error) on the σ_w term. If we eliminate the $T70$ term, we obtain contradictory results with constant- and current-dollar GNP: a 0.80 (0.14) coefficient on σ_w in the former case, compared to -0.68 (0.25) in the latter case. As the similar coefficients obtained with inclusion of $T70$ indicate, these differences reflect different treatment of the 1970s, when productivity growth was slow and inflation substantial. While the statistics support the current-dollar GNP equation ($R^2 = 0.853$ vs $R^2 = 0.810$), we believe the weak negative results given in the text with the $T70$ term provide a more accurate picture of what the data say.

REFERENCES

Bluestone, B., and B. Harrison. 1982. *The DeIndustrialization of America*. New York: Basic Books

Branson, W.H., and J.J. Rotemberg. 1980. 'International Adjustment with Wage Rigidity,' *European Economic Review* 13:308–22

Bruno, M., and J. Sachs. 1984. *Economics of World Wide Stagflation*. Cambridge, Mass: Harvard University Press

Cullen, D.E. 1956. 'The Interindustry Wage Structure, 1899–1950,' *American Economic Review* 46, No. 3 (June) 353–69

Dunlop, J.T. 1948. 'Productivity and the Wage Structure.' in *Income, Employment and Public Policy (Essays in Honor of Alvin H. Hansen)*. New York: Norton

Freeman, R.B., and J.L. Medoff. 1979. 'New Estimates of Private Sector Unionism in the United States,' *Indusutrial and Labour Relations Review* 32, No. 2 (January) 143–74

– 1983. *What Do Unions Do?* New York: Basic Books

Garbino, J. 1950. 'A Theory of Interindustry Wage Structure,' *Quarterly Journal of Economics* 44, No. 2 (May) 282–305

Gordon, R.J. 1982. 'Why U.S. Wage and Employment Behavior Differs from That in Britian and Japan,' *Economics Journal* 92 (March) 13–44

Hamermesh, D.S., and A. Rees. 1984. *The Economics of Work and Pay*, 3rd edition. New York: Harper and Row

Johnson, G. 1981. 'Changes over Time in the Union/Nonunion Wage Differential in the United States.' University of Michigan, February, mimeographed

Kendrick. 1983. *Interindustry Differences in Productivity Growth* (Washington, DC: American Enterprise Institute)

Meyers, F., and R.L. Bowlby. 1953. 'The Interindustry Wage Structure and Productivity,' *Industrial and Labour Relations Review* 7, No. 1 (October)

OECD. 1965. *Wages and Labor Mobility*, Paris: OECD

– 1984. *Employment Outlook*. Paris: OECD.

Reynolds, L., and C.H. Taft. 1956. *The Evolution of the Wage Structure*. New Haven: Yale University Press

Sachs, J. 1979. 'Wages, Profits and Macroeconomic Adjustment: A Comparative Study,' *Brookings Papers on Economic Activity* 2:269–319

Salter, W.E.G. 1960. *Productivity and Technical Change*. Cambridge: Cambridge University Press

Wachter, M. 19—. 'Cyclical Variation in the Interindustry Wage Structure,' *American Economic Review* 40, No. 1, 75–84

Comments

DANIEL S. HAMERMESH

The common ground in these papers is their concern with adjustment in the labour market in the United States. Bloom and Bloom deal with institutional adjustment, while Bell and Freeman deal with employment and wage adjustment. The first paper builds a theory of how institutions change in response to underlying demographic and technological changes; the second tests the competitive adjustment of labour-market outcomes.

Bloom and Bloom postulate that labour-market institutions respond to changes in technology and tastes with lags that arise because of the presence of adjustment costs. Adjustment to a new equilibrium of institutions will be slower the greater are the costs, but the eventual change in the institutions will be greater the more rapid and substantial are the changes in tastes and technology. Bloom and Bloom claim that the tastes of American workers are becoming more diverse and point to (among other things) the increasing variety of fringe benefits as outcomes of the growing dispersion of tastes.

The basis for their theory is unobjectionable: any social-scientific theory that is to have positive value deals with the response to specified stimuli. However, there is unfortunately nothing falsifiable in what they propose. To state that institutions respond to changed stimuli with a lag is reasonable; it does not, though, distinguish between responses like the French Revolution and those like the substitution of Brian Mulroney for John Turner!

I believe their theory can be given positive content by making an analogy to the (well-developed) theory of factor demand. That theory shows that adjustment will be slower if the marginal cost of adjustment increases more rapidly with the magnitude of the change made in each time period. If they were to identify those factors that affect the marginal cost of increased rapidity of institutional change, they would then be half-way toward a theory with positive predictions. The remaining half would be attained if they could specify the likely eventual magnitude of the response of institutions to specific shocks.

Though the authors claim that current institutional change is the result of an unusually rapid increase in the diversity of tastes, surely there are other periods in US history when tastes diverged more rapidly yet institutional change in the labour market was minimal. The period of massive eastern and southern European immigration from 1880 to 1910 created a more diverse labour force far more rapidly than the small changes induced by the post-war baby boom; yet the institutions with which Bloom and Bloom are concerned changed remarkably little during that period.

The relatively small underlying change in demographics (and presumably tastes) cannot be easily rationalized with the change in institutions by their approach. I believe the institutional changes are explained by the rapidity of growth of real disposable income and the levels that it has attained. With a society of abundance has come the ability to sacrifice some income growth in exchange for an increased diversity of experiences, including how time is used and fringe benefits. That unionism, the institution that Bloom and Bloom are most concerned with, is on the decline in the United States, despite government policy that is not discouraging and union organizing expenditures that have stayed constant per non-union worker in real terms, may be explained by the view that the institutional arrangements it offers are simply not ones that we want as our income increases (Hamermesh 1984; Voos 1984).

The pervasive theme of Bloom and Bloom that current institutional change is too slow cannot be established without a good theory of adjustment costs and a specification of agents' perceptions of the path of future stimuli. In addition, because of their preoccupation with the collective-bargaining sector, a segment of the market covering slightly more than one-sixth of the US work-force, they have neglected the major institutional changes in the past thirty years which have been in the areas of industrial safety and retirement and disability policy. In order to understand these changes, which are imposed by government in response to the perceived wishes of the electorate, it is necessary to go beyond the unionized sector of the US economy.

Bell and Freeman present four empirical findings describing the US labour market in the past fifteen years. 1) The dispersion of wage levels has increased, though it has not done so in other industrialized countries. 2) As part of the first finding, there has been a positive correlation between wage levels and percentage wage increases by industry. 3) There has been a positive correlation between percentage changes in wages and productivity per worker across industries. 4) There has been a negative correlation between percentage changes in employment and productivity across the industries. Bell and Freeman consider the implications of these fascinating facts for the process of competitive adjustment in the labour market.

In a sense the finding of increased wage dispersion is even more impressive than it seems initially, since the increased incentives for low-wage workers to leave the labour force should have reduced wage dispersion (Butler and Heckman 1977). The increased dispersion, however, says nothing about labour-market flexibility: it merely demonstrates that there are forces that have caused industry wage levels to rise more in high-wage industries. Indeed, though Bell and Freeman are pessimistic about the degree of wage flexibility in the United States, it is difficult to explain the superior performance of the American economy during the oil shocks without reference to downward aggregate real wage flexibility. Perhaps relative wages, on which they focus, do not adjust well; but economy-wide wage levels, which are what is important for evaluating responses to aggregate shocks, have been more responsive in the United States than elsewhere.

I do not find it difficult to reconcile the facts that Bell and Freeman have produced; a labour-demand story does the job quite well. In their employment-demand equations they show that there is capital-labour substitution in the the United States (as there undoubtedly is in other industrialized countries). We also know that the substitution of capital for labour is accomplished by the substitution of higher- for less-skilled labour (Hamermesh 1986). Since Bell and Freeman do not hold constant (indeed, given the aggregate data they use, cannot hold constant) labour quality, the correlations of productivity change with wage and employment changes reflect these various substitutions. We have seen rapid productivity changes in high-wage industries produced by capital deepening and a relative increase in labour-force quality; these changes have taken place through the substitution of capital and skilled workers for less-skilled labour. Aside from rationalizing Bell and Freeman's facts, this explanation shows that these facts are quite consistent with a standard competitive explanation.

The main thrust of Bell and Freeman's paper – the 'testing' of competitive labour-market adjustment – harks back to papers by Ulman (1965) and Behman (1964). Both used simple correlations of changes in industry aggregates – employment, wages, etc – to make claims about the ability of the market to allocate labour. While the correlations were interesting, claims such as theirs and those of Bell and Freeman are inherently incapable of determining the efficiency of labour markets. First, we know that lags in labour-market adjustments are very long. More important, more careful structural modelling needs to be done before one can conclude that the correlations of Bell and Freeman are anything more than interesting facts.

The US labour market has seen remarkable changes in the past twenty years, chiefly induced by three phenomena: the rapid growth of female labour-force participation; the entry of the 'baby boom' generation into the labour force; and the increased demand for labour resulting from the huge rise in the relative price of one of its substitutes, energy. These changes have been at least partly responsible for most of the labour-market outcomes that have concerned economists, including the slowdown in productivity growth, the rapid drop in youth relative wages (and the rise in youth unemployment rates), and the failure of women's wages to rise much relative to men's. As Bloom and Bloom note, these changes are likely to affect future institutional development; and despite Bell and Freeman's inferences, the flexibility of the American labour market suggests that these and future changes will be accommodated fairly well by the market system. At the very least, we should be aware that, compared to earlier changes, the changed stimuli that affected outcomes in the recent past have been relatively unimportant. Past evidence suggests that both institutions and allocative mechanisms are able to adjust to such changes in ways that, compared to other industrialized democracies, minimize social tensions and economic dislocation.

REFERENCES

Behman, S. 1964. 'Labor Mobility and Increasing Labor Demand,' *Review of Economic Studies* 31 (October) 253–66

Butler, R., and J. Heckman 1977. 'The Government's Impact on the Labor Market Status of Black Americans: A Critical Review,' in Leonard Hausman et al, *Equal Rights and Industrial Relations.* Madison, Wisc: Industrial Relations Research Association

Hamermesh, D. 1984. 'Homogenization of Time Use.' National Bureau of Economic Research, Working Paper No. 1397

– 1986. 'Demand for Labour in the Long Run,' in O. Ashenfelter and R. Layard, *Handbook of Labour Economics.* Amsterdam: North-Holland Press

Ulman, L. 1965. 'Labor Mobility and the Industrial Wage Structure in the Postwar United States, *Quarterly Journal of Economics* 79 (February) 73–97

Voos, P. 1984. 'Trends in Union Organizing Expenditures, 1953–1977,' *Industrial and Labor Relations Review* 38 (October) 52–63

THOMAS A. KOCHAN

The Bell and Freeman paper addresses four key questions which I will take up in turn. 1) What explains inter-industry wage dispersion in the United States and why did this dispersion increase in the 1970s? 2) Why is the US experience different from that of Europe and Japan over this same time period? 3) Were US wages flexible in the 1970s? 4) Do flexible wages account for US employment growth since 1970?

To these questions, I will add a fifth and sixth which provide a bridge to the paper prepared by Steven and David Bloom. 5) Under what institutional or industrial relations system arrangements are flexible wages likely to produce employment growth? 6) Is the US industrial relations system adjusting in ways that: (a) wages are likely to be more flexible, and (b) employment growth will result from this flexibility?

What explains inter-industry wage dispersion? I have a very different, yet simple, hypothesis for the increase in inter-industry wage dispersion observed in the United States in the 1970s, particularly within the unionized sector of the economy. That explanation involves the growth of cost-of-living clauses in union contracts during years of high inflation and the expansion of both the union/non-union wage differential and the differential within the unionized sector between high-wage, strong-union industries and low-wage, weak-union industries. In this explanation, the relation between wage dispersion and increased productivity obtained in Bell and Freeman's analysis would be explained as an effect of managerial adjustments to higher wages, not as a cause of increased wage dispersion. To the extent that increased productivity is causing inter-industry wage dispersion, it is more likely to be doing so in the growth firms and industries in the non-union sector, since these firms and industries are in early stages of their life-cycles, where output is expanding rapidly and firms need to pay competitive wages for skilled technical and managerial talent in order to meet their expanding market opportunities.

Evidence consistent with this interpretation of wage determination and wage outcomes under collective bargaining in the 1970s is contained in a recent paper by Jacoby and Pearl (1984). Clauses covering cost-of-living allowances (COLAs) were found in 41 per cent of union agreements in 1960; however, during that decade unions lost interest in these clauses, and by 1970 only 25 per cent of major agreements contained escalator clauses. This changed again in the 1970s. By 1972, 41 per cent of agreements again contained escalators, and by 1980, 59 per cent of major agreements contained escalator clauses. Thus, the 1970s saw an expansion of cost-of-living coverage within the union sector.

Jacoby and Pearl (1984) use an aggregate time-series regression equation to estimate the effects of the interaction of price increases and cost-of-living clauses on inter-industry wage dispersion in the United States. The coefficient on their price increase – COLA coverage interaction term is positive and statistically significant and indicates that the effects of inflation on wage dispersion turn positive at about 32 per cent COLA coverage. This point was first exceeded in 1972. These results suggest that increased COLA coverage accounted for about a 13 per cent increase in inter-industry wage dispersion in the 1970s, or approximately half of the observed increase. Further, more disaggregate analyses are needed before these preliminary results can be viewed as conclusive. However, they are consistent with my simple explanation for wage dispersion generated by collective bargaining in the 1970s.

While there may be evidence that productivity-specific factors were the dominant wage-determining force in some sectors of the US economy, this does not fit our analysis of the way in which private-sector collective bargaining was operating in the 1970s. Indeed, in other work drawing on survey data collected by the Conference Board in the mid-1970s, we observed that the dominant criteria used in wage setting by major firms operating under collective bargaining were wage comparisons and COLAs (Freedman 1979; Kochan 1980). Further analysis of those same data showed a significant coefficient for cost-of-living coverage as a determinant of both wage levels and wage changes in the 1970s (Kochan 1980).

Why is European experience different? On this question I agree with the conclusion suggested by Bell and Freeman, namely that wage determination is more centralized in most western European countries, and European economies on average are more highly unionized than the United States.

Do these data indicate that US wages are 'more flexible'? Here I take issue with the use of inter-industry wage dispersion as an operational definition for the concept of wage flexibility. I do not dispute the fact that dispersion in wages across industries may be an indirect indicator or result of flexible wages; however, inter-industry variation does not necessarily imply that wage adjustments conform to the features commonly implied by the term *flexibility*, or its detested obverse, *rigidity*. Flexibility is normally defined as the adjustment of wages based on the specific economic performance or conditions of specific plant, business unit, or firm, or at more aggregate levels, an industry or even an overall society. It further implies that wages are adjusted in differential ways over the course of a business cycle or over the business life-cycle of a firm in response to competitive conditions within its product market. The term is decidedly not consistent with the adjustment of wages to keep up with wages elsewhere within one's industry or region, or between rival unions, or to keep up with changes in the rate of inflation. While these wage policies may result in wage dispersion, they do not have the desired economic properties sought by proponents of wage flexibility. Instead, these wage policies create more standardization of wages and less responsiveness to the specific competitive conditions within the wage-setting unit. As noted earlier, these standardizing tendencies were common features of collective bargaining in the United States in the 1970s.

In contrast, the definition of wage flexibility as described above has come to the United States not in the 1970s under collective bargaining but in the concession-bargaining era of the early 1980s. Indeed, a replication of the Conference Board survey in 1983 found that the dominant wage criteria favoured by firms in the 1980s were no longer wage comparisons or standardization or increases in the cost of living, but the specific productivity and profit performance of the business or bargaining unit involved (Freedman 1985).

Did flexible wages in the United States create jobs? If my analysis is correct, that the United States is experiencing greater flexibility than existed in the 1970s, it is difficult to argue that flexibility created the job boom that dates back to the previous decade. Therefore, I agree with the basic conclusion of Bell and Freeman that the wage-setting patterns of the 1970s were not responsible for the job creation experienced during that time period.

Can flexible wages contribute to employment growth? The question remains: is it possible for flexible wages to contribute to employment growth in the US economy? The answer depends basically on the ability of the US industrial relations system to adjust in ways that effectively link the strategic investment decisions made by management and, to some extent at a more aggregate level, the federal government with the decisions made in setting wages at the level of collective bargaining. That is, wage concessions, gain-sharing, profit-sharing, and bonuses, as opposed to fixed wage increases and so on, are all means of introducing greater wage flexibility into collective bargaining. But whether these new forms of flexibility translate into domestic employment growth depends on the extent to which increased profits are fed back into new investments or are taken in the form of catch-up wage increases.

Are institutional changes in US industrial relations moving in this direction? This leads to the final and most important question and links us directly to a discussion of the variety of institutional changes in the industrial relations system described by Bloom and Bloom. My answer here is that despite the variety of changes that have occurred, in only isolated cases are labour and management linking wage flexibility to new investment. The US system of industrial relations separates decisions made at the level of collective bargaining from the strategic business decisions made within firms and from government policies that can effect investment decisions and structural adjustment for workers displaced by the direct effects of technological changes and increased productivity. For example, in the vast majority of firms that have engaged in concession bargaining, only a small fraction have agreed to trade-offs with their unions for ploughing the cost savings back into investments designed to enhance the productive capacity or employment potential of existing plants (Cappelli 1982). Moreover, because strategic investment decisions are made by American managers far removed from the influence of labour leaders, and because unions have been unable to organize new facilities in the domestic economy to which investment dollars have been flowing, there is little reason to believe that union leaders and their members will continue to be willing to divert wage increases to investment opportunities in which they are unlikely to share. Moreover, most US labour leaders view the crisis of collective bargaining experienced in the 1980s as a temporary pause or deviation from the type of bargaining that characterized the 1960s and 1970s. There is little enthusiasm among US labour leaders for continuing to make sacrifices at the bargaining table so that firms can divert saving and investment dollars either to the growing non-union sector or to overseas opportunities.

Yet there are a number of exceptions to this general pattern that illustrate potential paths to reform. For example, some firms and unions have begun to discuss and share information on longer-term strategic and competitive problems and to engage in very hard bargaining over the conditions under which new investments will be made in existing plants or in plants where unions are granted representational rights. General Electric Company and the International Union of Electrical Workers recently concluded this type of agreement over the 'factory of the future' in Lynn, Massachusetts. Earlier, this same union negotiated with Packard Electric Corporation in Warren, Ohio, over the conditions under which the firm would agree to expand job opportunities in that location and open new plants as oppose to moving plants and work to the Sun Belt or to Mexico. The recent 1984 agreement in the auto industry between the United Automobile Workers and General Motors and Ford illustrates a slightly different type of strategic bargain. In this case, the company agreed to a comprehensive set of training and adjustment benefits and programs for workers affected by technological change or out-sourcing of work and created some venture-capital funds to aid workers and communities affected by these structural adjustments and dislocations. Yet these are all isolated examples rather than the common pattern. They demonstrate that a series of institutional adjustments is possible that can have the potential of trading wage flexibility and flexibility of other terms of the employment contract for greater commitment to investment and job-creation activities. These types of significant institutional innovations in industrial relations will be required for wage flexibility to produce employment growth.

It is unlikely that this type of strategic bargaining will dominate the US industrial relations system in the 1980s. The federal government unfortunately lacks the political will to promote labour policies that encourage these types of bargains, management continues to guard its prerogatives and its autonomy to make its own investment decisions and to avoid unionization of new facilities, and the labour movement continues to bargain in a defensive and tactical posture without a long-term strategy.

REFERENCES

Cappelli, P. 1982. 'Concessions Bargaining and the National Economy,' in Barbara D. Dennis (ed), *Proceedings of the Thirty-fifth Annual Meetings of the Industrial Relations Research Association*, 362–71. Madison, Wisc: Industrial Relations Research Association
Freedman, A. 1979. *Managing Labor Relations*. New York: Conference Board
– 1985. *Changes in Managing Employee Relations*. New York: Conference Board
Jacoby, S.M., Pearl, M.Y. 1984. 'Wage Dispersion and Labor Market Contracting.' Unpublished paper, Graduate School of Management, UCLA
Kochan, T.A. 1980. *Collective Bargaining and Industrial Relations*. Homewood, Ill: Richard D. Irwin

CANADA

DAVID K. FOOT and JEANNE C. LI

Demographic determinants of unemployment

The determinants of unemployment are many and varied. Besides the well-recognized demand-side influences – macroeconomic business cycles, productivity growth, changing industrial and occupational structures, etc – supply-side factors have exerted an important influence on the level and composition of unemployment. While the role of labour-force participation rates, especially increasing female participation, has received considerable attention in the literature (e.g. Department of Finance Canada 1980; Robinson and Tomes 1982), demographic factors, although clearly recognized, appear to be considered somewhat less important in the determination of unemployment. Yet, over the 1960s and 1970s Canadian labour-force growth averaged in excess of 3 per cent per annum, over a full percentage point above its long-run growth path, and almost three-quarters of this growth was attributable to source population growth, a reflection of the entry of the 'baby boom' generation into the Canadian labour market over this period (Foot 1983).

The impact of demographic change on unemployment has been explored in studies concerned with the determinants of the natural rate of unemployment, where it has been suggested that the entry of the baby boom generation into the labour force over the 1960s and 1970s has exerted upward pressure on the natural rate (Fortin and Newton, 1982).[1] In a more direct examination of the effects of demographic change on unemployment rates in Canada, Reid and Smith (1981, 351) concluded: 'Changing unemployment rates in growing labour force groups rather than changing aggregation weights still constitute the major demographic contribution to a higher national average rate of unemployment.' They then noted: 'There appears to have been a substantial rise in structural unemployment as a result of the changing demographic composition of the labour force.'[2] The emergence and apparent persistence of this phenomenon[3] suggests that traditional market forces cannot be solely relied upon to effect a satisfactory resolution, at least within a 'reasonable' period of time.

This paper is motivated by these considerations. First, it briefly explores the demographic influences on unemployment in Canada. Second, it demonstrates that the aggregate effects reflect offsetting compositional influences and hence mask far more dramatic changes in individual age-sex categories of the labour force. Third, it argues that these compositional issues are likely to become a permanent feature of future unemployment and therefore that future-market policies should be developed accordingly.

From an examination of data on the growth of population, participation rates, the labour force, and employment in Canada, it is apparent that, in spite of the recent dramatic increases in participation rates, population growth has dominated participation-rate growth in the determination of post-war Canadian labour-force growth. Moreover, it has been the inability of employment growth to match this labour-force growth that has resulted in increases in unemployment rates. In this sense, therefore, population growth appears to have exerted a major influence on Canadian unemployment rates since 1945.

The growth of the Canadian labour force since 1945 has been accompanied by a noticeably changing age-sex composition. Especially over the 1960s and 1970s, the Canadian labour force has been characterized by an increasing proportion of women, primarily as a result of increasing female participation rates, and an increasing proportion of youth, primarily as a result of the coming of labour-force age of the baby boom generation (Foot 1982; 1983). Since both of these groups tend to have higher unemployment rates than prime-aged males, increasing their proportion of the labour force has placed upward pressures on the unemployment rate. To measure the impact of demographic change on unemployment, consider the labour-market identities (for any individual group i):

(1) $LF_i = PR_i * SPOP_i$ and

(2) $UR_i = 1 - (E_i/LF_i)$,

where PR denotes the participation rate, SPOP the source population, and E employment. Consequently,

(3) $1 - UR_i = E_i/(PR_i * SPOP_i)$,

and hence the change in UR_i can be approximated by

(4) $\Delta UR_i = (1 - UR_i)(\dot{SPOP_i} + \dot{PR_i} - \dot{E_i})$,

where a dot over the variable denotes a time-based derivative. Here the influence of demographics on individual group unemployment rates is explicitly identified in the SPOP_i term. The effects on the total unemployment rate can then be obtained from the usual aggregate identity

(5) $\quad \text{UR} = 1 - E/\text{LF}$,

where total employment (E) and total labour force (LF) are defined respectively as

$$E = \Sigma_i E_i \quad \text{and} \quad \text{LF} = \Sigma_i \text{LF}_i = \Sigma_i \text{PR}_i * \text{SPOP}_i.$$

This method explicitly recognizes the growth of source population as a demographic influence on unemployment and explores the influence of demographic change on the aggregate unemployment rate through the effects on individual group unemployment rates, thus enabling the compositional issues to be confronted directly. This approach is in contrast to studies (e.g. Flaim 1979 in the United States; Ram 1981 in Canada) that ignore the effect of demographic change on the separate group rates, and which thereby find that demographic factors did not contribute much to the unemployment rate over the 1970s.

Unlike these previous approaches, which have attributed a 'residual' unemployment rate to demographic factors, the empirical implementation of equation (4) can be used to estimate directly a demographically determined unemployment rate, initially for each group and subsequently for all groups. This attributes de facto the residual difference between this hypothetical rate and the actual or observed rate to 'other' (primarily macroeconomic demand) factors. In this way both the effects of population growth and changing labour-force composition are isolated as the demographic determinants of unemployment.

To estimate a demographically determined unemployment rate the following assumptions were made. First, unlike the previous studies, the effects of changing labour-force participation rates on unemployment are removed:[4]

(I) $\quad \dot{\text{PR}}_i = 0 \quad$ for all i.

Second, the cyclical impact of macroeconomic demand on unemployment must be removed. Note that the growth component should not be removed because long-run employment growth can be expected in any economy characterized by population growth. Therefore, a common non-cyclical employment growth is assumed for all age-sex groups:

(II) $\dot{E}_i = \dot{E}$ for all i.

Assumptions (I) and (II) effectively isolate the effects of SPOP_i on UR_i. Lastly, to empirically implement this procedure, a third assumption is necessary to determine $\dot{E}$. This can be achieved by using a constant employment population ratio, which implies that[5]

(III) $\dot{E} = \dot{\text{SPOP}}_i$.

Although the levels of the calculated unemployment rates are clearly sensitive to the choice of $\dot{E}$, the composition remains largely unaffected. In the calculations that follow, a constant non-cyclical employment growth rate of 1.51 per cent per year was used for all age groups for the period 1971-96. This represents the average annual growth in the total source population over this period. Data on source population growth are presented in Table 1 for six individual age groups for each sex and total labour-force source population for the period 1961-2001. A striking picture of the demographic effects of population growth and aging on the Canadian labour force emerges. First, source population growth reached a maximum over the period 1966-71 and has since been declining, a characteristic of Canadian demography that is projected to continue. As noted by Foot (1982) and others, slowing population growth is a characteristic of an aging population. Over the period 1981-6, source population growth for both sexes averages approximately 6.9 per cent over five years, while over the period 1991-6 this declines further to approximately 5.3 per cent over five years. This declining source population growth places downward pressure on unemployment rates – see equation (4).

Second, the growth in source population is dramatically different in each of the age groups, and a clear pattern emerges from the data presented in Table 1. Consider first the youth, aged 15-24. This group grew very rapidly over the 1960s as the baby boom generation began to enter the labour force and continued at above-average rates into the early 1970s as the remainder of the generation was absorbed into the labour force. By the late 1970s, the growth rate for this group had fallen below average, and this characteristic is expected to be maintained throughout the remainder of this century. In contrast, the 25-34 age group grew relatively slowly over the early 1960s. Rapid growth for this group was delayed until the early 1970s, which is hardly surprising given the inevitable aging of the baby boom generation. Consequently, the rapid growth of the youth group over the 1960s became the rapid growth of young adults over the 1970s. Above-average growth for this latter group was likely to be maintained over the early 1980s, after

TABLE 1
Source population growth by age and sex, Canada 1961–96 (percentage)

Period	Age group (years)						All ages
	15–24	25–34	35–44	45–54	55–64	65 +	
Men							
1961–66	25.8	−0.7	7.0	8.6	13.6	6.3	10.4
1966–71	21.7	16.9	0.9	8.8	12.3	9.1	12.7
1971–76	12.2	24.7	2.3	8.3	11.2	12.0	11.9
1976–81	4.2	15.5	13.8	2.5	11.1	15.5	9.8
1981–86	−7.1	8.5	24.8	2.1	10.2	14.1	6.7
1986–91	−11.6	5.4	14.2	12.8	2.9	16.4	5.2
1991–96	−3.1	−6.8	8.1	38.1	2.8	13.9	4.7
Women							
1961–66	26.4	0.9	5.8	12.7	16.0	14.8	12.5
1966–71	21.0	15.8	−2.2	11.8	19.2	17.0	13.4
1971–76	11.6	25.9	3.3	7.6	13.5	17.1	13.2
1976–81	3.8	17.4	14.7	−0.4	13.2	19.8	10.8
1981–86	−8.9	8.8	24.2	2.9	7.7	16.6	7.1
1986–91	−12.1	3.2	16.1	14.1	0.1	16.3	5.4
1991–96	−3.0	−8.8	8.4	23.9	3.0	12.0	4.8

SOURCE: Calculations by the authors from Statistics Canada, Catalogue Nos. 91-512, 91-518, 91-519, and 91-520

which the declining growth patterns experienced in the youth age group ten years previously should have become prevalent.

Exactly the same sort of repeated pattern is experienced by the 35–44 group delayed ten years. Here the rapid growth occurs over the early 1980s as the leading edge of the baby boom generation enters these age groups. They then become 45–54 years old over the early 1990s. Similarly, the comparatively weak growth of the population aged 25–34 in the late 1950s and early 1960s becomes reflected in comparably weak growth in the 35–44 group over the late 1960s and early 1970s, in the 45–54 group over the late 1970s and early 1980s, and in the 55–64 group over the late 1980s and early 1990s.

These quite dramatic patterns, the logical consequence of population aging, can be expected to be reflected in the unemployment rates of individual age-groups. These unemployment rates are, therefore, affected by changing population growth and composition and hence should not be taken as exogenous when one attempts to assess the impact of demographic change on unemployment rates.

As a final observation, because of the gradually increasing relative longevity of women,[6] an aging population is characterized by increasing female dominance, especially in the upper age groups. This is reflected in generally higher growth rates for women compared to men, especially in the higher age groups.[7] As a result, demographic change can be expected to place upward pressure on the unemployment rates in these higher-age female groups.

The results[8] are presented in Tables 2 and 3. Table 2 summarizes the impact of demographic change, both historical and projected, on the levels of unemployment rates over the period 1971–96 for the major aggregates. Unemployment rates increase rapidly with the continuing entry of the baby boom generation into the labour force over the 1970s to a peak in the early 1980s, after which they decline as decreases in source population growth take effect (see Table 1). The calculations indicate that, under the given employment assumptions, demographic factors alone would have accounted for a substantial 5.5-percentage-point increase in the unemployment rate over the decade 1971–80. Projected declines in labour-force source population growth as a result of slowing population growth and population aging are likely to reduce future unemployment rates. The calculations suggest that the decline over the decade 1986–95 may well be slightly larger than the increase over the historical decade 1971–80.[9]

These changes are greater for women than for men. This arises not because of increased participation rates.[10] Rather, it can be attributed to the higher source population growth rates for women, especially in the older, relatively low-participation-rate groups, and the earlier peak in the female participation rate profile.[11] These calculations indicate that between 1976 and 1981 over two percentage points of increase in the male unemployment rate and 1.5 percentage points of increase in the female unemployment rate can be attributed to demographic factors. Over the subsequent five years, the unemployment rate declines by 0.7 percentage points for men but more than double this amount for women. By this time, the bulk of the baby boom generation is moving into slightly lower-participation-rate age groups for women, but slightly higher-participation-rate age groups for men. This intensifies the unemployment problem for men. Population aging, however, continues to place relatively more people in the relatively lower-participation-rate older age groups for both sexes.

146 Canada

TABLE 2
Demographically determined unemployment rates, Canada 1961–96 (percentage)*

Year	Men	Women	Total
1971	6.8	6.0	6.5
1976	10.0	10.3	10.1
1981	12.1	11.8	12.0
1986	11.4	10.3	10.9
1991	9.2	6.9	8.2
1996	5.8	2.7	4.5

*Calculations by the authors based on 1983 data – see text for details.

TABLE 3
Composition of unemployment by age and sex, Canada 1971–96 (national average = 1.00)

Year	Age group (years)						All ages
	15–24	25–34	35–44	45–54	55–64	65 +	
Men							
1971	4.02	0*	0.23	2.14	0.12	0	1.06
1976	2.68	0.56	0	1.41	0.38	0	0.99
1981	2.21	1.00	0.14	0.82	0.56	0.04	1.01
1983	1.88	1.02	0.68	0.62	0.69	0.19	1.02
1986	1.33	1.15	1.24	0.44	0.80	0.55	1.04
1991	0.40	1.28	2.23	1.10	0.52	1.57	1.11
1996	0	0	4.11	4.40	0	3.88	1.29
Women							
1971	3.35	0	0.06	2.67	0	0	0.92
1976	2.44	0.31	0	1.69	0.17	0	1.01
1981	1.82	0.92	0.20	0.86	0.54	0	0.99
1983	1.43	0.96	0.78	0.67	0.67	0.14	0.97
1986	0.68	1.20	1.40	0.55	0.58	0.56	0.94
1991	0	0.97	2.59	1.37	0	1.59	0.84
1996	0	0	4.82	5.03	0	3.59	0.59

*A zero indicates that under the chosen assumptions group employment is constrained by the group labour force – see text for details.

The changing composition of unemployment is deomonstrated in Table 3 where the ratios of the individual group unemployment rates to the total unemployment rate are presented. In 1983, unemployment rates for male youths were 88 per cent above the national average unemployment rate, while those for female youths were 43 per cent above the same figure. These calculations suggest that from a demographic perspective these percentages are on a downward trend and that by the 1990s there could well be more jobs for the youth than there are youths available to fill them. In other words, changing demographics is gradually 'solving' the youth unemployment problem (Kaliski 1984; Foot and Li 1985). But this unemployment is emerging elsewhere – in the young adult age groups (25–34 years) over the 1980s and in the 35–44 and 45–54 groups over the 1990s. These calculations suggest that, as a result of demographic changes, the unemployment rate in the 35–54 groups could be over four times the national average by 1996, up from around 70 per cent of the national average in 1983. This is a substantial increase and suggests considerable challenges for labour-market policy in the years ahead.

Another trend suggested by these calculations is the possibility of gradually increasing unemployment rates among the elderly as a result of demographic change. Whether or not this emerges as a labour-market problem will likely depend on developments in the myriad of other social incentives and programs provided to this group. However, the rapid growth in the numbers in these age groups in the years ahead suggests that employment opportunities for the aged could well be an emerging policy issue on the horizon.

Finally, these calculations suggest that the future unemployment problem could be somewhat more severe for men than for women. The evidence for 1983, where the male unemployment rate is 5 per cent above the female rate, indicates that this problem could be emerging. Changing demographics alone could gradually increase the policy concern with employment opportunities for men relative to women. However, this is not the case among the prime working-age groups (35–54 years), where female unemployment rates remain relatively higher than male rates. Consequently, continued policy concern with employment opportunities for women in these age groups would appear justified.

Whether or not these issues emerge, however, depends on the demand side of the labour market and on the possibilities for labour substitutability in the future Canadian labour market. The calculations in Table 3 are implicitly based on the assumption of no substitutability in employment. Such an assumption has its basis in the theory of labour-market segmentation, as opposed to orthodox theory (Cain 1976). Evidence has been emerging in recent years suggesting limited substitution possibilities in labour markets in Canada and elsewhere.[12] The calculations for men and women in Tables 2 and 3 outline the implications of sex but not age segmentation in the labour market, while the 'total' calculations in Table 2 implicitly assume sufficient possibilities at the margin that all available employment opportunities are filled. In this sense, therefore, aggregation across age-sex groups, as has been employed by previous authors, is based on the implicit assumption of orthodox rather than segmented labour-market theory. Recognition of limited labour-labour substitution possibilities, however, suggest calculations along the lines outlined in this section.

With the coming of labour-force age of the baby boom generation in Canada and elsewhere over the 1960s and 1970s, demographic change has become an increasingly important determinant of unemployment rates. Recent analyses have explored the impact of changing demographics on Canadian unemployment rates, but the method usually adopted treats individual group unemployment rates as exogenous, and hence the demographic influences on unemployment may have been underestimated. Alternative estimates provided in this paper indicate a more substantial impact. Perhaps more important, the paper shows that these aggregate effects encompass offsetting compositional influences and hence mask more significant changes in the unemployment rates of individual age-sex groups in the labour force. The aging of the baby boom generation is shown to play a major role in determining the past and likely future unemployment rates of individual groups in the labour force. Moreover, these compositional issues are likely to become a permanent feature of future unemployment in Canada. Policies to reduce unemployment are not likely to be successful if these effects are ignored.

NOTES

1 Fortin and Phaneuf (1981) estimated that demographic factors in Canada were responsible for an increase in the natural rate of approximately one percentage point over 1955–75. See also Cousineau and Green (1978).
2 Similar calculations can be found in Ram (1981), both in a historical and in a projection perspective, and for the United States in Flaim (1979) and Russell (1982). See also Antos, Mellow, and Triplett (1979).
3 This impact of demographic change on unemployment is only a relatively recent phenomenon. With a lag of at least a decade and a half before births

affect the labour force and hence unemployment, the inevitable effects of the dramatic fluctuations in post-war fertility rates did not emerge in force in the labour markets until the late 1960s and the 1970s.

4 Actually, removal of any differences in the translation of total population 15 years and over into the labour-force source population by subtracting the institutionalized and, in Canada, Indians on reserves and residents of the Territories is the initial step in the calculations. Note that assumption (I) does not impose a constant aggregate participation rate (*PR*) since

$$PR = \frac{LF}{SPOP} = \Sigma_i \frac{SPOP_i}{SPOP} \frac{LF_i}{SPOP_i} = \Sigma_i \ s_i PR_i$$

and the s_i changes over time.

5 Because it abstracts from the participation-rate decision, the employment/population ratio has been considered as an alternative to the unemployment rate as an index of the cyclical performance of the economy. Shiskin (1976) argues in its favour, and Cain (1979), after reviewing the extensive evidence, comes out against its use. Note that given these assumptions, there is nothing in this method to constrain employment to be less than the labour force, although assumption (III) ensures that this will likely be the case in the aggregate. This feature could be removed by incorporating an unemployment-vacancy relationship into the calculations.

6 In Canada in 1931 life expectancy for men and women was 60 and 62 years, respectively. By 1981 these had risen to 72 and 79 years, an increase of 12 and 17 years, respectively.

7 In the lower age groups, the higher incidence of male births and the slightly male dominance of net immigration works to offset these effects.

8 These calculations are based on the 1983 Canadian unemployment rates for the six age groups for each sex, when the overall unemployment rate was 11.9 per cent. Rates for males were slightly higher and those for the youth considerably higher (see Statistics Canada, *Catalogue No. 71-529 Occasional*, Table 1).

9 Of course, different employment growth assumptions yield different figures. For example, setting $\dot{E}$ equal to the lower average annual total population growth over the 1971–96 period (of 0.89 per cent) yields an increase of 11.5 percentage points over 1971–81 followed by only a 0.8-percentage-point decrease 1986–96. A more rapid employment growth assumption would have the opposite effects.

10 In fact, the aggregate participation rate declines gradually by 1.7 percentage points over the 25-year period. See note 5.

11 Female participation rates for the sex age groups in 1983 were 62.8, 67.6, 66.9,

58.2, 33.7, and 4.6 per cent, respectively. The comparable male rates were
69.2, 93.7, 95.1, 92.6, 72.3, and 13.0 per cent.

12 There are now several papers suggesting imperfect labour-labour substitution
across sex and age groups. See Hamermesh and Grant (1979) for a review,
Merrilees (1982) for Canadian evidence, and Foot and Li (1985) for further
details.

REFERENCES

Antos, J., W. Mellow and J.E. Triplett. 1979. 'What Is the Current Equivalent
to Unemployment Rates of the Past?' *Monthly Labour Review* 102, No. 3
(March) 36–46

Cain, G.C. 1976. 'The Challenge of Segmented Labour Market Theories to
Orthodox Theory: A Survey,' *Journal of Economic Literature* 14, No. 4
(December) 1215–57

– 1979. 'The Unemployment Rate as an Economic Indicator,' *Monthly Labour
Review* 102, No. 3 (March) 24–35

Cousineau, J.M., and C. Green. 1978. 'Structural Unemployment in Canada:
1971–1974. Did it Worsen?' *Relations industrielles / Industrial Relations* 33,
No. 2, 175–92

Department of Finance Canada. 1980. *Participation and Labour Force Growth in
Canada*. Ottawa: Department of Finance Canada

Flaim, P.O. 1979. 'The Effects of Demographic Changes on the Nation's Unemployment Rate,' *Monthly Labour Review* 102, No. 3 (March) 13–23

Foot, D.K. 1982. *Canada's Population Outlook: Demographic Futures and Economic Challenges*. Toronto: James Lorimer & Co. for the Canadian Institute
for Economic Policy

– 1983. 'The Impacts of Populations Growth and Aging on the Future Canadian
Labour Force,' in *Canadian Labour Markets in the 1980s*, 50–64. Kingston:
Industrial Relations Center, Queen's University

Foot, D.K., and J.C. Li. 1985. 'Youth Unemployment: A Misplaced Priority?
Policy Study No. 85-7, Institute for Policy Analyses, University of Toronto

Fortin, P., and L. Phaneuf. 1981. 'Why Is the Unemployment Rate So High in
Canada?' Working Paper 8115, Department of Economics, Laval University

Fortin, P., and K. Newton. 1982. 'Labour Market Tightness and Wage Inflation
in Canada,' in M.N. Bailey (ed), *Workers, Jobs and Inflation*, 243–75. Washington, DC: Brookings Institution

Hamermesh, D.C., and J. Grant. 1979. 'Econometric Studies of Labor-Labor
Substitution and Their Implication for Policy,' *Journal of Human Resources*
14, No. 4 (Fall) 518–41

Kaliski, S.F. 1984. 'Why Must Unemployment Remain So High?' *Canadian Public Policy* 10, No. 2 (June) 127-41

Merrilees, W.J. 1982. 'Labor Market Segmentation in Canada: An Econometric Approach,' *Canadian Journal of Economics* 15, No. 3 (August) 458-73

Ram, B. 1981. 'The Effect of Changing Age and Sex Composition of the Labour Force on the Unemployment Rate in Canada: Recent Trends and Future Prospects,' in *Demographic Trends and Their Impact on the Canadian Labour Market*, 145-68. Ottawa: Statistics Canada and Employment and Immigration Canada

Reid, F., and D.A. Smith. 1981. 'The Impact of Demographic Changes on Unemployment,' *Canadian Public Policy* 7, No. 2 (Spring) 348-51

Robinson, C., and N. Tomes. 1982. 'Family Labour Supply and Fertility,' *Canaian Journal of Economics* 15, No. 4 (November) 706-34

Russell, L.B. 1982. *The Baby Boom Generation and the Economy*. Washington, DC: Brookings Institution

Shiskin, J. 1976. 'Employment and Unemployment: The Doughnut or the Hole?' *Monthly Labour Review* 99, No. 2 (February) 3-10

W. CRAIG RIDDELL

Reducing unemployment: medium- and long-term considerations

High unemployment levels represent one of the most serious challenges facing economic policy-makers today. In discussing this challenge, it is useful to distinguish between short- (or possible medium-) term macroeconomic policy and longer-term choices. The latter – the focus of the second part of this paper – involves consideration of structural or institutional changes that may enable us to attain lower unemployment rates in the future, but which may be of little use in speeding the current recovery.

Few would deny that a combination of expansionary monetary and fiscal policy would lead to a reduction in unemployment.[1] The issue is the consequences of such a switch to a more expansionary policy for other goals, in particular for inflation and for the deficit. First, let us examine the inflationary consequences.

The question of whether unemployment can be reduced in the short to medium term without adverse consequences for inflation raises two key issues. The first is how close the economy is to its level of potential output or natural unemployment rate, for reducing unemployment below the non-accelerating inflation rate of unemployment (NAIRU) would risk increasing inflation.[2] The second has to do with the effect of a more expansionary policy on inflation expectations and the credibility of the government's commitment to non-accommodation of inflation in the future. These issues are discussed in turn.

A common (indeed, mainstream) view is that the natural unemployment rate rose through the 1960s and 1970s primarily because of demographic trends and some important changes in labour-market legislation. This view is based on a body of empirical research that would place the NAIRU at 6–8 per cent today, well below current unemployment rates of 11–12 per cent.

Further, this literature indicates that the natural rate should at least not increase and quite possibly even decline in the future, at least in the short- to medium-term horizon being considered here. For these two reasons – the gap between current and natural unemployment rates and the probable future decline in the natural rate – there may be little inflationary danger in a more expansionary policy than is currently planned.

A detailed survey of this empirical literature will not be provided here, but some indication of the degree of consensus may be useful. Fortin and Newton (1982), using data covering the period 1957–78, estimated the NAIRU at 6.5–7 per cent in 1977–8 but indicated that, according to their model, it would have fallen to about 6 per cent in 1981. More recent studies by Guindon (1984) and Fortin and Prud'homme (1984), using a similar method, estimate the natural rate at 6.7 per cent in 1981 and 6.5–7 per cent in 1982. Riddell and Smith (1982) obtained estimates of 6.5 per cent in 1972–9 and 6.2 per cent in 1980. Other estimates include 7.2 per cent in 1975 (Freedman 1976), 7 per cent in 1977 (Aubry, DiMillo, and Cloutier 1979), 6.6 per cent in 1978 (Fortin and Phaneuf 1979), and 6.5 per cent in 1979 (Gosselin 1980). These estimates, then, are quite similar, placing the NAIRU at 6–8 per cent, well below current rates of unemployment.

To see why the NAIRU is expected at least not to increase and quite possibly decline, we need to examine the reasons given for the rise in unemployment in the 1960s and 1970s. The demographic trends have been widely discussed. The population of working age grew rapidly, and the participation rates of women (especially married women) and younger workers increased. Because of these trends, the proportion of youths and women in the labour force increased substantially. For a variety of reasons, elaborated below, these demographic trends are thought to have raised the natural unemployment rate.

The most important legislative changes were the profound alterations made in the Unemployment Insurance (UI) system in 1971–2, which substantially increased the coverage of the program, raised the benefit rate (but made benefits taxable), lowered the minimum number of weeks of work required to qualify for benefits, raised the maximum number of weeks for which benefits could be drawn, altered the relation between weeks worked and benefit weeks, and established an extension period tied to the regional unemployment rate. Another factor that several studies have found to have increased the NAIRU was the rise in minimum wages relative to prices and other wages that occurred during the 1968–76 period. In addition, the coverage of minimum wage legislation was expanded throughout this period in most jurisdictions.

As noted by Fortin and Newton (1982) and Kaliski (1984), most of these factors would suggest that the NAIRU should decline in the future. The rate of growth of the source population has slowed. Growth in the source population of youths has been declining since 1976 and turned negative in 1981. Revisions to the UI system in the latter half of the 1970s, especially in 1978-9, while modest in comparison to the 1971-2 changes, made the system less generous. Minimum wages have been declining in real terms since the late 1970s in most jurisdictions. The only factor pushing in the other direction (at least among those mentioned above) is the continued rise in the participation rate of women, especially married women. However, this effect is unlikely to offset the other factors tending to reduce the natural unemployment rate.

An alternate view – that unemployment cannot be reduced in the near future without considerable risk of a resurgence in inflation – is based on the belief that the NAIRU is in fact considerably higher than the above studies would suggest, so that there is little scope for expansionary policy. The hypothesis with the most empirical support, advanced by Lilien (1982) for the United States, is associated with the rate of change of industrial structure. That is, in recent years the variation in the growth of industries has increased – some growing rapidly, other declining – and such variation across industries may have increased unemployment, as people who experience the job losses have to be matched with the newly created jobs.

Samson (1983) and Charette and Kaufmann (1984) have examined this hypothesis for Canada, estimating the natural rate respectively as 10.6 per cent and 11.0 per cent versus an actual unemployment rate of 11.0 per cent for 1982. Thus according to these studies the rise in unemployment in recent years is structural, not cyclical, and there is presumably little or no scope for more expansionary policy.

There is no doubt that Lilien (1982) has identified a potentially important source of temporary structural unemployment, which previously received too little attention. Incorporation of this structural-change hypothesis in models of inflation and employment is likely to lead to significant improvements in our knowledge. However, I have serious reservations about the claim that the natural rate has risen, albeit temporarily, to approximately 11 per cent. I discuss these reservations in order of importance.

The variance of inter-industry employment changes – the measure of structural adjustment used by Samson (1983) and Charette and Kaufman (1984) – has risen substantially in each recession in the post-war period. But did this 'cause' the recession, or vice versa? To address this question, we need to distinguish between changes in the inter-industry composition of employment that are later reversed and changes that are more lasting. To the extent that the reduction in employment in each sector is temporary, the unemployment associated with the downturn can be described as cyclical. To the extent that it is permanent, the unemployment can be described as frictional or structural. This differs from the usual definition of structural unemployment, which requires unemployment in some occupation or region and unfilled vacancies in another occupation or region. According to this new definition, there is structural unemployment in industry A when there will be, following economic recovery, job vacancies in some other industry but not in industry A. At the time of the downturn, however, there need not be offsetting job vacancies elsewhere. Perhaps this type of unemployment should be called 'dynamic' or 'temporary structural.'

Economic downturns may well differ in the extent to which the reductions in employment in each sector are temporary or permanent. Probably the most important factor accounting for this difference will be whether the downturn was caused by a real or a nominal shock. A real shock will cause a change in relative prices and in equilibrium output and employment of different sectors. Employment will fall in the contracting sectors, and some time will be required for employment to rise in the expanding sectors. If the real shock is permanent, so too will be the reduction in employment in the contracting sectors.

In contrast, a nominal shock is expected to lead to changes in employment in each sector that will be reversed. However, some industries are more sensitive than others to the cyclical fluctuations associated with nominal shocks. Thus we expect that the variance of inter-industry employment growth will respond to nominal demand shocks; that is, nominal shocks have real effects across industries in the short run.

The equations estimated by Lilien (1982) for the United States and Samson (1983) and Charette and Kaufmann (1984) for Canada contain a term that is intended to control for nominal demand shocks – the amount of unanticipated money growth. However, our ability to measure expected money growth is limited. Thus their measure of structural change across industries may 'pick up' the rise in unemployment associated with the nominal demand shock, thus attributing the rise in unemployment to structural rather than cyclical factors.

Perhaps the clearest implication that this in fact occurs is the behaviour of the variance of employment growth across industries and the estimated natural rate in 1981-2. It is widely acknowledged that the recent recession was brought on by restrictive monetary policy. Yet the variance of employment growth across industries rose dramatically from 1981 to 1982, as employment fell much more in some sectors than in others.[3] Further, the unexpected money growth variable did not 'control for' the nominal shock, as is evidenced by the equality or near-equality of the actual unemployment rate and the estimated natural rate in 1982.

To examine this issue more systematically, Table 1 provides data on the evolution of employment shares by industry.[4] The first column is the cumulative change index (CCI), which compares the share distribution to the base year (1947). For example, the value of 1.5 in 1948 for the CCI means that 1.5 per cent of the distribution of employment shares changed sectors from 1947 to 1948. In 1949, the CCI equalled 2.7, indicating that a further 1.2 per cent of the employment distribution changed from 1948 to 1949. Column 2 gives year-to-year changes in the CCI. Column 3 contains the year-to-year Change Index (CI), which compares the share distribution to that of the previous year.

A comparison of columns 2 and 3 is instructive. Year-to-year changes in the share distribution that are subsequently reversed will cancel out in the CCI, so that the sum of the CIs will exceed that of the CCIs. Thus when CI exceeds that year's change in CCI, the difference is a measure of the extent to which the year-to-year change in share distribution is temporary rather than permanent. However, when CI equals the year-to-year change in CCI, the change in share distribution is permanent in nature.[5]

Each of the post-war recessions (indicated by an asterisk in Table 1) is characterized by a relatively high value of CI. Comparison of columns 2 and 3 indicates clearly that each of these recessions is also associated with the large difference between CI and the change in CCI. That is, much of the year-to-year change was temporary. Yet inspection of the Samson (1983) and Charette and Kaufmann (1984) studies indicates that the estimated natural rate rose dramatically in each of these recession years. This analysis, while admittedly imprecise, suggests that the estimating equation is not able to distinguish between temporary and permanent changes in industry structure. This suggests that the evidence supporting the view that the economy was operating at approximately potential output in 1982 is weak.

The discussion of this section suggests that sharp movements in the dispersion of employment changes are probably associated with cyclical movements in economic activity. However, the trend in the variance of employment growth across industries may be an important indicator. The appearance, albeit slight, of an upward trend from 1960 to 1982 does suggest that this may be a factor tending to raise the natural unemployment rate and thus offset the demographic and other factors discussed earlier. In

TABLE 1
Changes in share distribution of employment (12 sectors)

Year	CCI	ΔCII	CI	CI − ΔCCI
1948	1.5	–	1.5	–
1949	2.7	1.2	1.3	0.1
1950	4.1	1.4	1.6	0.2
*1951	5.6	1.5	2.6	1.1*
1952	7.2	1.6	1.6	0.0
1953	8.4	1.2	1.4	0.2
1954	8.1	− 0.3	1.7	2.0*
1955	9.4	1.3	1.4	0.1
1956	10.8	1.4	1.4	0.0
*1957	11.9	1.1	1.5	0.4*
*1958	13.3	1.4	2.1	0.7*
1959	14.4	1.1	1.4	0.3
*1960	15.3	0.9	1.7	0.8*
1961	16.4	1.1	1.4	0.3
1962	17.2	0.8	1.1	0.3
1963	17.8	0.6	0.6	0.0
1964	18.3	0.5	0.8	0.3
1965	19.2	0.9	1.2	0.3
1966	20.0	0.8	1.2	0.4
1967	20.6	0.6	1.2	0.6
1968	21.8	1.2	1.3	0.1
1969	22.7	0.9	1.0	0.1
1970	23.8	1.1	1.4	0.3
1971	24.5	0.7	0.8	0.1
1972	25.2	0.7	0.9	0.2
1973	25.6	0.4	0.9	0.5
*1974	26.1	0.5	1.1	0.6*
1975	27.3	1.2	1.3	0.1
1976	27.8	0.5	0.5	0.0
1977	28.6	0.8	1.1	0.3
1978	28.7	0.1	0.8	0.7
*1979	28.8	0.1	0.8	0.7*
*1980	29.2	0.4	1.0	0.6*
1981	30.0	0.8	0.9	0.1
*1982	31.4	1.4	1.9	0.5*

Average annual change in the share distribution

Total	1.26
Structural	0.90
Cyclical	0.36

addition, there may well be an interaction between the UI changes of the 1970s and the slight upward trend in the variance of employment growth across industries in that the net effect of the UI changes was to slow down labour-market adjustment. Thus, for a given dispersion, we should perhaps expect a higher level of structural unemployment in the 1970s than in earlier periods. These conjectures may be worth exploring in subsequent research.

The above discussion suggests scope for reducing unemployment: the economy is well below the level of output and employment at which wage and price inflation would begin to rise. Current forecasts call for a very slow return to these normal levels of output and employment. Should the return be hastened? There is not an easy answer. On balance, my view is that we should accelerate the recovery; however, there are potential costs and risks associated with this approach. A policy mix that would minimize these risks is needed.

One consequence of a faster recovery is that we would be more likely to accept current rates of inflation. The memory of high inflation rates is fresh, and while short-term inflationary expectations may have fallen with actual inflation rates, expectations may well be quick to respond to a slowing in the decline of inflation. In this situation, the economy is probably more prone to a resurgence in inflation than was the case in the 1950s and 1960s, when expectations apparently responded slowly to increase in inflation (Carlson 1977).

The power of inflationary expectations is strong. Not long ago (spring 1984) most published forecasts called for continued slow economic recovery, with unemployment remaining high throughout the remainder of the 1980s, and steady inflation of 6–7 per cent. Although these forecasts were clearly inconsistent with the natural-rate hypothesis (which predicts declining rates of inflation when the economy is maintained below potential output), they were evidently widely believed. The persistence of high real interest rates is consistent with the view that expectations of inflation over the medium and longer term remain high. These expectations may in turn be associated with a view that large government deficits will eventually be financed by monetary creation.

In the short term, the inflationary consequences of a more expansionary policy would not likely be large. There is already considerable downward momentum in wage and price increases. This inertia may be slowed but is unlikely to be quickly reversed by a more expansionary policy.

However, the longer-run consequences of a more expansionary policy cannot be ignored. In retrospect, monetary and fiscal policy was on average overly expansionary in the late 1960s and early 1970s. The consequences were lower unemployment at the time but a deeply imbedded inflation that has proved difficult and costly to reduce. Of course, the supply shocks of the 1970s exacerbated the inflation problem significantly, but, even without these, reducing inflation would have been the challenge of the late 1970s and possibly early 1980s. A repetition of this mistake would not be desirable.

Of course the situation today is much different. There is evidently little risk of being overly expansionary in the sense of unemployment falling below the NAIRU. However, a more expansionary policy would reduce the pace of the current disinflation. The long-run consequence of a relatively rapid return to normal levels of output and employment would thus be some continuing inflation, possibly in the 3–4 per cent range (assuming no adverse inflationary shocks). While inflation of 3 to 4 per cent is relatively mild in comparison to recent experience, this rate of price increase was considered a serious problem in the 1950s and 1960s.

A related risk is that a more expansionary policy would undermine the credibility of the government's commitment to a policy of non-accommodation of inflation in the future. Since the mid-1970s, the Bank of Canada has attempted to wind down the inflation built up over the previous decade, first using a gradualist approach (combined with wage and price controls) and, subsequently, following the lead of US monetary authorities, employing a more determined policy of monetary restraint. These policies, particularly the latter, have achieved considerable success in reducing inflation. The willingness of the authorities to continue with the policy in spite of its adverse consequences may have enhanced the credibility of their stated commitment to non-accommodation of inflation. In order to prevent this credibility from being undermined, it is important to make clear that the intention is one-time expansion designed to return the economy more quickly to normal levels of output and employment rather than a continuing expansionary stance. A one-shot expansion of this nature is needed to solve the 're-entry problem' and for this reason need not reduce the credibility of the longer-term commitment to non-accommodation of inflation.

The policy mix is also important. Because of the size of the deficit, a more expansionary fiscal policy would not be appropriate. Thus one-shot expansion in aggregate demand should be brought about by a combination of a more expansionary monetary policy and a moderately less expansionary fiscal policy.

This package is designed to accelerate the return to normal levels of output and employment while minimizing the adverse consequences for inflation and the deficit. The risk of adverse effects on inflation could be further reduced by adopting norms for wage and price increases that involve planned continuation of current disinflation. Because one of the key obstacles to a more expansionary policy is fear of a resurgence in inflation, taking steps designed to ensure continuation of current disinflation would alleviate this concern.

I recognize that the chances of reaching voluntary agreement on such norms are slim. Both the Canadian labour movement and business associations are highly fragmented and decentralized and thus cannot commit their constituents. Nonetheless, it should not be impossible to obtain some commitment to wage and price restraint. There is much more awareness of the costs of disinflation via monetary restraint than in the past. There is more recognition of the true choices we face and that rapid reflation is not an option. And there is a new government committed to co-operation and consultation on economic policy. There is also the recent Australian experience in which extremely high unemployment evidently played an imortant role in bringing about the 'National Accord.'

At the very least, the choice should be put to business and labour, as well as other groups. Simply recognizing that we have some options, and placing these options in front of employers and employees through their representatives, would be worthwhile. Some commitment to wage and price restraint would enable a more rapid return to potential output and normal levels of unemployment. In the absence of this agreement, the moderate one-time expansion of aggregate demand recommended above is the best that can be done.

The early post-war period was characterized by increasing confidence in the ability of governments to stabilize output and employment and thus protect citizens from the vicissitudes of the business cycle. However, in recent years there has been increased recognition of the limited ability of governments to foresee and offset economic shocks in a manner that will stabilize cyclical fluctuations, as well as of the possible inflationary consequences of doing so on a continuing basis. For these reasons, many analysts suggest that monetary and fiscal policies should be directed more toward longer-run goals. This in turn implies that it is desirable to consider structural changes such that the various disturbances that cause cyclical fluctuations result in shorter and less severe deviations from full employment.

The degree of wage and price inertia plays a central role in modern explanations of the magnitude and duration of cyclical fluctuations. The momentum in the inflationary process also accounts for the high cost of reducing inflation by demand restraint. This section briefly notes the contribution that certain institutional features of our wage determination system make to wage and price inertia and raises the issue of structural reforms that might lead to improved economic performance.

Three key features of wage determination in North America appear to be important sources of inertia: the length of wage contracts (often 2–3 years in the unionized sector), the fact that these contracts typically overlap (i.e. at any time some are being renegotiated while others are still in effect), and the fact that contracts typically fix the wage in advance. By way of contrast, in Japan labour contracts are much shorter (one year), are renegotiated in a highly synchronized fashion (the annual spring wage offensive), and contain an important 'bonus payment' component that relates wages paid to realized economic conditions.

The reasons why wage-setting mechanisms differ so widely across countries are not well understood. The tendency for firms and unions in North America to negotiate long-term, overlapping fixed-wage contracts appears to derive in part from an attempt to minimize the costs to both sides of a strike or lockout. However, in choosing this form of contract, the parties may impose an important macroeconomic externality on the rest of the economy. They thus contribute to wage and price rigidity, and so the brunt of economic disturbances falls more on output and employment than would otherwise be the case. Society as a whole may be better off with more flexible wage-setting arrangements such as those employed in Japan. The wisdom of making changes to North American institutional features – in particular, shorter contracts, synchronized negotiations, and gain-sharing and other flexible compensation systems – should be priority issues for research and debate.

NOTES

1 Though in this era of despair about the inability to reduce unemployment, it may be worth stating this basic proposition. Such 'simple truths' tend to be forgotten in difficult times. For example, in the stagflation of the 1970s, we heard numerous claims to the effect that the standard tools of demand restraint were no longer effective in dealing with inflation and that new tools were needed. Surely the experience of 1981 has at least silenced those claims.

2 I will use the terms *natural unemployment rate* and NAIRU (non-accelerating inflation rate of unemployment) interchangeably to refer to the unemployment rate at which a stable rate of inflation can be maintained and below which inflation will tend to increase.

3 For a detailed breakdown of the cyclical behaviour of employment across industries during the 1981-2 recession and the recovery in 1983 see Department of Finance, *Economic Review*, 1984, 38.
4 These data are based on the twelve-sector or one-digit industrial breakdown and are described in more detail in Charette, Kaufmann, and Henry (1985), from which this table is taken. More detailed breakdowns are also examined in their paper.
5 Of course all of this is conditional on the two base periods, 1947 and the previous year.

REFERENCES

Aubry, J.P., J. DiMillo, and P. Cloutier. 1979. 'An Estimation of the Natural Rate of Unemployment in Canada.' Bank of Canada
Carlson, J.S. 1977. 'A Study of Price Forecasts,' *Annals of Economic and Social Measurement* 6:27–56
Charette, M.F., and B. Kaufmann. 1984. 'Short Run Variation in the Natural Rate of Unemployment.' Mimeo, University of Windsor
Charette, M.F., and B. Kaufmann, and R.P. Henry. 1985. 'The Evolution of the Canadian Industrial Structure: An International Perspective.' Background paper prepared for the Royal Commission on the Economic Union and Development Prospects for Canada
Fortin, P., and D. Prud'homme. 1984. 'La courbe de Phillips canadienne contre vents et marees.' Université Laval, Cahier de recherche 84-06
Fortin, P., and K. Newton. 1982. 'Labour Market Tightness and Wage Inflation in Canada,' in M.N. Baily (ed), *Workers, Jobs and Inflation*. Washington, DC: Brookings Institution
Fortin P., and L. Phaneuf. 1979. 'Why Is the Unemployment Rate So High in Canada?' Paper presented to the Canadian Economics Association, Saskatoon
Freedman, C. 1976. 'The Phillips Curve in Canada.' Bank of Canada, RM-76-189
Gosselin, M. 1980. 'Modifications apportées à l'équation des salaires et estimation du taux de chomage natural.' Bank of Canada, RM-80-39
Guindon, D. 1984. 'Wage Growth and Price Formation in Canada.' paper presented at the CEA Meetings, Guelph 1984
Kaliski, S.F. 1984. 'Why Must Unemployment Remain So High?' *Canadian Public Policy* 10 (June 1984), 127–41
– 1985. 'Trends, Changes and Imbalances: A Survey of the Canadian Labour Market.' Background paper for the Royal Commission on the Economic Union and Development Prospects for Canada

Lilien, D.M. 1982. 'Sectoral Shifts and Cyclical Unemployment,' *Journal of Political Economy* 90 (August) 777–93

McCallum, J. 1983. 'A Generalized Credibility Hypothesis: Theory and Evidence.' Université du Québec à Montréal, Département de science économique, Cahier 8309

Riddell, W.C., and P.M. Smith. 1982. 'Expected Inflation and Wage Changes in Canada,' *Canadian Journal of Economics*, 15 (August) 377–94

Samson, L. 1983. 'A Study of the Impact of Sectoral Shifts on Aggregate Unemployment in Canada.' Mimeo, University of Western Ontario

MORLEY GUNDERSON and
NOAH M. MELTZ

Labour-market rigidities and unemployment

While there have been short-term differences in performance, over the long term the Canadian and American economics have tended to follow similar patterns. This is not surprising in view of the high degree of interrelationship between the two economies based on geographic, trade, investment, and cultural connections. The marked contrast in the experiences of the two countries during and since the 1981–3 recession has raised the question of whether some fundamental changes have occurred within Canada to alter the long-run relation or whether what we are observing is merely another of the short-term differences that have appeared from time to time.

The differences that have been observed are the much greater depth in Canada of the recent recession and the much slower recovery. Starting from almost identical unemployment rates in 1981 (7.5 per cent in Canada, 7.6 per cent in the United States), the rate in the United States peaked a year earlier than in Canada (1982 versus 1983) and at a much lower annual average (9.7 per cent versus 11.9 per cent). Since then, the US rate has fallen sharply to a mid-1984 figure of 7.5 per cent, while in Canada the figure is 11.4 per cent. This difference of almost four percentage points is by far the most that the Canadian rate has ever exceeded the US rate in the more than 30 years for which unemployment data are available from the two countries.

One possible explanation for the differential performance is the greater flexibility of labour markets in the United States, associated with a number of interrelated phenomena such as deregulation (e.g. trucking, airlines), wage concessions by unions (e.g. automobiles, steel, meat packing, trucking, airlines), and the general lower strength of the labour movement (Meltz 1985). This greater flexibility of labour markets in the United States may have facilitated adjustments to 'shocks' such as changes in energy prices, trade patterns, technology, and demography and deindustrialization.

The purpose of this paper is to consider whether labour-market rigidities appear to be primarily responsible for the sluggish growth of employment and the limited decrease in the unemployment rate since the depth of the 1981-3 recession. We deal with the question in two ways. First, we explore the effects of the various impediments to the labour-market adjustment process and why these impediments or rigidities arose in the first place. Second, we explore aggregate measures of the net effect of these impediments in the context of the differences in the behaviour of unemployment rates in the two countries. Our conclusions are that available measures do not seem to imply that a recent increase in rigidities in Canada or the removal of rigidities in the United States is responsible for the differences in labour-market performances in the two countries between 1981 and 1984. The major factor appears to be much lower aggregate demand in Canada, a finding consistent with Kaliski's (1984) assessment of the problem. In addition, our discussions suggest that care must be taken in considering the efficiency effects of labour-market rigidities, since institutional arrangements that appear as impediments to market adjustments usually arise for some reason and may have an efficiency as well as redistributive rationale (hence, their possible 'survival value').

While there are a variety of ways of categorizing labour-market rigidities, most can be classified as arising from the optimizing behaviour of individual agents, from union practices, from public policy initiatives, or from the absence of competitive forces.

Certain institutional features of labour markets may give the appearance of rigidities in that they impede the labour market from functioning in an otherwise unimpeded, classical fashion. Nevertheless, these arrangements may be the outcome of the optimizing behaviour of individual agents subject to very real constraints involving transactions costs, imperfect or asymmetric information, monitoring costs, or quasi-fixed costs of recruiting and hiring. In such circumstances, the private parties may develop joint value-maximizing strategies that appear as constraints or rigidities but that really evolve out of otherwise well-functioning markets.

For example, wage rigidity over the business cycle – the classic impediment to reducing unemployment – may have an efficiency rationale. In situations of asymmetric information, where employers have better information than employees on the true nature of demand shocks in the product market, there may be an incentive for employers to pretend that demand is declining in order to get wage concessions. Not knowing whether this information is true, employees may bargain for rigid wages even if that may lead to employment reductions in times of declining demand because employment (as opposed to wage) reductions are also costly to employers (e.g., loss of quasi-fixed hiring and training expenditures). Alternatively stated, employers are less likely to bluff about adverse demand conditions when bargaining is over employment rather than wages. In such circumstances, real demand shocks may be absorbed in employment declines rather than wage reductions, even when workers are risk-averse and hence would otherwise seem to prefer small price (wage) reductions to the risk of all-or-nothing quantity (employment) reductions.

Obviously, there are a myriad of other possible rationales for rigid wages that may lead to demand shocks being absorbed by employment fluctuations. For example, the private cost of employment fluctuations may be offset by state-supported unemployment insurance or borne by workers who are best able to absorb the costs or perhaps have no say in union decisions that are determined by median voters. Nevertheless, rigid wages may also be part of an implicit or explicit contractual arrangements that emerges as a bargaining strategy to elicit truth-telling in a market subject to costly asymmetric information and quasi-fixed hiring costs. Similarly, implicit contracts on the part of the parties in the employment relationship may also give the appearance of a labour-market rigidity, yet they may have an efficiency rationale. Risk aversion on the part of workers and a difficulty in diversifying the risk associated with the loss of human capital coupled with a greater ability of firms to diversity risk (both through product market diversification and through the stock market) may imply a contractual arrangement whereby firms provide a degree of income (both wages and employment) security in return for a lower compensating wage. This could imply the retention of redundant workers, as well as their wage levels, during a downswing; firms provide earnings insurance with the insurance premium being transacted through the compensating wage mechanism. The moral-hazard and adverse-selection problems of insurance markets are mitigated by the fact that the employer controls the layoff decision. In such a contractual arrangement, the risk becomes efficiently located with the party – the employer – best able to control and absorb the risk. This efficient location of risk bearing may imply a contractual arrangement that appears as a labour-market rigidity and that does inhibit the short-run adaptiveness of the labour market, albeit it may imply long-run efficiency.

In addition to reflecting the optimizing behaviour of private individual agents in a competitive market environment, many so-called labour-market rigidities may emerge as a result of collective bargaining on the part of unions. Whereas the rigidities that arise from the competitive market will reflect the preferences of the marginal worker with the threat of 'exit,' those that arise in the unionized environment will reflect the preferences of the median union voter.

The median union voter, in turn, is likely to be older and less mobile than the marginal worker and is less likely to be a woman or a minority group member. Such median voters are thereby more likely to pressure for rules like seniority, job security for incumbent workers, and wage rigidity, even if that means employment cuts (which would not likely fall on median voters). In the extreme, median union voters may favour two-tier bargaining, whereby their wages are protected but new workers can be hired at competitive market rates.

Many of the private-market rigidities discussed in the previous section are more likely to emerge in a unionized environment independent of the bargaining power of the union. Unions can serve an important communication function, ascertaining and articulating the collective preferences of the work-force and determining the internal union trade-offs within their membership. They can also monitor the arrangements and convert implicit contractual arrangements into explicit ones through the collective agreement. As an illustration, seniority rules, which at first glance appear as rigidities preventing efficient layoff and promotion policies, may also have an efficiency rationale, even in competitive markets. Both firms and workers incur considerable quasi-fixed costs in an employment relationship – firms because of recruiting, hiring, and training, and employees for these reasons and because employment decisions are intricately tied to other aspects of behaviour involving the family and community. Severing an employment relationship, either through a quit or a firing, can involve a substantial loss of such costs, which are not really 'sunk costs' (in which case they would be irrelevant for the efficient allocation of resources) but rather 'start-up costs' – they would have to be incurred again in any new employment relationship (hence, they have efficiency as well as equity implications). Especially for workers, such 'fixities' (associated with such factors as house purchases, the building up of social and community networks, the school location of children, and the employment location of one's spouse) are likely to increase with wages and length of service. Severing a particular employment relationship may involve substantial costs associated with these other aspects of behaviour. In such circumstances, both employers and employees may mutually agree to an explicit or implicit contractual arrangement such as seniority so as to avoid continuous 'start-up' costs. While seniority and the merit principle may often conflict in individual cases, they need not conflict as personnel policies in this broader context in a world of substantial quasi-fixed costs of employment.

Union-induced rigidities can be particularly prominent given the avowed purpose of the trade union movement 'to take labour out of the labour market,' the clarion call of the movement being 'labour is not a commodity.' In essence, unions have arisen as a security response against what otherwise may be the arbitrary and even capricious treatment of labour, and such a security response obviously may involve factors that can be interpreted as labour-market rigidities. The business of unions may well be to create rigidities that afford their members a degree of protection from the vicissitudes of market adjustments, especially in an economy that they regard as riddled with other imperfections, protected for employers, and subject to state-induced unemployment. The challenge for policy-makers, of course, is to ensure that such legitimate union objectives are required to confront the equally compelling objectives of consumers for inexpensive products, employers for survival, and non-union workers (including possibly minorities and new labour-force entrants) for jobs.

The issue of union-induced rigidities is particularly important in Canada, given the level and growth of unionism, at least relative to the United States. In Canada, approximately 40 per cent of the non-agricultural work-force is unionized, with about 50 per cent of the work-force being covered by a collective agreement. This is substantially higher than the corresponding figures in the United States, currently at roughly 22 per cent. More important, there does not appear to be the decline in unionization in Canada that is going on in the United States (Meltz 1985 and references therein).

Related to these facts, concession-bargaining does not appear to be as prominent a feature of Canadian as opposed to American industrial relations. This may be interpreted as a manifestation of the Canadian labour market being more rigid and less responsive than its US counterpart to demand pressures. This differential concession response may reflect differences in a variety of factors underlying the pressure for concession bargaining, such as deregulation, deindustrialization, foreign competition, regional relocation opportunities, non-union competition, government income support programs, and contract characteristics pertaining to such factors as length and existence of cost-of-living escalators. Whatever the underlying reasons – still largely unresearched in Canada – the difference appears to reflect the Canadian labour market's being more rigid and less responsive to changing demand pressures. From a trade-unionist perspective, of course, this would be interpreted as an ability to hold the line on wages over profits in spite of massive state-induced unemployment.

In addition to labour-market rigidities resulting from the optimizing behaviour of private actors as well as those induced by trade unions and professional associations, labour-market rigidities may arise as a by-product of public policies usually designed to serve some other social objectives, including that of income security.

For example, unemployment insurance, which obviously can serve a viable insurance function against the risk of being unemployed, can also reduce the adaptiveness of labour markets. As with most insurance markets, a moral-hazard problem may arise; in this case, by reducing the cost of being unemployed, the parties may not take proper precautions against the risk of being unemployed, and workers may enter the state of unemployment more often and remain there longer than they would otherwise. In the long run, however, this may facilitate job search and mobility that leads to a better job match, highlighting the importance of considering the long-run consequences of policies that may discourage short-run adaptiveness. To the extent that the moral-hazard issue remains a problem, however, it may be mitigated by experience rating.

Policies requiring severance pay, advance notice, and proof of 'just cause' in the case of permanent layoffs or dismissals can also inhibit the adaptiveness of labour markets by making it more costly to lay off redundant workers. This in turn can make firms reluctant to hire workers for fear of having to incur these possible termination costs. However such policies obviously serve other important social objectives, especially the mitigation of the consequences of layoffs on workers. In addition, they can facilitate adaptation by providing workers with advance notice so that they can look for a new job, and, by providing compensation, they may reduce the resistance of workers to changes that may lead to job losses.

The previously discussed rigidities were examined in the context of the imposition of specific constraints into what otherwise would be a competitive market. Many rigidities in labour markets, however, are associated with the absence of competitive forces.

More generally, those who believe in the prominence of dual, segmented, and internal labour markets perceive the absence of competitive forces as being the rule rather than the exception in labour markets. Competitive pressures may exert some influence, especially at the 'ports-of-entry'; however, administered pricing mechanisms and rules tend to insulate the internal labour markets of firms from the forces of competition. (The extent to which these administrative rules are consistent with competitive forces in a world of such realistic constraints as imperfect or asymmetric information, risk aversion, and monitoring cost remains an open question in need of further research.)

In the dual, segmented labour markets perspective, the primary labour market is segmented from the lower-wage secondary labour market by such factors as discrimination, custom and tradition, union rules, and the administrative work rules of the internal labour market. In a sense, of course, such factors are really just descriptions or manifestations of non-competitive factors; they are not really explanations of the rigidities or why they may persist under competitive pressures.

There appear to be two opposing policy responses that emanate from the dual labour-market perspective. One is to endeavour to break down the barriers that inhibit workers moving from the secondary to the primary market. This, of course, would be consistent with facilitating labour-market adjustment by removing rigidities. The other perspective, however, perceives that many of the barriers provide a degree of protection and security to those in the primary labour market and that removing these barriers is unlikely to be feasible or desirable; hence, the policy recommendation is to extend those protective measures through government policies (e.g. wage-fixing and labour-standards legislation) to the unprotected sector. Needless to say, this would involve increasing the rigidities in the labour market largely through legislative fiat.

Rigidities associated with the absence of competitive forces also may be associated with the public sector, where the political constraint replaces the profit constraint as the motivating factor for employers (Gunderson 1985). This may give rise to public-sector wage premiums, evidence of which has been found in both Canada and the United States. The political constraint is expected to be less binding than the profit constraint, especially when the labour costs can be deferred to future generations of taxpayers (who do not have a say in the current voting mechanism) through such compensation practices as job security, liberal pensions and early retirement, and deferred wages guaranteed through seniority – all of which tend to be characteristic of public-sector employment. Market pressure would ensure a competitive floor on public-sector wages (otherwise workers would leave); however, they need not ensure a competitive ceiling, and it is this asymmetry that can give rise to, and sustain, a public-sector wage advantage. This is especially the case in countries like Canada where the high degree of unionization in the public sector facilitates a wage advantage.

Since interest arbitration of wages is a prominent feature of public-sector labour markets (especially when the right to strike is banned), then features of the interest arbitration process may also explain some of the public-sector wage advantage. Specifically, in the wage-determining criteria used by interest arbitrators (usually lawyers experienced in grievance arbitration), little attention is paid to economic criteria such as queues or shortages of applicants (Gunderson 1983). For this reason and others, public-sector labour markets may exhibit considerable inflexibility in their responsiveness to economic and other changes.

The previous discussion of labour-market rigidities suggested that, from a pure efficiency point of view, not all rigidities should be removed. Many may be efficient outcomes of bargaining between private actors in competitive markets subject to constraints involving imperfect or asymmetric information, risk, transactions and monitoring costs and quasi-fixed costs in the employment relationship. This was illustrated with respect to such practices as seniority rules, wage rigidity, implicit contracts, and rules pertaining to due process and layoff protection. In the case of non-competitive markets, the issues may be as much political as economic. The policy dilemma in the competitive sector becomes one of ascertaining when these rules may be efficient outcomes of optimizing behaviours and when they may be inefficiencies associated with rent-seeking behaviour.

Without being able to provide a precise estimate of the impact of each and every impediment, one can get an impression of their overall impact by examining some aggregate data that distinguish between structural and frictional unemployment on the one hand and deficient-demand unemployment on the other hand. If, on balance, there was an increase in labour-market rigidities, then one would expect to find an increase in structural and/or frictional unemployment.

One way to ascertain whether such an increase has taken place is through the use of the vacancy-unemployment (V-U) relation (Reid and Meltz 1979). If there has been an outward shift in the V-U relation, then structural and/or frictional unemployment has increased. That is, there would be a higher unemployment rate for any given level of vacancies or jobs offered by firms; alternatively stated, for a given level of unemployment, more jobs are being offered as vacant and not filled by the unemployed. In contrast, a move along a V-U curve, where the vacancy rate is increasing and the unemployment rate decreasing, represents an increase in aggregate demand for labour, since the reduced unemployment is coming about from the greater number of job offers (vacancies) from firms.[2]

In exploring the V-U relation we have to distinguish between the short run (recent developments over the past four years) and the long run. Results on the long run (i.e. the post–Second World War period) suggest a net increase in structural and frictional unemployment in Canada (Reid and Meltz 1979; Kaliski 1984); that is, the V-U relationship in the 1970s appears to have shifted out relative to the 1950s and 1960s. The outward shift resulted from changes induced by more generous unemployment insurance programs and from demographic changes (the increase in the proportion of women and youth in the labour force). In contrast, the recent years of 1982 and 1983 appear to be an upward and leftward movement along the same outward V-U curve, suggesting that the recent high unemployment is demand deficient, not structural or frictional, in origin. This may reflect high wage demands or wage rigidities leading to fewer job offers (vanancies) and higher unemployment; however, our assessment is that such rigidities are not likely to emerge in such a short period.

How do we account for the dramatic increase in Canadian unemployment since 1981 and its failure to decrease as did the rate in the United States? Since the V-U data are available only for Canada, we have used help wanted indexes (available only since 1980) and unemployment rate data as proxies for V-U relations in the two countries.[3] The results for the period 1980-4 indicate that in both countries there is the expected inverse relation between vacancies (represented by the help wanted index) and the unemployment rate.

The post-1981 years in Canada appear as an upward and leftward move along the same V-U curve (suggesting demand-deficient unemployment), whereas the post-1981 years in the United States appear as a mild upward shift in the curve (suggesting a slight increase in frictional or structural unemployment) and/or a movement downward and to the right along the same schedule (suggesting expansionary, demand-increasing job offers and hence reducing unemployment). By 1984, the US curve had returned almost to its 1980 position, whereas the Canadian unemployment rate remained exceedingly high and job offers (vacancies) exceedingly low. For both countries, the curves exhibit the expected upward loop following a recession (e.g. Hansen, 1970). The fact that the American V-U relation is on a similar path as that in Canada but at a much higher help wanted rate suggests that the dominant factor in the difference in unemployment rates between the two

TABLE 1
Employment in selected industries, Canada and the United States 1980–4 (thousands)

	1980	1981	1982	1983	1984*	1984 as % of 1980 × 10
Canada						
Meat and poultry products	44	50	48	49	45	102
Primary metals	140	151	128	116	131	94
Transportation equipment	200	199	171	173	223	112
Motor vehicle manufacturers	61	61	58	64	74	121
Air transportation	53	55	50	49	48	91
Trucking	167	160	150	151	167	100
United States						
Meat products	391	362	358	342	338	86
Primary metals	1,175	1,154	925	804	830	71
Transportation equipment	2,128	2,136	1,931	2,247	2,432	114
Motor vehicles and motor vehicle equipment	1,007	1,012	853	997	1,143	114
Air transportation	534	556	502	477	522	98
Trucking	1,368	1,380	1,360	1,427	1,555	114

SOURCE: Canada: unpublished data from the Labour Force Survey; United States: *Employment and Earnings* US (Department of Labor, Bureau of Labour Statistics, January 1983, January 1984); *Labor Force Statistics Derived from the Current Population Survey: A Databook*, Volume 1 (Bulletin 2096, Washington, DC, US Department of Labor, Bureau of Labor Statistics, September 1982); and unpublished data from the Bureau of Labor Statistics.
*The June figure for Canada and the second quarter average for the United States.

countries is the result of deficient demand in Canada. Kaliski (1984) reaches the same conclusion.

Another way of approaching this problem is to examine changes in employment in Canada and the United States in those industries that were most characterized by deregulation and concession-bargaining in the United States: automobiles, steel, meat-packing, air transportation, and trucking. Table 1 contains average annual employment figures for 1980–3 and employment for the second quarter of 1984 for these industries in the United States, together with data for roughly comparable industries in Canada. In meat packing, primary metals, and motor vehicle manufacturing there was less of a decline or a greater increase in employment in Canada than in the United States, while in transportation equipment, air transport, and trucking the reverse occurred. These data on employment by industry therefore indicate a mixed record of employment growth for industries that experienced a reduction in labour-market rigidities in the United States relative to Canada. It is certainly not the case that the apparantly greater flexibility in the US labour market led to relatively more employment opportunities, at least as evidenced by the aggregate data.

While there are specific instances of greater rigidities in the Canadian relative to the US labour market, the aggregate data still seem to portray a deficient-demand rather than a structural-frictional explanation of the recent high level of unemployment in Canada relative to the United States. In addition, some basic theoretical considerations suggest that many of the so-called rigidities may have an efficiency rationale even though at first glance they appear as impediments to the efficient operation of labour markets. At least for these two reasons, the case for policy initiatives to whole-heartedly remove such rigidities has yet to be made.

NOTES

1 The data presented in Table 1 are based on each country's definition of labour force, employment, and unemployment. A recent study by Statistics Canada, *The Labour Force* (August 1984) 93–118, shows that the two surveys use effectively identical definitions, that both address the civilian non-institutional population, and that both used stratified area samples. The only difference is the minimum age, which in Canada is 15 and in the United States is 16. Removing 15-year-olds in Canada lowers the unemployment rate by at most 0.1 percentage points.

2 In his comments earlier in this volume, Richard Lipsey observes that a movement along a V-U curve could also be the result of an increase in wage demands or wage rigidities leading to reduced job offers (vanancies) and higher unemployment. Mancur Olson also raised this point in a private conversation. While this is a possibility, the question we will ask is whether the magnitude of the changes that we observe suggests that this has a high probability of occurring over the short period we examine. As Lipsey suggests, this is clearly a subject for further research. If only Statistics Canada had not discontinued the Job Vacancy Survey (Meltz 1982)!

3 In his paper earlier in this volume, Neil Martin Baily shows that the relationship between the help wanted index and unemployment for the United States follows a roughly similar pattern to that of the V-U relation for Canada. In spite of Baily's reservations – which we share – about the quality of the data, the results do suggest the same trend toward a long-term increase in structural and frictional unemployment.

REFERENCES

Gunderson, M. 1983. *Economic Aspects of Interest Arbitration*. Toronto: Ontario Economic Council
- 1985. 'The Public/Private Sector Compensation Controversy,' in M. Thompson and G. Swimmer (eds), *Conflict or Compromise: The Future of Public Sector Industrial Relations*, 5–43. Montreal: Institute for Research on Public Policy
Hansen, B. 1970. 'Excess Demand, Unemployment Vacancies and Wages,' *Quarterly Journal of Economics* 84:1–12
Kaliski, S.F. 1984. 'Why Must Unemployment Remain So High?' *Canadian Public Policy* 10, No. 2, 127–41
Meltz, N.M. 1982. 'Labour Market Information in Canada: The Current Situation and a Proposal,' *Relations industrielles / Industrial Relations* 37, No. 2, 431–7
- 1985. 'Labour Movements in Canada and the United States,' in T. Kochan (ed), *Challenges and Choices Facing American Labor*, 315–34. Cambridge, Mass: MIT Press
Reid, F. 1982. 'Wage-and-Price Controls in Canada,' In J. Anderson and M. Gunderson, *Union-Management Relations in Canada*, 482–502. Don Mills, Ont: Addison-Wesley
Reid, F., and N.M. Meltz. 1979. 'Causes of Shifts in the Unemployment-Vacancy Relationship: An Empirical Analysis for Canada,' *Review of Economics and Statistics* 61:470–5

Comments

S. F. KALISKI

The principal question that appears to be emerging from these studies is: are current unemployment levels caused by structural problems or demand deficiency and how can (should) they best be reduced?

Foot and Li return to the theme of demographic structural unemployment, already raised by Baily and Fortin. They argue that previous measurements are biased downward and propose an alternative calculation. That alternative calculation is certainly illuminating but, I think, overstates the case.

It really is not the case that previous studies looked at the impact of changing labour-force weights and attributed the rest to demand deficiency. As the authors acknowledge, Reid and Smith (1981) attempted to measure unemployment caused by mismatches of the demographic structure as well. So did Fortin (this volume). I do, however, applaud the authors' recognition that earlier studies mislead us when they treat participation-rate changes as an element of supply rather than as an endogenously determined result of labour-market interaction.

I quite accept that there is imperfect substitutability in the labour market and that we should not rely on relative wage changes to look after everything. But it is a long way from that proposition to accepting that demand is rigidly segmented for as many as six age groups for each sex. Granted that a 25-year-old woman cannot become a 45-year-old man; need that matter? I presume the authors intend the working out of the implications of their assumption simply as a vivid counter-example to the assumption of homogeneity, which also, presumably, no one takes quite literally.

Related to this, I am less sanguine than the authors about the prospects for youth unemployment. There are difficulties to absorbtion into the labour force of new entrants (or of married women returning after a prolonged absence) that do not present similar barriers to substitution in the opposite direction, or between other age-sex groupings.

I also think that these interesting calculations could mislead us badly about what has happened in the recent past and is likely or desirable for the near future. As the authors acknowledge (note 10), their essentially arbitrary choice of $\dot{E}$ greatly affects their results. They argue persuasively that $\dot{E}$ might best be equated with SPOP but choose average $\text{SPOP}_i = 1.51$ per cent per year over the very long period 1971–96. Yet, as they explain, this is an average of rather rapid growth of around 2 per cent for 1971–81 and much slower growth thereafter. Thus the matching growth in E for 1971–81 should also be higher, and less of our current unemployment is therefore structural than would appear from their figures.

Also, the choice of 1983 unemployment rates by age-sex group for projections and backcasting is unfortunate. The average level and structure of rates in that year are certain to be heavily influenced by cyclical variability. Moreover, as has already been pointed out, it is one thing to project a stable growth path and quite another to use the same rate of growth to project the near future from a situation of much below potential output and employment.

Both Gunderson and Meltz and Riddell suggest that our principal difficulty is demand deficiency, although both pay proper attention to institutions and other structural considerations. Gunderson and Meltz review the various structural problems and find that, while they had the result of raising unemployment in the past, they are now tending to decline in importance and should not inhibit us in the near future. Riddell, too, takes this view. He views possibilities for non-inflationary expansion in the near term as favourable and endorses Fortin's recommendation (this volume) for a more expansionary monetary policy accompanied by gradual reduction of the deficit. He also recommends an incomes policy to contain any resurgence of inflationary expectations, while recognizing both the obstacles to a voluntary policy and the problems with a compulsory one.

Gunderson and Meltz, like Baily (this volume) and other American authors on whom he reports, study the Beveridge curve and find it for Canada drifting out till the mid-1970s. Since then the movement appears to be along a curve. I recognize Lipsey's (this volume) valid objection that one cannot by this means distinguish between demand deficiency and classical unemployment à la Malinvaud caused by above-equilibrium real wages. I would, however, add two comments.

First, as I understand Helliwell's (1983) interpretation of the results of his macroeconometric model, the Anti-Inflation Board (AIB), with its asymmetrical impact on the wage and other components of price inflation, has helped to save us from this problem of real wages being above equilibrium. Second, if we do have the problem, the once-and-for-all increase in the price level that would accompany the Fortin-Riddell increase in the quantity of money and currency depreciation might well cure it. Can we be sure that the above-equilibrium real wage is a once-and-for-all problem? Clearly, as both Lipsey and Riddell stress, there can be no ironclad guarantees. However, and here I am being very neo-classical, surely the recent major reorientation of macro policy in much of the world from combating unemployment to fighting inflation must have constituted a major policy surprise; and surely Riddell's and Fortin's examination of the wage-round process suggests that it is nominal, not real, wage increases that are subject to inertia. These two considerations lead me to suppose that part, at least, of any rise of the real wage above equilibrium is the result of an error in forecasting price inflation resulting from the policy surprise.

For the longer run Riddell suggests a move to synchronized shorter con-tracts to reduce wage inertia. Like Gunderson and Meltz, he worries that the existence of the present arrangements suggests that they might be privately optimal; but both papers also contain evidence that private and social optimality may not coincide here. Thus, private optimality, even if it exists, is not a good reason for continuing the contractual arrangements.

Finally, both papers consider and largely discount the possibility that unemployment may be structural as a result of increasing rates of change in industrial structure, as measured, for example, by the dispersion of the rate of change of employment by industry. Like some other papers reported upon by Baily, (this volume) Abraham and Katz (1984) examine this prob-lem in the American context. They propose a simple test: if demand defi-ciency caused both the higher unemployment and the larger dispersion of employment changes, the relation between the dispersion and vacancy rates should be negative; if the results are structural, it should be positive. For Canada, since 1962, the relationship turns out to be negative (with the sole exception of 1975–6) based on data on structural unemployment arising from the dispersion of employment growth across industries (given in Rid-dell's paper) and on vacancies (given in the Gunderson-Meltz paper). This provides further evidence of the predominance of deficient demand as opposed to structural unemployment.

REFERENCES

Abraham, K.G., and L.F. Katz. 1984. 'Cyclical Unemployment: Sectoral Shifts

or Aggregate Disturbances?' National Bureau of Economic Research Working
Paper No. 1410
Helliwell, J.F. 1983. 'Stagflation and Productivity Decline in Canada, 1974–82,'
Canadian Journal of Economics 17:191–216
Merrilees, W.J. 1982. 'Labour Market Segmentation in Canada: An Econometric
Approach,' *Canadian Journal of Economics* 15:458–73
Reid, F., and D.A. Smith. 1981. 'The Impact of Demographic Changes on
Unemployment,' *Canadian Public Policy* 7:248–51
Welch, F. (1979). 'Effect of Cohort Size on Earnings: The Baby Boom Babies'
Financial Bust,' *Journal of Political Economy* 87, No. 2, S65–97

KEITH NEWTON

A dominant theme of this conference has been the rivalry between competing explanations of North America's high unemployment rates and the policy implications that are associated with them. The Canadian papers all bear directly on this important question of structural versus aggregate demand interpretations.

Gunderson and Meltz examine a long list of ostensible impediments to labour-market adjustment and explore aggregate measures of the net effect of these impediments with respect to the divergent unemployment performances in the United States and Canada. A large part of their paper involves the setting up and more or less vigorous destruction of a series of 'straw man' rigidities. For example, they examine some labour-market manifestations of a class of efficient outcomes in a principle/agent framework characterized by such factors as risk, uncertainty, and asymmetric information. And they do quite validly point out that a number of important labour-market institutions such as minimum wages and unemployment insurance may have overwhelming rationalizations that owe nothing to efficiency considerations. The proportionately small part of the paper devoted to measuring the impact of rigidities looks at the relation between help wanted and unemployment indexes. Curiously enough, the emphasis here seems to be on the period 1980–4. I would have thought that coming to grips with the question of the origins of recent increases in unemployment would require scrutiny of a somewhat longer period (though, of course, Meltz and Reid did in fact analyse the Canadian U-V curve up to 1976). In any case, I would like to mention two other recent studies that are relevant. The first, by Siedule and Newton (1983), suggests the possibility of a retreat of the U-V curve in the late 1970s. The second, by Betcherman (1984), concludes that the main story is one of overwhelming cyclical slack in recent years.

I found these two parts of Gunderson and Meltz's paper disconnected. Some theoretical development as to the links between the various rigidities considered in the first part of the paper and their manifestation in U-V space would have been helpful. Nevertheless, I like the principal conclusion of the paper, which is quite consistent in spirit with the paper by Riddell and, in turn, with the other important Canadian paper, by Fortin.

Riddell, in asking whether we can and should reduce unemployment in the short to medium term, examines the evidence supporting the structuralist argument and finds it lacking. I felt that in this connection the examination of some dispersion indexes of the kind described by Baily would have been helpful. In this regard I might mention the calculations that appear in chapter 5 of the Economic Council of Canada's recent (1984) *Twenty-First Annual Review*. They suggest modest downward trends in the indexes for the age-sex and regional dimensions, a modest increase in the occupational dimension, and some slight but discernible increase in the industry dimension in recent years.

In any case, Riddell's conclusion is generally consistent with the now-familiar theme that the important characteristics of recent Canadian unemployment is its cyclical origin. Indeed, Riddell's policy conclusions are remarkably close to Fortin's, with the exception that Riddell cautiously combines expansionist recommendations with complementary wage and price policy.

Foot and Li perform a valuable service in suggesting that previous assessments of the contribution of demographic factors to unemployment in Canada may have been underestimated. Their important message is that we must not necessarily take comfort in projected demographic trends, because ostensibly salutary aggregate outcomes may mask troublesome compositional features. This may serve to remind us that, however seductive the emerging consensus at the aggregate level, there remains a series of complex micro adjustment problems that Canada must face.

In this context I offer one simple illustration that has been virtually ignored in our discussions of labour-market adjustment at this conference. It is the issue of technological change which, at the aggregate level, one may view with equanimity or, as in the case of Tobin's keynote address, virtually dismiss as an issue entirely. At the micro level it is an issue of concern that causes painful and costly distortions. Therefore, the structuralist and aggregate demand diagnoses of Canadian unemployment are not either/or but and/and propositions. This is the element that links all of these papers, and it is nicely characterized by Riddell's distinction between the short-run and long-run aspects of the diagnosis and treatment of unemployment. It seems quite consistent that we should address the urgent cyclical problem through short-term aggregate demand policy while also considering carefully the array of institutional impediments documented by Gunderson and Meltz, the demographic composition problems highlighted by Foot, and the sources of wage inertia identified in the latter part of Riddell's paper. Our policy package must therefore reflect balance and complementarity in acknowledging explicitly the coexistence in Canada of substantial unemployment problems deriving from both cyclical and structural sources.

REFERENCES

Betcherman, G. 1984. 'Matching People and Jobs: Labour Market Efficiency in Canada, 1966-1983.' Ottawa; Economic Council of Canada, mimeographed
Economic Council of Canada. 1984. *Steering the Course, Twenty-First Annual Review*. Ottawa: Supply and Services Canada
Siedule, T., and K. Newton. 1983. 'The Relationship between Unemployment and Job Vacancies in Canada: Theory and Evidence.' Ottawa: Economic Council of Canada, mimeographed

INDUSTRIAL RELATIONS

JOHN DUNLOP

Industrial relations and unemployment

In this volume you can see advocated virtually every possible position on the relation between unemployment and industrial relations. Some argue that industrial relations are irrelevant to unemployment, which is determined alone by macroeconomic considerations such as fiscal and monetary policy. Others suggest that industrial relations are a major contributing factor to unemployment through creating rigidities in market adjustment and fostering unwise public social policy. And still others urge that industrial relations mitigate unemployment through training and improving the performance of the labour market. Economists are to be found on all sides of the issue.

In the past decade in the Western world a number of conservative governments have come to power believing the old adage: 'General unemployment exists when asking too much is general.' In order to reduce unemployment, they advocate reductions in wages and a shift to profits; destandardization of wages and elimination of wage solidarity; reductions in unemployment insurance and social programs; cuts in public programs for retraining and redeploying workers; reductions in restraints and costs imposed on plant closures; and some changes in industrial relations rules to shift power to management (Sengenberger 1984).

These politicians, as politicians everywhere, have their gaggle of supporting economists who view the labour market as essentially like any other market, and they spell out detailed programs for renewed worker competition to reduce unemployment. As stated by Sengenberger (1984, 327): 'The risk-bearing associated with economic change is seen as the individual responsibility of each worker.' Or, as indicated by Olson (1982, 201): 'The main group that can have an interest in preventing the mutually profitable transactions between the involuntarily unemployed and employers is the workers with the same or competitive skills.'

In view of such politically popular judgments, I trust that the writers here do not intend to rule out the potential of industrial relations for *increasing* unemployment! I do not refer alone to the views of the far right that regard labour organizations and governments as unfortunate intrusions in labour markets that are much in need of deregulation. As reported in the *New York Times* (19 June 1984, 14), the Closing Declaration of the London summit on 9 June 1984 stated that the leaders of the seven nations agreed to reduce obstacles to the creation of new jobs, including encouraging the efficient working of the labour market. One senses the official notion that industrial relations systems have created inefficiencies – that would not otherwise exist – and have discouraged new jobs by 'measures to preserve obsolescent production and technology.'

However, industrial relations measures are not appropriately used as a substitute for the optimum mix of general or macroeconomic policies. While there may be no political alternative on occasions to using the industrial relations system to try to offset the macroeconomic policies advanced by general economists or used by political operatives, the more direct approach is to institute a more appropriate set of macroeconomic policies.

I recognize that it is most difficult to secure concurrence on technical grounds alone as to the appropriate mix of four areas of macropolicies – public expenditures and taxes, monetary and interest rate policies, foreign exchange rates, and the complex of trade policies – to assure long-term growth or to move an economy from deep recession or a state of overheat to a long-term growth path. Nonetheless, it is essential both in analysis and public policy decisions to identify explicitly the most appropriate mix of macro policies, because there is a considerable tendency and temptation in politics to substitute specific regulatory measures, including price and wage controls or incomes policies, labour-market measures, industrial policy, or sectoral activity for the most appropriate macro-policies (Dunlop 1944, 286).

James Tobin (1983, 113) has stated this view strongly, perhaps too pre-emptively: 'Macro physicians do not deny that the economies of the United States and the rest of the world also face some challenging macro-economic adjustments. They do, however, deny that these are of such unusual magnitude that, given a clement macro climate, they could not occur via the normal processes of private and public initiatives in our mixed economies.' That statement leaves open both the meaning of merciful or lenient macro policies and the range of measures envisaged in 'the normal processes of private and public initiatives.'

I am quite prepared to render unto macro policies a great deal of the level and fluctuation in employment (and unemployment), and prices and wages, but not all of it. And I insist on rendering to more specific industrial, labour-market, and industrial relations policies a share of the action, not to neglect the critical role of industrial relations in compensation, incomes policy, and work-place productivity. Moreover, the political process refuses to await the outcome of endless technical debate and indecision over appropriate macro policies and their mix. We live too often in a second- or third-best or even a least-best world.

An indispensable tool, for me, in thinking about industrial relations and employment (unemployment) is the internal labour market (Dunlop 1966; Doeringer and Piorie 1971). Movement among the categories of employed, unemployed, and outside the labour force constitutes movement among enterprises, or self-employment, and movement across the boundary line between being within or outside the labour force. These movements within the 'external' labour market constitute a small proportion of the total complex of changes that takes place each day, most within the 'internal' labour market of the enterprise.

The administration of policies established by management alone or through collective bargaining determines the patterns of movement involved in hiring, promotion, transfer, layoff (temporary or permanent), and relocation arrangements; leaves, discipline, and discharge; and retirements and disabilities. Some of these movements are purely internal to an administrative unit and others affect the external market in different ways, as in decisions respecting hiring, retirement, and permanent layoff. The internal labour market is thus an administrative unit in which movements within the unit or with the outside are patterned by formal rules or custom. The unit may involve only some job classifications of an establishment or may include a number of enterprises as in multi-employer hiring halls or multi-plants of a single company. The internal market may be narrow, involving a single occupation in a single enterprise, or broad, as in the civil service.

Internal markets are concerned with such topics as seniority, seniority districts for various purposes, retirement policies, hiring and recruitment policies, promotion rules and standards, layoff criteria in a temporary or permanent mode, absentee policy, health care regulations, equal employment opportunity and age discrimination, as well as dispute resolution over these complex rules and their consequences for management and employees.

The discipline of economics has no knowledge or room for the field of internal markets; it is as given to economic theory as are engineering and technical production coefficients.

The cumulative consequences of all these internal movements on exterior labour markets is substantial. This judgment establishes a unique role for industrial relations in employment (unemployment), apart from any ideal macroeconomic policies, or apart from the interests of industrial relations in exterior markets, compensation-setting, or incomes policy. Internal labour markets, with their alternative designs, rules, and administration and their effects on external labour markets, constitute a vast and somewhat neglected field for research even among industrial relations specialists.

Internal labour markets help us to understand the training that takes place within enterprises. There is a spectrum ranging between training on the job and informal formal training.

Internal labour markets and their rules, which govern the movement of workers, are the fundamental determinants of the quality of a work-force and the training that it acquired over a period of time on the job. Internal labour markets put substance into the importance ascribed to on-the-job training. What qualities and training does an employee have on entry? What skills and experience does an employee achieve through transfers and promotions? What additional experience is acquired when other employees are late, absent, sick, or on vacation? How broad or narrow are job classifications and their duties and how limited or extensive are seniority units or districts? How much hiring from outside or contracting-out of work takes place?

The rules and practices responsive to these questions are critical to the range of work operations that an employee performs and the training that he or she acquires. The flexibility of the work-force – its adaptability to technical change, shifts in work processes, new quality and work standards, and new products – is likely to be mightily influenced by its previous work experience and applicable internal rules. Clearly also, the adaptability and employability of those exiting to the exterior labour market is likewise materially influenced by this internal experience and training. In no two workplaces, even in the same industry, are the complex of these rules and resulting training identical.

In recognition of the rapid changes taking place in the 1980s – in demography, proportion of women in the work-place, and technology and product markets – parties to collective bargaining or management alone must re-examine these traditional internal rules of movement to assess their impact on training, mobility, flexibility, quality, employment security, and efficiency (with necessary trade-offs).

I am not sanguine about generalized advice concerning rearrangements of internal markets and rules, on account of the wide diversity of these arrangements. Some pundits argue that job classifications should be broadened and seniority districts widened or shortened. But there are dangerous generalizations, since the quality of performance, earnings, costs, and efficiency may be adversely affected. Historically, management has tended to prefer narrower seniority districts, particularly for promotions and short-term reductions in force, and unions have tended to urge broader districts, particularly for permanent layoffs. Management was concerned that broader districts might result in higher costs of experience training, costs of movement as in railroad districts, and difficulties of supervision arising from changes in the composition of the work group. The preferences of unions reflected the interest in greater job security. In recent years, these seniority district preferences seem to have generally continued, although significant permanent layoffs have encouraged limited transfer rights (as in the five- and ten-year rule that developed in meat packing), and the concern with equal employment opportunity, as in steel, whether directed by court order or not, has provided for cross-district limited promotion rights.

Academics could help the parties by making some case studies and some comparative studies in a sector, as to the consequences of various internal market organizations and patterns of movement. They have done little or nothing, probably because data are difficult and methods may be too inelegant to attract current professional interest. But training derived from the internal market is decisive to internal efficiency and external unemployment (employment); the structure and operation of the internal market are a tool available to private parties to influence employment and unemployment and the quality of those exiting to the external markets. Internal markets are more significant than formal training to which the discussion now turns.

The mutual interests of workers and enterprises in formal training are illustrated in apprenticeship programs with on-the-job and formal education components. Such training is on a market or multi-employer basis in some skilled occupations and on a single-enterprise basis in other cases. These programs have been expanded to include upgrading, retraining, and training for new skills or technologies. The limited but long-established tuition aid programs of some companies have been designed to enhance vocational skills, although some are intended also for liberal education (Barton 1982). The last generation also has seen an enormous growth in technical, professional, and executive training for managers and professional employees.

Apart from governmental training programs, private parties have in some cases embarked on formal training and retraining programs, for production and maintenance employees. The well-known negotiated programs of the United Auto Workers and Ford and General Motors cover employees who are unemployed or likely to be out of employment, whether they are preparing to work for the automobile companies or to take employment elsewhere (American Society for Training and Development 1984, 1). No one has a complete inventory of all these activities or even an adequate overview of formal training in all its dimensions. These innovative programs confront many difficult issues – the willingness of employees to move geographically, the difficulties in predicting company decisions with respect to locations of operations, and the vast uncertainty of product demand. While most businesses, a recent survey finds, are not opposed to retraining workers whose skills have become obsolete, they are not certain how to go about the appropriate training, and as a result 'most firms currently tend to replace workers who have inadequate skills with more qualified individuals (Bureau of National Affairs 1984, A-4 to A-6).

Industrial relations could make a more significant contribution to the economy if appropriate training programs could become a routine subject of collective agreements, or on employer policies, over the next decade, in the same way that health and welfare and private pension plans have become standard in the past generation, or apprenticeship programs have historically existed in some industries.

Formal training costs money, and there are also large costs not readily apparent in informal training. Moreover, training presents the same enigma as fixing the leaky roof: there is little pressing need to do so when unemployment abounds, and it is too late to do so in times of labour shortage. Some employers prefer to hire away workers rather than do formal training themselves. Small firms are on the whole less likely to engage in formal training programs.

One of the major challenges to our industrial relations is how to transform our federal-state unemployment insurance program so that it can be used to make a contribution to training. It has now been made clear that being engaged in bona fide training is not to constitute grounds to deny unemployment insurance benefits because one is not available for work. But only several states have yet integrated training into their unemployment insurance programs.

Clearly, in providing more accurate and prompt flow of labour-market information, industrial relations can ameliorate frictional or seasonal unemployment. Moreover, various industry-specific measures, like weathering control in construction, can smooth seasonal patterns of unemployment. But cyclical and structural unemployment is of greater interest at these meetings. Moreover, the major concern is the role of industrial relations in aggravating or mitigating unemployment derived from international competition, technoligical change, longer-term structural adjustments in demand for a sector, periodic cyclical fluctuations, and competition between organized and unorganized enterprises.

Industrial relations influence competitiveness in a number of ways, most notably through compensation levels and productivity, the latter at the enterprise and work levels. Moreover, the adaptability of industrial relations to changing competitive environments is no less significant and perhaps of major concern to management confronted with rapid changes in markets, financial constraints, government policies, technologies, and opportunities. Sectoral and enterprise compensation, plant-level productivity, and adaptability in compensation and work rules are tools of industrial relations, rather than of general economics.

It has been argued that adaptability can be enhanced by one-year collective bargaining agreements and by the institution of profit-sharing as a significant component of compensation. Flexibility may also be enhanced by defined-contribution pension plans rather than defined-benefit pension plans; we are seeing many conversions from the first to the second type.

As to the duration of collective agreements, I recall setting in the Manchester Library in England in the winter of 1938–9 reading a hundred years of the *Cotton Factory Times*. The early collective agreements, or more accurately the piece-rate lists, were written without specific limit of time so that either the owners or the unions oculd ask at any time on reasonable notice for a change in piece rates with a change in the demand for the product, primarily from overseas. Collective agreements have a longer duration in North America than elsewhere. Perhaps we need to develop sophisticated standards and procedures for reopenings in export industries. Year-to-year agreements, to most parties, are too expensive in time, effort, uncertainty, and potential conflict to be practical. As to profit-sharing, far too many factors affect profits however defined – and that is a major problem – to make a large element of compensation for most workers depend upon profits.

Collective bargaining has always been significantly influenced by the state of demand and competitiveness in the relevant product markets (Dunlop 1944). In recent years in the United States, there have been changes, unprecedented since the Depression, in product market competition as a consequence of international competition (automobiles and basic steel), deregulation of governments rate-setting (master freight trucking and airlines), marketing changes and geographical locations (meat packing), and the rapid growth of non-union enterprises (certain construction branches and locations), all within the setting of a deep recession and an administration regarded as hostile by unions. It is not clear in any particular case how much adjustment is mandated by irreversible structural change and how much is likely to be reversible with high employment and a more settled economic outlook.

Some predict the disappearance of collective bargaining, as we have known it, and the emergence of negotiations solely on an enterprise or establishment basis. I regard such predictions as seriously misguided. I see no reason to doubt that collective bargaining, with some lags, will respond constructively to the new environment in these troubled sectors.

I do expect that as long as loose labour markets persist, collective bargaining parties will constrict to some degree the scope of parties or activities covered by agreements and develop separate agreements with different terms.

In construction, for example, we are seeing the emergence of separate agreements, with separate wages and work rules, in industrial construction, commercial construction, heavy and highway, pipelines, transmission lines, refractory work, maintenance, and so on. Moreover, separate jurisdictional rules have emerged. These branches are separate product markets with distinctive competitive forces.

As further illustration, I recently had occasion to settle a local dispute involving Bricklayers and their employers in Beaumont, Texas, with the participation of the international union and the national contractor organization. We set separate rates in the metropolitan area, a lower rate for outlying counties, a separate schedule for housing, and refractories in the territory of a local union that previously had a single uniform posted rate. The avowed purpose was to enable competitive contractors operating under collective agreements to be more competitive. That sort of adjustment is going on in industry generally, to make for greater competitiveness in present and foreseeable product markets.

The quest for adaptability in compensation and rules in order to be viable requires, as a minimum, a continuing forum in which results of recent operations, projections of the future, and concerns over compensation, productivity, employment, markets, and so on can be shared and candidly reviewed. Such a forum requires access to the most intimate business data, and it flourishes in a style of management that is more co-operative and participatory than US management has generally been. Thus adaptability at the work-place requires major changes in management, nor merely changes in the rules of the work-place and collective agreements. Such forums are also appropriate at the sectoral and regional levels beyond the work-place or enterprise.

REFERENCES

American Society for Training and Development. 1984. *National Report for Training and Development*

Barton P. 1982. *Worklife Transition: The Adult Working Connection*. New York: McGraw-Hill

Bureau of National Affairs. 1984. *Daily Labor Report*, 19 November

Doeringer, P. and M. Piore. 1971. *Internal Labor Markets and Manpower Analysis*. Lexington, Mass: D.C. Health

Dunlop, J. 1944. *Wage Determination under Trade Unions*. New York: Macmillan

– 1966. 'Job Vacancy Measures and Economic Analysis', in *The Measurement and Interpretation of Job Vacancies*. New York: Columbia University Press

– 1984. *Dispute Resolution, Negotiation and Consensus Building*. Dover, Mass: Auburn House

Hamermesh, D. and A. Rees. 1984. *The Economics of Work and Pay*, 3rd edition. New York: Harper and Row

Heldman, D.J. Bennett, and M. Johnson. 1981. *Deregulating Labor Relations*. Dallas: Fisher Institute

Olsen, M. 1982. *The Rise and Decline of Nations, Economic Growth, Stagflation and Social Rigidities*. New Haven: Yale University Press

Sengenberger, W. 1984. 'West German Employment Policy: Restoring Worker Competition,' *Industrial Relations* 23 (Fall) 323–43

Tobin, J. 1983. 'Commentary,' in 'Industrial Change and Public Policy,' Symposium sponsored by the Federal Reserve Bank of Kansas City, 24–26 August

Comments

JOHN CRISPO

The conference began with a review of how the Reagan administration in the United States had inadvertently stumbled onto a temporary Keynesian solution to that country's unemployment problem, based on a bastardized and distorted supply-side rationale. While this review should have reinforced one's faith in Keynesianism, it did not necessarily have that effect among the Canadians present, as a result of recent experience in their country.

Unlike the Keynesian prescription of deficits in bad times and surpluses in good times, the last Canadian government ran higher and higher deficits over the past decade or so, regardless of the state of the economy. Its thinking appeared to be that while the country needed deficits in bad times it could afford them in good times, so that it might just as well run a deficit all the time. Even the staunchest Keynesian is likely to wilt somewhat in the fact of this kind of misapplication of Keynes's doctrines. At least this experience should help foreigners to understand the counter-cyclical concern among some Canadians over excessively high deficits at this time of double-digit unemployment.

Considerable time has been devoted to the wide variation in experience with unemployment across and between OECD and related countries. At one end of the spectrum are countries like Austria and Japan, which have maintained relatively high rates of employment regardless of experience elsewhere. At the other end are countries like Belgium and Britain – not to mention Canada – that have lived with high rates of unemployment for some time.

Among the explanations offered for this variation in unemployment were everything from effective fiscal and monetary policies, through labour-market and other structural policies, to all manner of incomes policies, including controls, guidelines, and social contracts. Also mentioned was Austrian-style neocorporatism and whatever Japan has going for it. So many combinations and permutations of explanations were tabled that virtually everyone could count on hearing something about their pet theory.

Some seemed to feel that the institutions of collective bargaining and industrial relations are close to being irrelevant because broader aggregate or macro forces are ultimately determinant. Others felt that such institutions are all to relevant because they are failing to adapt fast enough to new competitive, demographic, and technological realities.

All this background material set the stage for this final session involving two industrial relations practitioners and those who try to regulate their activities, both at the federal and provincial levels in Canada. What is to be learned from their presentations? First, there are wage adjustment and related work-rule data that suggest that the results of collective bargaining are eventually more flexible than might have been anticipated heretofore. However, it seems to take a high and sustained level of unemployment to bring about such flexibility. Moreover, sometimes relations between the parties are so rigidly structured that existing bargaining relationships have to be altered radically before accommodations to new realities can be implemented.

Overall, several sets of conclusions can doubtless be drawn. One could conclude that the ongoing search for any one school of thought to explain unemployment is quite fruitless and even counterproductive. At any given time in any country there is invariably a mixture of causes of unemployment. While one may be able to rank these causes, this ranking is likely to change almost as fast as it is produced. Further, just as the mixture of causes is probably constantly changing, so is a steadily varying mixture of remedies usually appropriate.

It seems to begin by assuming that a country must have an appropriate set of fiscal and monetary policies or it is bound to be in difficulty. In addition, such macro economic policies must normally be complemented by a host of compatible measures, ranging over everything from manpower to trade policies.

One feature not dwelled on at any length was the need for countries to become and remain more competitive. Presumably this concern tended to be neglected on the assumption that any such challenge will automatically take care of itself in institutions operating on a bottom-line basis in reasonably open market situations. However, there is no long-run solution to a country's unemployment problem – not to mention any aspirations it may have to grow and enjoy a higher standard of living – that can escape the need to become more competitive.

The challenge of becoming more competitive, if nothing else, brings one back to the focus of the last session of the conference. If labour and management are to assist in the reduction of unemployment through collective bargaining, they are going to have to work together to make both the country and its enterprises more competitive. Thus the need for joint action at both the macro and the micro level. This may seem a strange plea coming from one so known for his support of an adversarial system of collective bargaining. In the increasingly competitive world in which Canadians find themselves operating, however, it is imperative for labour and management to complement their adversarial relations with joint measures designed to ensure a large pie to divide.

It is easier to start this process at the micro level, where at least two major developments are required, neither of which is without significant precedent. First, if labour and management are to co-operate in making enterprises more efficient, innovative, and productive, and hence more competitive, gains-sharing plans akin to the Scanlon Plan must be introduced more widely to ensure a mutual incentive. It is also important to work on measures like the Domtar Industrial Conversion Adjustment Plan to ensure that the costs (as well as the benefits) of changes required to become more competitive are shared more equitably. As with a similar plan on the railways, the Domtar Plan involves a joint labour-management committee with sufficient funding to enable it to introduce adjustments tailor-made to those individuals adversely affected by changes of any kind brought about by efforts to make an enterprise more competitive. Both gains and adjustment-cost sharing are critical at the micro level if labour and management are to work together to meet the competitive challenge that confronts most Canadian enterprises.

Second, joint efforts by labour and management at the macro level are also required if only to help fashion an overall framework of public policies within which they can work together more effectively at the micro level. In the new Canadian Labour Market and Productivity Centre (CLMPC), labour and management now have an institution that can begin to work on such a framework of public policies, many of which are now in operation, though not on as complementary and co-ordinated a basis as could be the case.

Eventually, if successful, the CLMPC could set the stage for a more grandiose labour-management venture at the national level that would ultimately have to involve other interest groups as well. The idea of a national economic and social forum where all major interest groups could try to reach a general consensus on the economic facts of life should not be ruled out. Even a common data base and a shared perception of problems and prospects could yield more constructive relations between all manner of groups, not just labour and management.

Nothing much of consequence is likely to happen at the national level unless a great deal of attitudinal and institutional change takes place. Most important of all is the need to stop isolating and ostracizing the labour movement. Neither management nor government nor anyone else should expect trade unions to act more responsibly unless they are treated more responsibly. In return, of course, organized labour would have to learn to live with the party in power regardless of its own political preferences. And last but not least, the government would have to resist the temptation to exploit whatever labour-management co-operation emerged for its own narrow political purposes.

T.E. ARMSTRONG

It is certainly plausible, and somewhat tempting, to advance the thesis that collective bargaining is a reactive instrument, not related to employment creation; that employment is created (or not created) through fiscal and monetary strategies, industrial and trade policies, and other macroeconomic strategies; and that the business of collective bargaining, at least on the wage side, is simply to divide up the resulting product. However, to assert that proposition would be to adopt an idiosyncratic and narrow perspective on the way in which the world operates.

A more realistic view is that any system of wage determination has an important effect on employment and unemployment – and that along with fiscal and monetary policies, it forms a triad that makes the difference between growth and stagnation in an economy.

It is hard to think of an industrialized jurisdiction where wage behaviour is not a prominent consideration in economic policy-making. During the recent recession of 1981–2, virtually every Western country, in developing its economic recovery strategy, had something to say about the importance of wages and wage levels in achieving non-inflationary growth.

However, the way in which collective bargaining affects both the level and nature of employment and unemployment is much more difficult to address. In simplistic terms, if bargaining produces wage settlements that are too high – that is, which exceed the growth in productivity – it exercises an inflationary influence, which in due course causes weakening in competitiveness, loss of markets, and ultimately loss of jobs. In contrast, if bargaining does not yield a fair and equitable share of gross national product for workers, other equally troublesome problems arise, such as declining purchasing power, slack demand, failing enterprises, and unemployment – to say nothing of the social unrest consequent upon an inequitable distribution of income.

From the basic premise that collective bargaining is inextricably linked to employment creation, all sorts of subsidiary questions arise having to do with the efficiency, effectiveness, and fairness of collective bargaining. Some argue that it is one of the most unfairly maligned components of a free-market economy and that if left to function in a free and untrammeled way (e.g. without wage controls or compulsory arbitration) collective bargaining is a sensitive instrument reacting sensitively to market forces. At the other extreme, others contend that it is a blunt, unwieldy instrument, a series of disconnected events that too often produce quixotic and irrational results, having more to do with institutional power, accident, and/or good luck than anything else.

The truth surely lies somewhere between these two caricatures. I must confess that both as a labour practitioner and as a public servant, I have oscillated in my own views about the capacity of the system to produce fair, affordable, and equitable results. Over the last decade, collective bargaining has had a checkered history, but on balance its distinguishing feature has been its resilience and capacity to adapt to changing circumstances.

With respect to its capacity to influence employment, I would suggest that there are several ways in which collective bargaining can and does contribute in positive ways. On the wage side, it does respond to harsh market facts, albeit many would say that the reaction is too slow and that it takes cruelly high levels of unemployment for wages and prices to moderate. One of the problems is that despite this recent moderation in wage settlements, current unemployment remains unacceptably high. This does not prove that moderation was not necessary. It may fairly be asked where we would be, in terms of recovery and levels of employment, had this moderation not occurred.

Our recent experience with recession-induced moderation leads to some tough questions by trade unionists. How equitable have the sacrifices been? Have others – professionals, executives, dividend recipients, etc – shown the same degree of sacrifice as wage-earners have? And to the extent that wage moderation has not led to lower unemployment, what has gone wrong with other public policy instruments, principally our fiscal and monetary strategies? Have the savings achieved through wage moderation and bargaining concessions been channeled into job-creating investments? More fundamentally, if wage behaviour is so important an element in economic policy and is so inextricably linked to fiscal and monetary policies, why should labour not be included in advisory undertakings where these policies are discussed and options developed? Others have shown the positive correlation betwen social consensus among the labour market parties and the positive indices of economic performance, including levels of employment.

Recently we analysed the major current collective agreements in Ontario to determine the prevalence of provisions that, prima facie, appear designed to minimize work-force reductions. For example, we looked at what might be referred to as the incidence of 'work-sharing' provisions: i.e. collective agreements that contain provisions for reductions in weekly hours, division of work, and rotation of layoffs. Approximately 10 per cent of the agreements surveyed had some provisions for the reduction of weekly hours below normal schedules, with a view to spreading work and avoiding layoffs. Some 2.7 per cent of agreements had provisions for dividing work with a view to sharing earnings without reducing the numbers of employees; 2.1 per cent contain provisions requiring periods of layoffs to be rotated equally among employees. Other substantive employment-related provisions included the following: 32 per cent required employers to transfer employees slated for layoff to existing vacancies; 2.4 per cent prohibited or limited overtime during slack period; 45 per cent restricted or limited contracting-out during slack periods; and 20.9 per cent entitled employees affected by plant closures or relocation to move to another plant of the same employer. Some had provisions for some measure of employee protection as a result of technological change, ranging from the right to some form of consultation through measures relating to retraining, income, maintenance, relocation allowance, and attrition provisions. The incidence of these provisions varies widely depending upon the subject matter. For example, 32 per cent provided for some form of consultation, while only 2.1 per cent provided for relocation allowances. Twelve per cent provided for extended vacations to expand job opportunities and reduce the incidence of layoff.

On the face of it, these provisions should reduce unemployment at the enterprise level. What is unclear, however, is their effect on aggregate levels of unemployment. It might well be argued that provisions such as these operate to retard structural changes which, if allowed to occur without contractual impediment, could lead, in the long run, to greater aggregate employment in the economy.

Aside from this larger unanswered question, the data do, however, indicate that within the narrow confines of collective bargaining, there appears to be considerable scope for more bargaining over employment stabilization. In this connection, I would observe by way of example that despite organized labour's insistent message that policy-makers ought to legislate restrictions on overtime, only 2.4 per cent of the agreements surveyed contained such provisions. In fairness, this may reflect the strength of employer opposition to provisions of this sort, but it would be interesting to analyse the frequency with which such proposals are put forward by unions in bargaining.

Another less direct technique that can form part of collective bargaining is joint investment decision-making. I am speaking here about union participation in the administration of pension funds. No less than $86 billion is now held in Canadian trusteed pension funds. A large percentage of those funds are held in plans covering unionized employees. It is becoming increasingly common for unions to be given participation in the administration of those funds pursuant to collectively negotiated arrangements. In those situations, union and employer trustees are able to explore investment strategies that not only provide market returns on investment but also create jobs in Ontario and Canada.

For all these reasons, I conclude that collective bargaining does have a role to play in employment creation. That role can be positive. Regrettably, however, collective bargaining and collective bargainers are too often insufficiently aware of the creative role that can be played. Moreover, as I have argued above, the labour-market parties in Canada are not sufficiently involved in economic policy-planning mechanisms and systems.

BERND K. KOKEN

To answer the question posed to this panel, I was strongly tempted to give a short and simple 'no' and let it go at that. The temptation became even stronger when I tried out the question on a senior official of one of the major unions we deal with and he came up with exactly that answer. The more I thought about it, however, the more I realized that the real answer – as so often – is both 'yes' and 'no.'

Let me illustrate what I mean by some real-life examples drawn from experiences of my own company. Two years ago we concluded that our pulp and paperboard mill in Jonquière, Quebec, would no longer figure in our plans for future development. So we decided either to close it down with the consequent loss of over 400 jobs – or sell it. There were many good reasons why continued operation did not make sense for us, but these did not necessarily apply to other possible owners. We therefore put the operation up for sale. A buyer was found, and the mill has continued to run to this day without missing a beat.

No amount of collective bargaining could have changed our corporate decision to 'sell' or 'close.' However, the process of collective bargaining definitely had an impact on the prospective buyer's decision as to whether or not the mill could become a viable entity.

The buyer saw an opportunity as long as certain preconditions could be met. One of these was achievement of an acceptable agreement with the labour unions in the mill. Through the process of collective bargaining just such an agreement was reached – the sale went through – and something in excess of 400 people directly involved and hundreds more indirectly involved did not end up on the unemployment rolls. And let me hasten to reassure representatives of labour, this was a good deal for the work force. Its members did not end up as poor cousins. They still enjoy an enviable package of wages and benefits. The point is that every employee at this location could have ended up losing his or her job had not a spirit of harmony and co-operation been applied to the process of collective bargaining. An almost identical situation occured in our paper mill at Sault Ste Marie in 1984.

The general conclusion that can be drawn from these examples is that in survival situations, the proper use of collective-bargaining initiatives can be very effective in reducing or preventing prospective increases in unemployment.

Now, let me make three basic observations relating collective bargaining to the maintenance of – or creation of – employment, stemming from the experience of our industry. 1) The Canadian forest products industry can provide more employment by being competitive in international markets. The converse of that is, of course, that unemployment is created by being non-competitive. 2) Collective bargaining, in an overall sense, affects directly and significantly our ability to be competitive, and the process must therefore be carried out in the most rational, least adversarial, and most co-operative manner possible. 3) Productivity is the key to being competitive, and there are many opportunities in the collective-bargaining relationship that can affect productivity in a positive way – as well as, unfortunately, in a negative way.

I am glad to say that in recent years we have been making progress toward a more co-operative, productive bargaining relationship than had been the case in our industry in the past. Beginning in the mid-1970s there is evidence that a sour and confrontational collective-bargaining relationship, particularly in the newsprint sector of our business, created a very negative reputation for us among our US publisher customers. This perception of poorly managed labour relations combined with a proliferation of work stoppages that disrupted newsprint supply was, in large part, responsible for our US customers encouraging – and indeed participating – in more US mill expansion. The results? Canada's share of US demand tumbled from 68 per cent in 1974 to 57 per cent last year, implying a loss of about 5,000 Canadian jobs.

If we are to grow – or indeed survive – cost competitiveness with other producing countries is imperative. The partners in collective bargaining have a contributing role to play in the equitable resolution of issues that affect cost competitiveness. Such issues include technological change, profit- or gain-sharing, shorter work weeks, multi-skill trades, and, of course, the subject of wage levels. With a positive approach to these and other issues of mutual interest, the collective bargaining partners have an opportunity to affect favourably the unemployment rate in Canada.

JOHN FRYER

'Does the present industrial relations system assist in reducing unemployment?' The answer is 'No.' However, Canada's industrial relations system could be used to reduce unemployment. I think it could, provided that we are prepared to make some basic changes to the system.

Recent wage settlement data from Labour Canada show that the average wage settlements of all contracts signed in the second quarter of 1984 hit a record low of 3.2 per cent, down from 3.9 per cent in the first quarter and still well below the inflation rate, which was running above 4.5 per cent at the time. Even with a slowdown in the rate of inflation in 1984, workers' real earnings continued to fall. Calculations by the Industrial Relations Centre at Queen's University indicated that 1984 would be the eighth consecutive year of decline in the purchasing power of Canadian wages. Since 1977, real wages – adjusted for inflation – have fallen by a total of 12 per cent. The effect on the whole economy has amounted to a staggering $423 million in lost purchasing power each week, or $22 billion annually.[1]

The labour movement is still finding itself involved in concession bargaining. Taking advantage of high unemployment levels, employers are still trying to wring concessions from employees. According to Labour Canada, of the 169 major contracts signed during the second quarter of 1984, more than 25 per cent called for a wage freeze or cut in the first year of the contract. In August, 5,000 employees struck Burns Meats when the employer demanded wage concessions ranging from $1.15 to $5 per hour. Two months later, Dominion Stores locked out 450 employees at its Windsor supermarkets for not agreeing to a 5-per-cent wage cut and a relaxation of seniority provisions.

Not only are we seeing an assault on workers' wages, but governments across Canada are changing the rules of collective bargaining to weaken the already weak bargaining power of unions. In Ontario, for example, the union bargaining team must take the 'employer's final offer' to the membership for a vote. In British Columbia decertification votes are now necessary when supported by only 45 per cent of the bargaining unit, and there is no automatic certification when the majority of employees express their wishes to join a union. Every certification application must be accompanied by a vote, regardless of the percentage of employees who have signed certification cards. In Newfoundland, if provincial government employees choose not to go on strike at the end of a mandatory seven-day strike notice, they cannot legally go on strike for another month. In addition, the strike must be continuous, making rotating strikes illegal. If workers return for any reason, the strike vote process – including the seven-day notice – must be started all over again. Added to these attacks on trade unions in our country is the attack on the public sector, involving downsizing, privatization, and controlling wages of public-sector employees.

For these and other reasons the labour movement is clearly on the defensive. It is in for the fight of its life as its stagnating level of membership devotes all its energies and resources to fending off attackers from all sides. Unions tend to feel they are in a corner – and when you are cornered you are inclined to come out scratching, clawing, and fighting for survival. Such behaviour does not lend itself to devising innovative problem-solving techniques concerning the major economic problems of the decade.

Although the labour movement is on the defensive, industrial relations can play an important role in reducing the massive unemployment we are experiencing. However, this will require some major amendments in our political, social, and economic systems, of which the industrial relations system is a part.

One new objective must be full employment. There is only one proper framework within which it is possible to reduce unemployment to acceptably low levels, and that is a commitment to full employment. Let me quote from a recent speech by Senator Michael Pitfield: 'The whole system of our society is predicated on jobs. Maybe we are coming to a leisure society but we are not there yet. Individual self-respect, domestic resource allocation and national prosperity are critically dependent on the availability of useful employment. This is the key to our social system. There is no alternative.'[2]

In the White Paper on Employment and Income of April 1945, the federal government pledged itself to the maintenance of a 'high and stable level of employment and income ... as a primary object of policy.' The white paper went on to state that the government, in setting this goal, 'is not selecting a lower target than full employment.'

Every government since then, and every budget statement, have paid lip service to the goal of reducing unemployment. In fact, our last government deliberately planned to increase unemployment in pursuit of other economic goals. This backing away from a commitment to full employment is totally unacceptable to labour. It leads inevitably to a perverse distribution of income. It weakens the economy by undercutting vital consumer spending, and the associated costs are too high. The creation of jobs and the reduction of unemployment must become the number 1 priority of the government in Ottawa and the ten provincial governments.

As well as seeking full employment, Canada must look closely at the impact of technological change in our society. Technology in Canada seems to be treated with alternative doses of hope and terror. The enthusiasm of technological advances is followed by nightmare visions of widespread layoffs, worker alienation, and ingenious new forms of exploitation. On the whole, technology has been introduced as an enemy of working people. This is especially true of working women, who are prime victims for displacement from office and clerical work. Almost half of my union's membership, up to 100,000 people, 80 per cent of them women, are realizing that technology threatens their skills, their status, and their livelihood.

In the words of the personal computer salesman, we must make technology 'user-friendly.' We must guarantee an expansion of workers' rights through legislation, thereby establishing mandatory mechanisms of consultation, adequate compensation, and the right to retraining.

In addition to seeking full employment and technological change, Canada will have to consider effective national labour-market policies. We must recognize that labour-market planning is the cornerstone upon which to build job creation and fiscal policies.

Information on labour markets in Canada is inadequate. Until we have better information on the availability of specific jobs, it will be impossible to match the supply of trained workers with the demands of the labour market. One way to help overcome this problem is to require employers to list all job vacancies with Canada Employment centres. We should consider increased wage subsidies to employers who retrain workers and increased aid to relocate workers and their families where jobs are available.

The recent establishment of the Industrial Labour Market Institute has been a step in the right direction. For the first time, the major actors in the labour market have a mechanism within which to gather detailed information on the demand and supply sides for skilled labour. Perhaps more important, for the first time business and labour have a joint body within which to debate and discuss labour-market trends and economic issues.

A good example of an innovative labour-market policy is the Quebec Federation of Labour's Solidarity Fund. Launched in February 1984, the fund has already collected nearly $1 million. The fund will invest in Quebec industries to create and maintain jobs in small and medium-sized companies. It will also assist in the education of workers in economics and related matters to enable them to become qualified members of the boards of directors of companies in which the fund has invested money. Workers buying shares will receive a 35-per-cent tax break from the Quebec government. On top of that, the shares can be transferred into Registered Retirement Savings Plans, providing further tax breaks. The Quebec government passed special legislation to set up this Solidarity Fund, giving it a $10-million loan at interest rates below market value.

The initiation of quality-of-working-life (QWL) projects could be used as another vehicle through which the industrial relations system could address unemployment. What is could afford to organized labour is the opportunity to work jointly with management in solving problems that emerge in the work-place. It could also provide a mechanism through which management may surrender some of its prerogative to control the method, means, and processes of production.

The people who are doing the job day in and day out often have useful suggestions on how the work could be performed more efficiently. Earlier this year my union commissioned an attitudinal survey of our membership and one of the questions we asked was: 'In your own department, where do you think the best ideas for improving productivity and efficiency would usually come: management or workers?' Two-thirds of those polled said workers would have the best ideas, and just 26 per cent felt their managers were better equipped to make suggestions in these areas.

Many segments of labour are extremely distrustful of QWL programs because management has attempted to impose them without involving or even consulting officers of the local. In my opinion, QWL projects must remain within the collective-bargaining system. Arrangements should be made with management and the union before embarking on a QWL project, specifying what changes or redesign must be negotiated within the collective agreement.

Productivity is another area within industrial relations that merits more discussion. Labour is not opposed to looking at productivity pacts, unless of course the hidden agenda is purely how to cut jobs. To become more productive is a desirable goal for a trading nation like Canada. However, productivity pacts must be arrived at in the context of collective bargaining containing specific provisions protecting jobs or guaranteeing retraining as well as a formula to ensure that employees will share in the benefits of productivity.

I think one of the major challenges of labour and management in Canada today would be to explore ways to lessen the adversarial system of labour relations. If unions could find a way out of the corner that I spoke about earlier, they would be much more amenable to considering new, innovative approaches. We should consider more co-operation, with the objective of improving communication between unions and employers and attempt to develop new ways to shed more light and less heat in labour relations. If this were done, the emphasis in labour relations would shift to mutual problem-solving, rather than our present confrontational mode.

However, I am not naive enough to think that the adversarial approach can be completely eliminated. Labour and management will continue to grope with some fundamentally divisive issues. Most contentious will be the different views on the distribution of wealth. Until someone develops a more effective mechanism for dealing with fundamental differences, we will rely on collective bargaining, which, with all its warts, has worked reasonably well.

Fundamental to the effectiveness of any strategies we develop to reduce unemployment is our ability to work together to achieve common goals. One of the most obvious ways in which the various sectors of our society can work together is through consultative mechanisms. A recent study done for the C.D. Howe Institute by John Crispo builds a strong case for more meaningful national consultation and emphasizes the important role that labour should play in national consultation.[3]

I agree wholeheartedly with Crispo and believe that a national consultative process can help solve the unemployment crisis facing Canada. However, previous experiences of this kind have not been all positive from labour's viewpoint. Often labour is consulted after the fact – after the key economic decisions have already been made. The other two sectors – government and business – are most anxious and willing to consult with labour on how to share the poverty during difficult economic times. If labour is to be a true partner, it must also play an equal role in discussions on how to share the wealth during more prosperous times. If we are going to improve the industrial relations system in Canada, then trade unions must be seen and treated as equals with business and government.

NOTES

1 Canadian Labour Congress, *Economic Bulletin*, September 1984, No. 101
2 Senator Michael Pitfield, Address to the Society of the Plastics Industry of Canada, Ottawa, 24 September 1984
3 John Crispo, *National Consultation – Problems and Prospects* (Toronto: C.D. Howe Institute, 1984)

RAY PROTTI

The extent to which collective bargaining can assist in reducing unemployment depends upon the adaptability not only of institutions but also of the individuals (management and labour) who run the collective bargaining system. Such flexibility in the Canadian wage-determination process in 1983–4 can be illustrated from evidence from Labour Canada's data bank of collective agreements involving 500 or more employees. Close to 40 per cent of the non-agricultural labour force is unionized, but somewhere between 50 and 55 per cent of the Canadian labour force has its terms and conditions of employment determined by some form of collective agreement.

The following developments occurred in 1983–4 in Canada.
1 In the third quarter of 1984, effective average annual wage increases – including allowance for cost-of-living allowance (COLA) clauses – were 3.1 per cent, the fourth consecutive quarter in which this data series (which has been compiled since 1967) hit a record low. This was sharply down from the record high of 13.6 per cent in the fourth quarter of 1981.
2 The national aggregate numbers masked a good deal of regional variation. Alberta and British Columbia settlements, most notably, in the first nine months of 1984 were averaging 1.8 per cent while the rest of Canada was double that average, at 3.7 per cent.

3 Some 28 per cent of all agreements signed in the first nine months of 1984 provided for wage freezes or cuts in the first year of the agreement. Of these, 12 per cent featured either freezes or absolute cuts through the full life of the agreement.

4 In 1983 and the first nine months of 1984, 40 per cent of major collective agreements that were bargained and previously contained COLA clauses had them dropped or reduced in impact. Only 2 per cent of negotiated agreements introduced new COLA clauses.

5 There were major changes in the structure of bargaining, notably in meat packing, which have as a result introduced a measure of variability in regional wage rates in what previously was a uniform national rate.

6 There were a wide variety of innovative responses to reflect the particular circumstances of industries and occupations. There were work rule changes designed to increase productivity in return for wage increases. There were agreements with wage freezes in return for guarantees of job security and employment maintenance. COLA benefits were lowered or dropped in favour of a shorter work week allowing more to share in employment than would otherwise have been possible. In the construction industry, union contracts were negotiated in which wage rates could be reopened on particular projects to permit unionized contractors to compete with non-union firms.

7 Finally, there was a significant drop 1981–4 in work stoppages. In spite of the public's perception of Canada as a strike-prone country, work stoppages in 1984 were only about a third of what they were in 1980 and 1981 in terms of days not worked as a percentage of total working time.

Those who believe that such responsiveness and adaptability are required as a pre-condition for a return to a more efficient and competitive economy, and subsequently to a strong resumption in employment growth, would thus be inclined to argue that the collective bargaining system, if adaptable, can help maintain and eventually stimulate employment.

Is it sufficient? Did it work quickly enough? Like other authors of earlier papers, I have no bench-mark to judge. However, in a highly decentralized system, the consequences of not adapting are felt most severely and most immediately by those most responsible for making the system work.

Canada is at the decentralized end of the spectrum, having 799 unions and over 22,000 collective agreements. I found very interesting Ellman's comments on the relatively good macroeconomic performance of Norway, Sweden, and Austria relative to their European partners and Tarantelli's observations on the benefits of centralized bargaining structures and their seeming ability to effect a more acceptable trade-off between inflation and unemployment. As well, there have been passing references to the well-known Japanese success in this regard.

There are a number of common threads that run through the system of those countries that have experienced more favourable macroeconomic performance than Canada. These countries are all characterized by the amount of time and effort, particularly in the Japanese case, that is devoted on a regular and continuing basis to exchanging information and building consensus at all levels in the society. In Japan, there exist the following levels of consultation: at the shop level through quality control circles; at the plant level through union-management consultation, grievance-handling procedures, and a collective-bargaining structure; at the industry level, where industry and union federations are involved in regular meetings and wage negotiations during the annual spring wage offensive; and at the national level, where management and labour operate the Japan Productivity Centre and union, employer, and government representatives participate in regular tripartite consultations.

These countries are all characterized by the fact that wages are negotiated on an annual basis. This practice contrasts with the Canadian experience. In the first nine months of 1984, which had an unusually heavy bargaining agenda, over 90 per cent of private-sector agreements were multi-year. This can lead to a lack of continuous communication and information exchange among the players in the system. In such circumstances, it may be worth considering much more frequent and regular contact between employee and employers. Certainly those countries that have used collective bargaining most successfully to help manage adjustment and adaptability do so under annual negotiations.

In summary, then, it is difficult to manage collective bargaining in an era of economic slowdown and high unemployment without a lot of discussion between the parties and a high degree of information exchange representing meaningful, and combined, information inputs by all parties. Indeed, adaptability is the key link to the collective-bargaining system assisting to reduce unemployment.

REMEDIES

FRANK REID

Work-time reduction

It is somewhat paradoxical that a significant fraction of the Canadian labour force is involuntarily unemployed at the same time that many individuals are over-employed in the sense that they would prefer to reduce their work time. The effects of cyclical contractions in demand are concentrated in layoffs and unemployment of a few rather than being shared more equally in the form of small reductions of hours worked across the labour force. For example, if average hours in the 1982 recession had been reduced by 1.3 hours per week, the unemployment rate would have remained at its 1981 level of 7.5 per cent rather than rising to 11.0 per cent during 1982.

Public policies to encourage employment-sharing through work-time reductions could lead to greater efficiency through reduced public expenditures on unemployment insurance, welfare, and health services, the latter arising from the stress problems associated with layoffs or the prospect of layoffs. In addition, work-time reductions spread over the work-force are more equitable than unemployment concentrated on an unfortunate few.

The purpose of this paper is to assess the feasibility of three related employment-sharing policies that involve reductions in work time: legislated or negotiated reductions in the standard work week; policies to encourage individual employees to engage in job-sharing, longer vacations, sabbatical leaves, and early retirement; and short-time compensation (STC) policies, in which unemployment insurance benefits are used partially to compensate workers for temporary reductions in the work week to avoid layoffs.

Reducing the standard work week from say 40 to 35 hours could be accomplished either through collective bargaining or through amendments to employment standards legislation. As a complementary policy, the conventional overtime premium of time-and-one-half could be increased to double

time to discourage employers from increasing overtime in respons
reduction in standard hours.

Most Canadian workers, however, are already working well below the
standard work week of 44 hours or more that prevails in employment standards legislation covering most Canadian workers. Thus a substantial
reduction in the legislated standard would be required to obtain a reduction
in aggregate hours worked. Such a reduction may be difficult to enforce
when it conflicts with the preferences of both employees and employers
when they mutually agree to a longer work week. In addition, a widespread
reduction of the standard work week through collective bargaining is
unlikely, given decentralized bargaining in Canada; such a concerted action
would be more likely as part of a national accord in countries with more
centralized bargaining structures.

Reductions in the standard work week to combat deficient-demand
unemployment may also be difficult to reverse when the economy recovers;
therefore, if implemented, such a policy should be temporary and geared to
the state of the economy, perhaps through the inclusion of a 'sunset' clause
in the legislation. Western European experience also suggests that there is
enough 'slack' in the routine of most organizations that small reductions in
the standard work week (about one hour per week) can be accommodated
without increasing employment. These apparent productivity increases,
while perhaps desirable in themselves, can offset much of the need to
increase employment to compensate for the reduction in hours. However,
more substantial reductions, for example from 40 to 35 hours per week,
would likely lead to the need to increase employment.

A legislated or negotiated reduction in the standard work week could
also lead to an increase in unit labour costs because of person-specific
employment costs such as health insurance premiums or because of the need
to continue overtime procedures to meet unanticipated demand fluctuations. Such higher costs could reduce the demand for labour, partially offsetting the employment gains from the reduction in hours.

A legislated reduction in the standard work week might substantially
reduce unemployment, but its attractiveness is reduced by the disadvantages
outlined above. Although it is debatable whether such a policy change is
desirable, it is clear from western European experience that a 'cautious'
reduction to, say, 39 hours per week would have a negligible impact – if
implemented at all, the policy should be a 'bold' reduction to, say, 35 hours
per week.

Survey evidence based on US data indicates that a substantial number of
full-time employees are over-employed: they would prefer to work fewer

hours with a proportionate reduction in income. About 60 per cent of those questioned wanted to engage in one or more of five types of work-time reductions (shorter work day, shorter work week, increased annual vacation, sabbatical leaves, and earlier retirement), although only about one-quarter wanted to engage in any single type of reduction. Calculations indicate that allowing those who voluntarily wished to reduce their work time (with a proportionate reduction in income) would result in a total reduction in work time of about 4.7 per cent. Because of the offsetting effects of enhanced productivity and increased unit labour costs, such a reduction would likely lead to an employment increase of approximately 2.0 per cent, a significant offset for the 3.5 per cent rise in unemployment that characterized the 1982 recession.

While such a voluntary reduction in work time is preferred by a substantial number of employees, it is inhibited by the lack of such arrangements offered by employers. This may reflect legitimate cost considerations on the part of employers. However, employers will consider only their private costs associated with such hours reductions; they do not fully consider the social costs (unemployment insurance, welfare, health services) associated with unemployment. In such circumstances, private-cost calculations militate against hours reductions to reduce unemployment when the appropriate social-cost calculations would dictate otherwise.

Thus it would be desireable from the viewpoints of both equity and efficiency to ammend employment standards legislation to give employees the right to voluntary work-time reductions such as job-sharing, a reduced work week, increased annual vacation, and sabbaticals, all with corresponding reductions in pay but not loss of seniority.

Conventional unemployment insurance (UI) is, in effect, available only to people who are unemployed and not to those whose hours of work are reduced by demand reductions. Short-time compensation (STC) reduces this bias toward layoffs by allowing eligible workers to draw UI benefits on a temporary basis if they all voluntarily accept a reduction in hours of work instead of having a few laid off. Such a policy, which has been in effect in Canada since January 1982, obviously benefits employees who otherwise would have been laid off, but it can also benefit workers who are not threatened with layoffs because they are able to reduce their work time without much reduction in take-home pay. Employees on a four-day week, for example, would receive 92 per cent of their normal weekly earnings – 80 per cent as earnings from their employer and 12 per cent in the form of STC benefits.

Although employers pay for the same total hours of labour under STC as under the layoff alternative, they may experience a slight rise in fringe-benefit costs, since some benefits are paid for on a per-person basis rather than as a percentage of earnings. There are offsetting savings, however, because the employer retains his or her complete work-force and avoids the costs of hiring and training replacements for those who do not respond to recall from layoff when full production resumes.

The government, in principle, pays the same total number of days of UI benefits. In the case of the four-day week, under STC it pays UI to five persons one day per week, and under the layoff alternative it pays UI to one person five days per week. Actual UI costs were somewhat higher under the STC program than conventional UI, due to some administrative peculiarities of the STC program (such as elimination of the normal two-week waiting period for benefits), which could easily be corrected.

The conclusion of this analysis is that the existing STC program is desirable in terms of both efficiency and equity. The program should be maintained and strengthened by extending the maximum benefit period to the same length as conventional UI benefits and by streamlining some administrative aspects of the program.

The three major employment-sharing policies analysed in this paper – a legislated reduction of the standard work week, providing the right to voluntary work-time reductions through employment standards legislation, and short-time compensation – are designed to increase employment during periods of deficient-demand unemployment, i.e. an overall shortage of jobs. They would not be required during periods of full employment.

There are, however, a number of institutional features of Canadian labour markets that provide unintended barriers to optimal employment patterns. Since inefficiencies are created by these barriers, there is a strong argument for eliminating them even if the economy is not experiencing deficient-demand unemployment. First, the ceiling on employer and employee payroll taxes should be specified in hourly rather than weekly (or annual) terms to prevent a cost increase when hours are reduced by employment-sharing. Similarly, privately negotiated fringe benefits and benefits provided through employment standards legislation should be prorated according to hours worked to ensure that provisions do not become an unintended barrier to employment-sharing for either employees or employers. Third, labour relations boards should place part-time and full-time workers in the same bargaining unit in order to minimize differences in contract provisions between full-time and part-time workers. Such differences could otherwise affect the willingness of employees to engage in employment-sharing.

The employment-sharing policies advocated in this paper should not be regarded as a substitute for aggregate policies designed to reduce deficient-demand unemployment. Employment sharing, however, is a realistic means of combating unemployment without a significant increase in government expenditure – a considerable advantage, given the concern about the size of the government deficit. Although employment-sharing is clearly not a panacea for unemployment, it can make a small but significant contribution to the resolution of this important problem.

SHLOMO MAITAL

Reducing unemployment

Why has Western society so often failed to realize, and capture, the large increment to employment and output that accrues to co-operative, pro-social behaviour in non-zero-sum macroeconomic games?

Ten times in the post-war period, the American economy has sunk into recession. Of these, the tenth was by far the worst, posting the highest rate of unemployment since 1940. This recession was exported to Canada through high US interest rates and sluggish demand for foreign goods. The American economy has recovered strongly, with unemployment dropping faster than anticipated; but in Canada and western Europe, recovery has been slow and unemployment has remained stubbornly high.

This paper treats macroeconomic variables as outcomes of a labour-management macroeconomic game. It is postulated that the game is non-zero-sum in nature; evidence is given to support this claim. The business cycle is attributed to immoderate wage and price behaviour that generates unemployment and inflation. To remedy this, a new social contract is proposed. The change in behaviour implied by a social contract is arguably both necessary and sufficient for reducing unemployment.

At any given moment, a wide variety of economic games are in progress (Maital and Maital 1984 a, b), played by individuals, families, small and large groups, unions, corporations, and even whole nations. Of those games, the one whose outcome most crucially affects the efficiency, stability, and fairness of the national economy is played by labour and management, vying for shares of national income. To capture the key elements of this game, it will be assumed that labour and management are each monolithic and must choose one of two strategies: steep wage or price increases, or moderate ones. Modelling macroeconomic conflict as a two-player, two-strategy game (Shubik 1952; Maital and Benjamini 1980) can help determine whether an equilibrium solution exists and, if so, whether it is Pareto-efficient and stable.

Let $U(\cdot)$ and $V(\cdot)$ be the utility functions of labour and management, respectively. Assume U and V are each linear functions of four main macroeconomic variables: the rate of inflation (π), the unemployment rate (u), the rate of increase in real wages ($\dot{\omega}$), and the rate of growth of output (g):

(1) $U(\cdot) = F(\pi, u, \dot{\omega}, g),$

(2) $V(\cdot) = G(\pi, u, \dot{\omega}, g),$

Equations (1) and (2) reflect the structure of preferences and map macroeconomic outcomes into utility. To determine the game matrix, it is also necessary to know the macroeconomic structure – the link between wage and price behaviour and the four outcomes: π, u, $\dot{\omega}$, and g. Let labour's decision variable be $L = 0, 1$, where zero indicates wage moderation and 1 indicates high wage demands. Let management's decision variable be $M = 0, 1$, where zero indicates price moderation and 1 indicates large price increases. A non-linear relation is postulated between L and M and the four outcome variables:

(3) $\pi = A_1 + A_2L + A_3M + A_4L{\cdot}M,$

(4) $u = B_1 + B_2L + B_3M + B_4L{\cdot}M,$

(5) $\dot{\omega} = C_1 + C_2L + C_3M + C_4L{\cdot}M,$

(6) $g = D_1 + D_2L + D_3M + D_4L{\cdot}M,$

where A_1, B_1, C_1, D_1, are constants, reflecting exogenous influences on the economy. The interactive terms (i.e. $L{\cdot}M$) reflect the fact, supported by strong econometric evidence, that jointly immoderate behaviour on the part of both labour and management is likely to produce more inflation and unemployment than the summed effects of large wage and price increases taken separately.

To determine the 2×2 outcome matrix, it is necessary to estimate the coefficients of equations (3)–(6). Each of the four outcome variables will have four values, one each for $L = 0, M = 0$; $L = 1, M = 0$; $L = 1, M = 0$; and $L = 1, M = 1$. To determine the 2×2 payoff matrix, one must know the utility functions in (1) and (2). Once the payoff matrix is known, the 2×2 macroeconomic game can be analysed in detail.

One approach to determine empirically the macroeconomic structure of labour management games is to simulate the effects of various wage and price behaviours with the aid of a large-scale econometric model. Such a situation was conducted with Ray Fair's 130-equation quarterly model of the US economy.[1] The paths of inflation, unemployment, and GNP growth were predicted for four different economic scenarios:

Base-line: This is Fair's basic extrapolation of current American fiscal and monetary policies to the end of 1986. It shows a gradually slowing economic recovery, with inflation climbing from 4 per cent in 1984 to 6 per cent in 1986 and unemployment rates levelling off at around 7 per cent.

Wage modertion: Suppose organized labour were to adopt a unilateral policy of wage moderation, so that money wages rise at a constant 3 per cent annual rate, instead of the 7–8 per cent rate projected in the base-line forecast, while business raised prices at 4–6 per cent yearly. How would labour and capital fare under this scenario?

Price moderation: Suppose employers and businessmen agreed to hold price increases to 3 per cent annually; at the same time, suppose labour received money wage increases of 6–7 per cent annually. How would the economy perform?

Social contract: Let both business and labour adopt moderate behaviour, in wage and price decisions, so that both money wages and prices rise by 3 per cent per annum. Would everyone gain?

'Moderate' policies are assumed to begin in the third quarter of 1983. The four scenarios are outlined in Table 1, with the subheadings indicating whether wages and prices are endogenous of exogenous and, if the latter, the assumed annual rate of increase.

Estimates of the coefficients of equations (3)–(6) based on the model of Fair are:

(7) $\quad \pi = 3.1 \quad + 1.1L + 0.3M + 1.9L \cdot M,$

(8) $\quad u = 5.1 \quad + 0.7L + 0.9M + 0.7L \cdot M,$

(9) $\quad g = 2.75 - 0.85L + 1.05M - 0.45L \cdot M,$

(10) $\quad \dot{\omega} = \quad 0 \quad + 3.7L - 1.3M - 0.6L \cdot M,$

with $L, M = 0, 1$. All the coefficients have the expected signs. Wage and price immoderation have strong interactive effects in worsening inflation and unemployment and lowering growth and the growth of real wages. The relatively large constant terms in the inflation, unemployment, and growth equations indicate that there are important exogenous forces at work, apart from what either labour or management does.

The coefficient estimates of equations (7)–(10) in turn can be used to

TABLE 1
Econometric simulation of wage and price behaviour, for four scenarios, United States 1983–6 (percentages)

Quarter	Baseline		Wage moderation		Price moderation		Social contract	
	Wage rise endogenous	Price rise endogenous	Wage rise exogenous 3%	Price rise endogenous	Wage rise endogenous	Price rise exogenous 3%	Wage rise exogenous 3%	Price rise exogenous 3%
1983 4	6.7	4.1	3.0	4.0	6.2	3.0	3.0	3.0
1984 1	7.0	4.5	3.0	4.3	6.3	3.0	3.0	3.0
2	7.2	4.9	3.0	4.4	6.3	3.0	3.0	3.0
3	7.4	5.2	3.0	4.6	6.4	3.0	3.0	3.0
4	7.6	5.5	3.0	4.7	6.4	3.0	3.0	3.0
1985 1	7.8	5.7	3.0	4.7	6.4	3.0	3.0	3.0
2	7.9	5.9	3.0	4.7	6.5	3.0	3.0	3.0
3	8.0	6.1	3.0	4.7	6.6	3.0	3.0	3.0
4	8.1	6.2	3.0	4.6	6.6	3.0	3.0	3.0
1986 1	8.1	6.3	3.0	4.6	6.6	3.0	3.0	3.0
2	8.1	6.3	3.0	4.5	6.7	3.0	3.0	3.0
3	8.1	6.3	3.0	4.4	6.7	3.0	3.0	3.0
4	8.1	6.3	3.0	4.3	6.7	3.0	3.0	3.0

TABLE 2
Simulation of wage and price moderation for US economy, 1983 (3) to 1986 (4) (percentages)

Labour	Business			
	No price moderation		Price moderation	
No	π	6.4	π	4.2
wage	u	7.4	u	5.8
moderation	$\dot{\omega}$	1.8	$\dot{\omega}$	3.7
	g	2.5	g	1.9
Wage	π	3.4	π	3.1
moderation	u	6.0	u	5.1
	$\dot{\omega}$	−1.3	$\dot{\omega}$	0.0
	g	3.8	g	2.75

NOTE: π is annual percentage rise in the GNP deflator; g is the annual percentage rise in real GNP, annual rate, averaged for the four quarters of 1986; u is the unemployment rate at 1986 (4); and $\dot{\omega}$ is the percentage change in real wages, averaged for the four quarters of 1986.

derive the outcome matrix found by solving the Fair model for each of the four combinations of wage and price behaviour. These are given in Table 2. As an illustration, price and wage moderation on the part of both business and labour leads to inflation and unemployment of only 3.1 per cent and 5.1 percent, compared to 6.4 per cent and 7.4 per cent when neither practices moderation.

At least three different types of macroeconomic game can emerge from the outcome matrix of Table 2, depending on the nature of utility functions. These three games are shown in Table 3. (Utility functions that imply each of the three games in Table 3 are given in the Appendix). Following a game theory convention, 4 represents the best outcomes for a given player, and 1 represents the worst outcome. The first number in each cell is labour's payoff; the second number is management's.

The first game, 'charity,' is the game matrix most likely to result from Table 3, for conventional utility functions. Business prefers the x, x outcome to x, y, and labour prefers x, x to y, x, because of aversion to unemployment (excess capacity) and inflation. This is a highly 'psychological' game, especially for many players, because it is a game of conformity, in that each player tries to do what he or she thinks other players will do. Perception creates a reality consistent with the perception. There are two stable equilibria, y, y and x, x. An interpretation of the stagflation of the 1970s is

TABLE 3
Outcomes of alternative wage and price strategies

		Business	
Labour		y	x
y		2,2	3,1
x		1,3	4,4

x = wage or price moderation.

y = present behaviour.

(a) 'Charity.' This game has two Nash equilibria: 2,2 and 4,4. At the 2,2 equilibrium, neither player has any incentive to change to 'moderation' unilaterally. For N-person games of this sort once a 'critical mass' of players perceives that others will switch to 'moderation,' everyone ultimately does.

	y	x
y	2,2	4,1
x	1,4	3,3

(b) 'Prisoner's dilemma.' Each player has 'y' as the dominant strategy, yeilding a stable Pareto-inferior equilibrium. Even if a social contract moves society to 4,4, it will be unstable, since each player has an incentive to 'defect' unilaterally.

	y	x
y	1,1	4,2
x	2,4	3,3

(c) 'Chicken,' This game has no equilibrium. Each player would prefer to yield to an opponent's threat of 'y' by playing 'x,' but misunderstandings and 'called bluffs' may lead to 1,1 outcomes.

the y, y equilibrium, with neither labour nor business willing to change its behaviour unilaterally. This is an optimistic view of society; the sole task of a social contract here is to persuade players to undertake a joint change in behaviour. Once done, the new equilibrium is a stable first-best for all.

'Prisoner's dilemma' (3b) is also a plausible game structure. To obtain it, simply interchange the 3s and 4s in Table 3a. This will happen when, for instance, labour values the higher real wages attained in y, x more than the lower inflation and unemployment in x, x, and business prefers the higher growth and lower real wages in x, y to lower inflation and unemployment in x, x. Prisoner's dilemma is the only 2 × 2 game with a single Pareto-inferior stable equilibrium: 2, 2. A large literature exists on how to resolve the dilemma, by altering the structure of the game, altering how people perceive it, changing the rules, by eliminating immoderate behaviour (Lipnowsky and Maital 1985). For this game structure, achieving a social contract is difficult, and maintaining it in the face of defections is even harder. (See Maital and Maital 1984 for an interpretation of business-labour-government games as three-person prisoner's dilemma.)

Finally, suppose labour finds that the higher real wages in the y, x outcome, compared with x, y, do not outweigh the higher inflation and unemployment. Suppose business believes similarly that higher real profits and growth in y, y do not offset higher inflation and unemployment, compared with x, y. This suggests interchanging the 1s and 2s of Table 3b. The new game matrix is 'chicken' (Table 3c). This game has no stable equilibrium. Neither player has a dominant strategy. Each now seeks to do the opposite of the other player. A credible bluff of 'y' by labour, if believed by business, will lead the latter to play 'x.' A called bluff can lead to a disastrous 1, 1 outcome. A social contract that leads society to x, x may face defections, as with prisoner's dilemma.

It is quite probable that in any economy, at any given moment, all three games are being played at any given moment. 'Chicken' best characterizes strikes. 'Prisoner's dilemma' typifies 'buy-in-advance' behaviour of consumers, who accelerate spending in anticipation of higher prices. 'Charity' is perhaps a fair description of wage-price bargaining, when both sides are aware that moderation is beneficial for all. It is, of course, not necessary for payoff orderings to be symmetric. The game structure may be 'charity' or 'chicken' for labour and 'prisoner's dilemma' for Business. When preference orderings differ for business and labour, there are 3!/2! = 3 more game matrices, some of which have equilibria and others do not.

I have argued that society has failed to capture large positive increments in well-being inherent in macroeconomic non-zero-sum games, because the structure of those games makes individual non-co-operative behaviour rational and because the benefits of jointly co-operative behaviour may not be perceived. In concentrating on manipulation of technical variables – government spending, taxes, money supply – economics has overlooked key aspects of the problem involving human relationships, feelings, attitudes, and perceptions. As George Katona (1979) noted, there is need for a 'macropsychology' or a psychology of macroeconomics.

The notion of a new social contract provides a unifying framework for such a psychology, one to which other disciplines such as philosophy, anthropology, and political science can contribute. Recently, Maital and Meltz (1985) surveyed leading business and labour leaders in both the United States and Canada, to determine whether they accepted the diagnosis and prescription described in this paper and in earlier books (Maital 1982; Maital and Maital 1985). We heard two main themes. One was that a new social contract, even if desirable, was not feasible. A second was that it is not desirable, because it represents an unwarranted, dangerous limitation on personal freedom – a complaint we heard most often from business leaders.

This suggests an important area of research on the psychology of interpersonal relations. Suppose, as do many economists, that macroeconomic instability is caused by 'externalities' (one individual's behaviour affects other people, for good or ill, outside the normal workings of the price system). With large, widespread externalities, personal freedom implies: 'I am free ... to harm your well-being, and you are free to harm mine.' This is closer to anarchy than to freedom. 'Employers and unions who contribute to inflation by their price and wage behavior are imposing costs on the rest of society,' Tobin (1984) has written; 'the remedies are well known: devices to force or induce agents to internalize the social costs.' The remedies may be well known, but implementing them demands psychological principles and practice that have so far not been called upon.

In some cultures, and among some individuals, 'well-being' is considered a private good, subject to the scarcity principle; it is perceived that 'more' for one person necessarily means less for another. This perception induces competitive non-co-operative behaviour and is inimical to social contracts. In other cultures, and among other individuals, 'well-being' is seen as a public good, where more for one is more for all (Foster 1965; L'Armand and Pepitone 1975). How, when, and why people shift from the perception of well-being as a private good to one that sees it as a public good are questions to which economics badly needs answers; psychology can help provide them.

'Chastened by ten years of stagflation and depression, both business and labor are hungry for sustained resumption of noninflationary prosperity and growth. They should be ready for a social compact in which all would agree to restrain wage and price increases in return for jobs and markets' (Tobin 1984, 54). Building and implementing such a social compact are a task in which economics and psychology must join forces.

Nations with some form of incomes policy have fared demonstrably better in the past decade than those without one. As McCallum (1982) illustrates, the Netherlands, West Germany, Austria, Norway, Sweden, and Japan have done measurably better in controlling both inflation and unemployment since 1973 than other industrial nations, and all had either a formal incomes policy or an informal one based on a national-consensus system of wage bargaining, as in Japan. But even these countries have been experiencing increasing social frictions in recent years. Incomes policy refers to a narrow system of voluntary or mandatory wage-price guidelines. Social contract refers to a much broader type of social consensus that is implemented whenever and wherever non-zero-sum macro games are played, from individual plants and even work teams up to the national economy and even co-ordination of economic policies among nations, with the objective of securing a jointly profitable outcome and retaining it.[2]

Unemployment is not, as is often said or implied, an act of nature. Unemployment is a result of certain types of human behaviour. If it is caused by people, then it can be cured by them – not by adjusting this technical variable or that, but by altering the way macroeconomic players behave. Sizeable, lasting reductions in unemployment will reward societites able to fashion a new social contract among their members.

NOTES

1 A version of this model has been developed for the IBM-PC computer and was provided through the courtesy of Urban Systems Research & Engineering, Cambridge, Mass.
2 Keynes referred several times to 'social contract' agreements. Keynes (1925) proposed replacing Churchill's deflationary policies, which caused severe unemployment, with a social-contract agreement among workers to reduce wages and prices by 10 per cent, in order to return to the pre-First World War sterling

exchange rate without inducing a depression. Keynes felt, however, that the idea was impractical. Since wages had to be cut some time before prices would respond and fall, workers would be unlikely to accept the situation for long.

REFERENCES

Blinder, A. 1980. *The Great Stagflation*. New York: Academic Press
Fair, R. 1974, 1976. *A Model of Macroeconomic Activity*, Vols. I and II. Cambridge, Mass: Ballinger
Foster, G. 1965. 'Peasant Society and the Image of Limited Goods,' *American Anthropologist* 67:293-15
Katona, G. 1979. 'Toward a Macropsychology,' *American Psychologist*, February
Keynes, J.M. 1925. 'The Economic Consequence of Mr. Churchill,' in *Essays in Persuasion*
- 1940. *How to Pay for the War*. London: Macmillan
L'Armand, K., and J. Pepitone. 1975. 'Helping to Reward Another Person: A Cross Cultural Analysis,' *Journal of Personal and Social Psychology* 31:189-98
Lipnowsky, I., and S. Maital. 1985. 'Tax-Based Incomes Policy as the Game of Chicken,' in I. Lipnowsky and S. Maital (eds), *Macroeconomic Conflict and Social Institutions*. Cambridge, Mass: Ballinger
Maital, S. 1982. *Minds, Markets & Money: Psychological Foundations of Economic Behavior*. New York: Basic Books
Maital, S., and Y. Benjamini. 1980. 'Inflation as Prisoner's Dilemma,' *Journal of Post Keynesian Economics*, Summer, 459-81
Maital, S., and S. Maital. 1984a. *Economic Games People Play*. New York: Basic Books
- 1984b. 'Psychology & Economics,' in M. Bornstein (ed), *Crosscurrents in Contemporary Psychology,* Vol. III: *Psychology and Its Allied Disciplines: Social Sciences*. Hillsdale, NJ: Lawrence Erlbaum
Maital, S., and N.M. Meltz. 1985. 'Labour and Management Attitudes toward a New Social Contract: A Comparison of Canada and the United States' in I. Lipnowsky, and S. Maital (eds), *Macroeconomic Conflict and Social Institutions*, 193-206. Cambridge, Mass: Ballinger
McCallum, J. 1982. 'We Need a Way as well as a Will,' *Financial Post*, 20 November
Shubik, M. 1958. 'A Business Cycle Model with Organized Labor Considered,' *Econometrica* 20, 284-94
Tobin, J. 1984. 'A Social Compact for Restraint,' *Challenge*, March/April